Peter Weiss in Exile
A Critical Study of His Works

Theater and Dramatic Studies, No. 37

Oscar G. Brockett, Series Editor

Leslie Waggener Professor of Fine Arts
and Professor of Drama
The University of Texas at Austin

Other Titles in This Series

No. 29 *Black Theater, Dance, and
Ritual in South Africa* — Peter Larlham

No. 33 *The Dance Theatre of Jean Cocteau* — Frank W.D. Ries

No. 35 The Drama Review: *Thirty Years
of Commentary on the Avant-Garde* — Brooks McNamara
and Jill Dolan, eds.

No. 36 *Political Violence in Drama: Classical
Models, Contemporary Variations* — Mary Karen Dahl

No. 38 *The Tournament Tradition and Staging*
The Castle of Perseverance — Steven I. Pederson

No. 39 *The Wooster Group, 1975–1985:
Breaking the Rules* — David Savran

No. 40 *Late Victorian Farce* — Jeffrey H. Huberman

No. 41 *Shakespeare at the Maddermarket:
Nugent Monck and the Norwich Players* — Franklin J. Hildy

Peter Weiss in Exile
A Critical Study of His Works

by
Roger Ellis

UMI Research Press

Ann Arbor, Michigan

Produced and distributed by
UMI Research Press
an imprint of
University Microfilms, Inc.
Ann Arbor, Michigan 48106

Library of Congress Cataloging in Publication Data

Ellis, Roger, 1943 May 18-
Peter Weiss in exile.

(Theater and dramatic studies ; no. 37)
Revision of thesis (Ph.D.)—University of California-
Berkeley, 1980.
Bibliography: p.
Includes index.
1. Weiss, Peter, 1916- . 2. Authors, German—
20th century—Biography—Exile. 3. Weiss, Peter,
1916- —Political and social views. I. Title.
II. Series.
PT2685.E5Z66 1987 832'.914 [B] 86-19241
ISBN 0-8357-1764-X (alk. paper)

For Jeremiah, Zan, and Kady

Peter Weiss, 1964
(*Photo courtesy of the Berlin Volksbühne*)

Contents

List of Figures   *ix*

Preface   *xi*

Acknowledgments   *xvii*

1   Art and Exploration, 1947–1963   *1*

2   Committed Writing and *Marat/Sade*   *23*

3   Art and Political Experience, 1965–1968   *43*

4   The Revolutionary Intellectual, 1969–1971   *81*

5   Dramatic Themes and Ideas   *119*

Appendix A: Biographical Outline of Weiss's Career   *141*

Appendix B: Interview with Gunilla Palmstierna-Weiss   *145*

Notes   *155*

Bibliography   *169*

Index   *177*

Figures

Peter Weiss, 1964   *Frontispiece*

1. *Marat/Sade*   28

2. *Marat/Sade*   35

3. *Marat/Sade*   36

4. *The Investigation*   47

5. *The Investigation*   49

6. *The Investigation*   52

7. *Song of the Lusitanian Bogeyman*   60

8. *Song of the Lusitanian Bogeyman*   62

9. *Song of the Lusitanian Bogeyman*   64

10. *Vietnam Discourse*   66

11. *Vietnam Discourse*   68

12. *Vietnam Discourse*   69

13. *How Mr. Mockinpott Was Cured of His Sufferings*   72

14. *How Mr. Mockinpott Was Cured of His Sufferings*   74

15. *Trotsky in Exile*   86

x   *Figures*

16. *Trotsky in Exile*   *90*

17. *Trotsky in Exile*   *93*

18. *Hölderlin*   *102*

19. *Hölderlin*   *106*

20. Peter Weiss, 1980   *118*

Preface

This study examines the career of the dramatist Peter Weiss and traces in his work the development of his central concern for the relationship between the writer and society. The question of the writer's social importance in the modern world has occupied the attention of many post-World War II playwrights, but few have explored the problem so persistently as Peter Weiss.

This issue provides the focus of the book because it influenced most of Weiss's literary development even from his earliest years as a writer. It inspired his first autobiographies, prose fiction, and plays. Weiss's growing political consciousness then quickly led to the brilliant theatrical success of *Marat/Sade*, eventually drawing him in the mid-1960s into a temporary commitment to revolutionary socialism. Finally, in his plays of the 1970s, Weiss continued to study the problem of the writer *engagé*, and found what appears to be a satisfying—if paradoxical—solution in his two final dramas about Leon Trotsky and Friedrich Hölderlin.

By common agreement Weiss's dramas rank among the most intellectually compelling works written for the modern theatre; and it is very difficult for readers or audiences to appreciate them without sensing beneath the vivid language and theatrical innovation his development as a socially concerned writer. By this I do not simply mean his notoriety as a radical politician. Certainly his political stance as a leftist playwright has troubled many critics who have remarked upon Weiss's penchant for revolutionary subjects, agit-prop moralizing, and socialist ideologies. Few critics, however, have related these characteristics of his plays to Weiss's repeated attempts to integrate successfully the roles of artist and social reformer in his own life.

The widespread view of Weiss as a "socialist" playwright has laid too much stress on the political advocacy of his dramas, and too little on the philosophical problem of absurdity which colors much of his work and stage practice. This study treats Weiss's political outlooks as *responses* to the absurdity he felt in his own life, and it emphasizes Weiss's personal search for meaning and value through artistic activity. Throughout his career, he always looked on his work as a challenging process of self-discovery, in addition to its value as a forum for political statement. Because of this, he has been able to address some of the most pressing social issues of our age while clarifying and validating for himself his own position as a socially concerned playwright in the postwar world.

The note of exile is particularly important when considering Weiss's achievements because the dislocation he experienced as a Jew during World War II strongly encouraged a dual focus in his work: the self-analysis of his literary influence and the sociopolitical analysis of his society. His background reveals how he first went into exile in 1934 when his family left Germany for Britain in order to escape Fascist persecution. Weiss spent two years in Czechoslovakia, between 1936 and 1938, until Hitler moved into that country; then he rejoined his family for a brief period in Göteborg, Sweden, before moving to Stockholm in 1940 to continue his career as an artist.

This experience of exile cut him off from many old friends and helped him to regard his personal circumstances as part of the dismal European political situation in general. Thus it was perhaps inevitable that as he continued his writing Weiss should move from a position of social observer to that of social critic. As he developed his artistic skills and gained more public success, he gradually became more aware of the influence he could exert through writing— an awareness he never abandoned after his first stage success, *Marat/Sade,* in 1964.

This book examines the subject of the writer's influence upon society by stressing three major themes in Weiss's work between 1947 and 1982. The first of these is the theme of absurdity, which is reflected in the condition of entrapment against which all of his dramatic heroes must struggle. The second theme is Weiss's positive appraisal of the writer's vocation, as seen in three of his plays which discuss the careers of revolutionary intellectuals. The third theme which this book emphasizes is Weiss's concern for artistic independence and the political choices which this stance affords modern writers. Those topics have surfaced repeatedly in Weiss's work, always assuming new forms and provoking new questions as he moved through his art towards a better understanding of himself, his world, and his own place within the world.

The book discusses these issues by dividing Weiss's work chronologically into three periods, the first of which is that of his early prose and dramatic works written between 1947 and 1963. This is a body of writing characterized by the author's growing awareness of absurdity, his need to rebel against his bourgeois upbringing, and his attempts to explore his social surroundings in detail. Dramatic works such as *The Tower, The Insurance* and *Night with Guests* express the writer's grim view of human nature and society; while the two novels, *Shadow of the Coachman's Body* and *Conversation of the Three Wayfarers,* reflect Weiss's concern for writing as a genuine social gesture of communication and sharing of experience. His autobiographies, *Leavetaking* and *Vanishing-Point,* mark a decisive stage in Weiss's career, because by 1962 when they were completed and published, Weiss was comfortable analyzing his personal past in the form of a public dialogue.

With the emergence of *Marat/Sade* in 1964, Weiss entered upon the second period of his career, during which he tried to explore his political influence upon audiences. Between 1964 and 1968 he temporarily abandoned his earlier skepticism and political indecision to test different ideologies against the fabric of history. He relied almost exclusively upon political-historical material, and during this time he wrote almost entirely for the stage. In *Marat/Sade* he conducted a dialectical discussion between individualism and socialism; in *The Investigation* he recounted the monstrous atrocities of the Nazi death camps and urged audiences to recognize their own responsibility for tolerating modern systems of political oppression. *Song of the Lusitanian Bogeyman* attacked Portuguese colonialism in Angola; the *Vietnam Discourse* took an equally uncompromising stand against French and American policies in Indochina; and the fable of *How Mr. Mockinpott Was Cured of His Sufferings* developed a dramatic treatment of capitalist society's oppression of the individual. It was with *Mockinpott,* however, that Weiss started to reject political advocacy and to display a certain ideological exhaustion. The play seemed imitative and simplified to the point of complacency, and its ideological optimism seemed unconcernedly directed at the believer rather than at the skeptic.

The third and final stage in Weiss's development contains two historical dramas, *Trotsky in Exile* and *Hölderlin,* written in 1969 and 1971, respectively; the monumental novel, *Aesthetics of Resistance;* and a revised version of Kafka's *The Trial* which he and Gunilla Palmstierna-Weiss co-directed in Stockholm in 1982. During this period the two poles of artistic freedom and revolutionary commitment became finally aligned in his thinking. The two major historical dramas which my study focuses upon demonstrate how the revolutionary artist and the revolutionary political leader play complementary roles in influencing historical change. *Trotsky* portrays the situation of a revolutionary writer who refused to take effective action when he had the opportunity to do so; but who continued his theoretical work in exile, preserving the classical tenets of Marxism during the repressive years of Stalinism. In *Hölderlin* Weiss argued again for artistic independence by affirming value for the visionary writer–poet who continued to work and to theorize despite the unpopularity of his views.

At the time of his death early in 1982, Peter Weiss was beginning a new phase in his career. A play on the subject of Dante was in the planning stage. Weiss was eager to continue working with actors at Stockholm's Scala Studio theatre, as he had done on the recent production of Kafka's *The New Trial.* And Weiss was also preparing revisions for *Trotsky* which would greatly expand the stage time devoted to the avant-garde artists in the Zurich coffeehouse scenes, in order to amplify his thoughts on the role of artists in revolutionary societies.

This final period, therefore, displays overall Weiss's dissatisfaction with strictly political solutions to social change. Instead he was insisting on the value of an independent stance for writers seriously concerned with influencing progressive social changes; and he was convinced of the value of a double approach to such change: revolutionary art and revolutionary action, as he had known it in his own career.

Note on Materials

It is, of course, particularly difficult to put in perspective the work of a writer so recently deceased and much of whose work is still untranslated for English-speaking audiences. Helpful materials such as autobiographies and reviews of key productions are often sketchy and singularly biased. Photodocumentary materials are scattered among a dozen individuals and theatre organizations. And the critic while going about his analytical job is always haunted by the thought that there is more to be discovered. While recognizing such limitations to the present study, however, there is still much to be gained from a critical appraisal of Peter Weiss at this time.

The most important result that might emerge from this book is perhaps to bring to the attention of English-speaking audiences the many unnoticed and innovative contributions Weiss has made to the postwar theater, and to do so in a reasonably coherent fashion by providing a total perspective on his career. There is also the significant task of preparing as complete a background as possible for future study of this writer by clarifying the many controversial ideas he has advanced which have not yet been fully explored. By common agreement, Weiss is the most important political playwright to have emerged during the 1960s and we can hardly pretend to have begun the systematic critical exploration of his work. A thorough analysis of his political thinking, a detailed study of his life and professional associates, a close examination of his personal papers and playscripts as well as the stage productions on which he and Gunilla Palmstierna collaborated, and the relationship of his work to that of Brecht are a few areas which this book can only touch upon and which will undoubtedly generate intense interest among critics as the impact of Weiss's work becomes more widely felt.

In discussing the theme of the writer and society, this book relies heavily upon Weiss's own statements in public, in both autobiographical and critical contexts. This has been done in order to identify the imaginative sources from which his plays have sprung, and not to use such material as criteria for assessing his work. In fact, if there is one aspect of this study which has posed more difficulty than any other, it is this point of critical evaluation if only for the fact that the test of time is a key criterion in any such assessment. Furthermore, an objective appraisal of the stageworthiness of his plays must necessarily depend to a large extent upon the reactions of critics to certain directorial interpretations—a fact which often hinders more than it helps to clarify the value of any particular drama. Due to the controversial reactions provoked by many of Weiss's plays, and Weiss's frequent harsh criticism towards the methods of directors who staged his plays, I do not rely exclusively upon the opinions of critics and reviews but try instead to strike a comfortable balance between public reactions, the playwright's intentions, and my own impression of the possibilities contained in his scripts.

I have excluded from my study any extensive treatment of Weiss's last two works, the drama *The Trial* (1975–82) and the novel *Aesthetics of Resistance* (1981). Neither of these pieces advances any new ideas which affect the theme of my book, nor challenges the interpretation of Weiss's work which I have derived from his pre-1971 writings. The *Aesthetics of Resistance,* while highly significant from a literary-philosophical point of view, merely extends Weiss's thoughts upon the dilemma of the writer *engagé* as seen within the context of pre-World War II European Fascism. Weiss described the novel as a "wishful biography" since he identified himself with the narrator, freely mixed documentary and fictional materials, and sought to imagine how different his life might have been had he been raised among the proletariat. Thus the book is mainly of value as a comparison or even as a companion-piece to his earlier autobiographies, but it does not reveal much towards an understanding of his plays and stagecraft.

The much-revised play, *The New Trial,* is an adaptation of Kafka's famous work. It was first staged unsuccessfully as *The Trial* in Bremen in 1975, then re-written and successfully re-staged in Stockholm in 1982 under the personal direction of Peter and Gunilla Palmstierna-Weiss; and later in East Germany by the Berliner Ensemble. Many critics were quick to point out its weaknesses by comparison with Kafka's original; Weiss had radically adapted Kafka's universal theme of alienation and entrapment by transforming Joseph K. into a victim of capitalist exploitation. Audiences in Stockholm and East Berlin, though, found the production very enjoyable, and even amusing in many sections. I have referred briefly to these works where their themes or where Weiss's public comments seemed pertinent to my larger study. But I have not dealt in detail with the Kafka play since the script is not yet available and is currently being prepared for publication.

Finally, an exhaustive bibliography on this playwright is readily accessible in other critical works, most notably in the collection by Volker Canaris in his 1970 study, *Über Peter Weiss.* The bibliography here is therefore selective and contains only those works specifically referred to in the text, recent significant pieces not included in Canaris's anthology, and all the related material which I have found helpful in my investigation. A complete bibliography is currently being prepared by Gunilla Palmstierna-Weiss who plans to make all of Weiss's work available to scholars in a single collection which will probably be located in Frankfurt a.M., West Germany.

Acknowledgments

I wish to thank a number of individuals and groups whose suggestions, assistance, and support have made this book possible. Major acknowledgments must go to Professors William I. Oliver and David Littlejohn of the University of California at Berkeley whose critical opinions inspired and guided my investigation at many points. The Research and Development Committee and the School of Communications at Grand Valley State College provided generous financial support for completing the text and making travel arrangements. Julia Hennig of Suhrkamp Verlag provided invaluable assistance in locating press materials. Special thanks are also due to the following individuals who generously donated their time and materials in assembling the photographic sections of this book: Isolde Ohlbaum and Kurt Julius from Munich; Dr. Levi Fox of the Shakespeare Birthplace Trust; Hildegard Levermann-Westerholz from Rostock; Dr. Winrich Meiszies of the Düsseldorf Theater Museum; the staff of the library archives at the Berlin Volksbühne; and Portia Uhlitzsche of the Volkstheater Rostock.

Finally I must gratefully thank Gunilla Palmstierna-Weiss, who collaborated with her husband on all of his plays. The time and assistance she gave me in Stockholm in speaking about Peter Weiss helped me to clarify numerous areas of my research and introduced me to points of view which I would otherwise have overlooked. Her own plans for a book which would describe in detail the extent of their collaborations together, as well as her own work as a scenographer, will hopefully shed more intense light upon the subject of Peter Weiss's achievements than this present study could ever accomplish.

1

Art and Exploration, 1947–1963

Early Prose Words and Autobiographies

Peter Weiss began his literary work in 1947 at the age of 30. At that time he was living in Stockholm, having emigrated there from Great Britain in 1939 in order to pursue an artistic career. Initially Weiss had wanted to develop his ideas through painting, ideas which had been strictly personal and which, according to his own report, had little to do with the political upheavals surrounding him. As he remarked in his autobiography about this period of his life:

> I came to Stockholm to live as a painter. . . . For me there were no lost home and no thoughts of return, for I had never belonged anywhere. . . . I had attempted to break my last link and had left my parents' home in order to concentrate upon my work. Political and ideological demands were insignificant beside the great work that awaited me. . . . My painting was action, an expression of life: I wanted to choose it consciously as my alternative to taking part in the war.[1]

Although Weiss was able to exhibit some of his early paintings in Stockholm in 1941, and thus receive some public recognition of his work, during the war years he began to feel that painting was insufficient for expressing the kind of troubled feelings which the war aroused within him: the fear of the Fascist menace which all Jewish refugees carried about with them, the sympathy for childhood friends in Germany who had been swallowed up in the death camps, and most especially the discomfort of his own uncertain place in a wartime society which seemed to expect from him some political commitment as an artist and as a Jew.

It was only towards the close of World War II that Weiss put aside his painting and turned increasingly towards literature. In doing so he wished to resolve the tension he felt between his conflicting needs for artistic self-expression and social involvement; he hoped that writing would enable him to speak in precise terms about his complex experiences as a Jewish emigré. In his autobiography he recalled the idealistic thoughts he had at that time about the social contributions he could make as a writer: "If I were once to succeed in noting exactly what had happened to me, it could become part of the events on the border of which . . . other vigilant selfless ones were standing."[2] Though he was convinced of his vocation as a writer, he was also confused. He wondered what *kind* of writing he should undertake and, more importantly, what social purpose it should serve.

He first began by writing poems and journalistic accounts based upon his recent experiences; one collection of prose poems was self-published in Swedish in 1946, *Fran ö till ö*. Weiss also found work as a postwar European correspondent for a Stockholm newspaper, and a series of features which he wrote at that time (1947) appear to be his first published works. Weiss also wished to examine his early life and family background because he felt that the key to understanding his present condition lay in understanding his personal past. Thus he started the first part of his autobiography, *Vanishing-Point*, around 1947–48, and he continued with this project though the decade of the fifties.

His relationship as a writer to postwar European society was a third subject which he began to develop in several novels and experimental plays written between 1947 and 1963. This was a more important theme than the other two since it would run throughout much of his work for the remainder of his career. He described his stance towards society in 1946 as that of a person who was only beginning to emerge from adolescent interiority, as standing "between two poles which had been there from the very beginning, the pole of the *Thief of Baghdad* and the pole of *Taboo,* the pole of irrepressible life and the pole of transience." As a young boy in Germany he had been captivated by the Douglas Fairbanks film: "I once wanted to live like the Thief of Baghdad, I wanted to overcome all obstacles wildly and adventurously, to laugh at mortal dangers, to defeat all enemies and to find the treasure chest, to release the princess and win her for myself."[3] Several years later, after further literary and artistic exposure, he saw Murnau's film *Taboo,* a popular historical melodrama of heroes, villains, and kidnapped heroines. Weiss recalls "constantly musing over the final scene when the hero swims into the open sea after his abducted beloved and sinks ever further behind the boat until, overcome by exhaustion, he drowns, and finally only his hand is sticking out of the water."[4]

Weiss's comment on these two films indicates the general direction which his novels and plays took after 1947. Both films were romantic: one optimistic and the other tragic; and in each of them the hero encountered great obstacles in his passionate quest of a beautiful woman. In the polarity of Weiss's feeling towards these heroes' circumstances, in the vacillation between optimism and despair, or "irrepressible life and transience," we can see how Weiss hesitatingly chose his own responses to the uncertain world of postwar Europe. He wished to come to grips with social experience through literature, just as intensely as his cinema heroes had plunged into adventures without regard for the consequences. In artistic terms, Weiss's writing came to focus upon the minute details of his social surroundings. He no longer ignored society by relying solely upon inner imaginative visions as he felt he had done in his painting.[5] He tried instead to confront experience, to record and to present it in order to create "a unity between inner and outer reality. . . . He portrays the immediacy, the directness of life, the raw material, the essence."[6]

The Shadow of the Coachman's Body and *Conversation of the Three Wayfarers*

Weiss wrote two novels during this period which show how intensely he sought to come to grips with his social surroundings through literature. The first of these, *The Shadow of the Coachman's Body*, written in 1952, takes the form of a six-day diary by a first person narrator who minutely records everyday events in a nonchronological associative manner. A temporal framework is thus established in which the reader moves through a continuum of time present and time past, with only occasional interruptions to achieve a minimum of literary distance.

The novel is Kafka-esque in its use of unexplainable incidents, of familiar objects presented with sinister aspects, and in its hallucinatory merging of perception and reality. The narrator speaks from the standpoint of a distanced observer describing his environment indifferently, alienated from it but giving it meaning by his observation (in this example, by the act of writing):

> I continue keeping to the sensations that crowd in on me in my immediate surroundings; my hand guides the pencil over the paper, from word to word and line to line. . . . what else shall I do? And from this question grows the insight that my other activities also remain without result or purpose. Tracing the occurrences in front of my eyes with my pencil in order to give an outline to what I've seen, to make what I've seen clearer, in short, to make seeing into an occupation.[7]

The reader is immediately struck by the writer's uncompromising viewpoint. For example, the narrator found his inspiration to write while defecating in the farmyard outhouse: "Sitting bent forward, one's feet propped on the ledge in front of the box, one gets absorbed in small, mixed-up fragments of time, in events without beginning or end, often divided crosswise or up and down." The writer's literary stimulus also began under drugs, or with table salt rubbed into the eyes as he lay abed at night—an activity which ultimately stretched no farther than the desire "to bring up images." As the salt induced tears from the narrator's eyes, the ordinary features of the room dissolved into a fantastical assortment of "curves, swellings, grooves like those that grow out of the clay on the wheel . . . dappled planes in purple or pink . . . and figures like castles from a game of chess or ballet dancers." The experience then climaxed in the naked figure of a voluptuous woman, whose nearness the writer felt "so strongly that I took the image for reality and made a hasty movement with my arms which immediately tore the image."[8] Surface reality is made to yield suggestive images which become as firm, as certain and as tantalizing as the object itself.

The solidity of images—hallucinations, dreams, madmen's ravings—later became a recurrent feature of Weiss's work. In his surrealistic 1953 film, *Hallucinations,* Weiss played an intricate visual game on the interchangeability of image and reality. His presentation of French history through the eyes of Charenton lunatics in 1964, or of German history from the mouth of the raving Hölderlin in 1971, are other examples of this tendency. This radical correspondence between dream and reality assumed its most complex form in Weiss's 1969 drama about Leon Trotsky, in which the entire history of the Russian Revolution passed expressionistically like a nightmare vision before the eyes of the dying hero (and the audience). The narrator in *Coachman's Body* was unable to find a pattern to the numerous objects, incidents, and lives of the people with whom he shared his existence. The novel thus presented a sort of "catalogue" of reality, with events and details recorded as if on a filmstrip, but seemingly without a pattern.

It was the narrator's search for such a pattern which motivated the writing. As Weiss described his approach, "the medium of film has been introduced into the medium of language."[9] Walking through a room, for example, Weiss's narrator "grazed the edge of the sewing machine which had faint silver reflections on its spools and metal parts, went by the round table in whose open drawer [he] more assumed than saw buttons, hooks, needles and thread." In the novel, human activities are recorded without apparent emphasis or selection. At dinner the narrator registers the movements of his fellow boarders as they "hand around the mug like a mound of earth . . . flat hand as a lid on the mug . . . hand sideways for drinking." Experience becomes the activity of looking from the outside into a strange reality, just as at one point the narrator peers through a keyhole in order to spy on a family argument. One of the participants suddenly shifts his gaze: "His eye had turned away from the father and fixed on the keyhole in the door as if he could see my eye in the darkness behind the keyhole."[10] In several such instances, the reader is jolted by the writer's unique perspectives.

Although the narrator's environment seems chaotic, it does produce a powerful emotional impact upon him, and it is in this area that the essential nature of reality manifests itself in Weiss's novel. The very title of the work in German, *Der Schatten des Körpers des Kutschers,* offers a key to understanding Weiss's literary approach, as do the tangled German titles for the later plays on the French Revolution and Vietnam. Speech sounds of glottals and glides explode and slither across the tongue to provide suggestions of physicality, a hint of sinister activity, and the mysterious imagery of "shadow" and "coachman." The title phonetically suggests the author's mood and the novel's tone. Of all Weiss's prose writings this one suffers the least in translation because it depends for its impact not so much upon the semantics of the language or upon syntax as upon the imaginative point of view. Consider the following treatment of a social tea in the housekeeper's room, wherein Weiss extracts grotesque possibilities from the situation:

> The housekeeper jumped up, knocking over the half-full coffee mug; the coffee ran over the table and into the lap of the mother who couldn't move away fast enough; the housekeeper heaved herself sideways past the father, Schnee, and the captain, and hit the glass the captain was holding in front of himself; and the contents of the glass, only a few drops, it is true, ran down the lapel of his cutaway; the mother, shaking her skirt and squeezing by the table, caught her foot on the leg of the table, losing her shoe; then she stumbled towards the father who had time enough to open his arms and catch her, but not time to put down the mug in one hand and the glass in the other, which made both coffee and liqueur splatter over both the mother's dress and the father's pants. The housekeeper, her hands ready to grab the key to the music-box (which was to come loose in her hand), in sweeping by caught the iron on the table with the bow of her apron strings; and the iron fell on something which had been withdrawn the moment the housekeeper ran by, but which immediately pushed forward again: Mr. Schnee's foot.[11]

That the novel seems to overwork such comic grotesque technique is ultimately less a literary judgment than a description of Weiss's view of the world. Just as in the plays of Samuel Beckett, where nonaction is turned into a dramatic value par excellence—and Beckett was one of Weiss's favorite writers—Weiss gains powerful emotional mileage by using perfectly ordinary material.

Another noteworthy feature of this novel is Weiss's handling of characters. By reducing the characters to the level of puppets who perform their actions like automata, Weiss intensifies the reader's sense of becoming another depersonalized and impotent individual, caught up in the mechanical flux of experience. It is important to note in this respect that all of Weiss's dramatic writings utilize puppets and mannequins in just this way. One thinks immediately of the figure of the Bogey in *Lusitanian Bogeyman,* the Punch-and-Judy clownlike characters in *Night with Guests* and *Mockinpott,* or the mannequin-like behavior of many of the Charenton inmates who are controlled by the puppet master, Sade.

After proceeding from one event to another over the course of six days, Weiss finalizes all his impressions in a single dense image which seems one of the finest passages in modern German prose. Late at night after the household is asleep, the narrator sees from his window the shadows of the coachman and the housekeeper in coitus. They become silhouetted in the flickering light of the kitchen lamp, and the novel concludes with a grim restatement of the allegory of Plato's cave:

> After a violent side movement of the bodies, the shadow of the coffee pot broke free from the shadow of the hand and fell down; for a few seconds, the shadows of the bodies came apart; the housekeeper's body with the arching breast line leaned back on the table; the coachman's shadow opened up and rose up high with wild gestures and as if flapping his

wings, throwing off the bulk of his coat's shadow. After the coat's shadow had slid off the shadow of the coachman's body, the shadow of the coachman's body thrust forward again, and the shadow of the housekeeper's body came to meet him with the shadows of the housekeeper's arms reaching into the shadow of the coachman's body, by and around it. . . . The shadow of the coachman's arms bent toward the shadow of his lower body and pulled out a rodlike shadow which, in form and position, corresponded to his sexual organ; this questing shadow he thrust in the heavy, full shadow of the housekeeper's body . . . and the shadow of the coachman's body threw itself with full force into the shadow of the housekeeper's body, whereupon the shadows of both bodies fusing, broke down and stayed stretched out on the shadow of the table, rising and falling in heavy respiration.[12]

Weiss's second novel, *Conversation of the Three Wayfarers,* pursued much the same tack as *Coachman's Body* in its stance towards a world randomly populated by objects, activities, and the comings and goings of anonymous people. Although it was completed nearly 10 years later, it was published by Suhrkamp together with *Coachman's Body;* and critics have usually approached the novels as complementary because of their surrealistic perspectives upon the material.

Three Wayfarers takes the form of a series of recorded conversations by three anonymous travelers in an anonymous European metropolis:

They were men who did nothing but walk, walk, walk. They were big, they were bearded, they wore leather caps and long raincoats, they called themselves Abel, Babel and Cabel, and while they walked they talked to each other. They walked and looked around and saw what there was to see, and they talked about it and about other things that had happened . . . since they looked alike they were taken for brothers by passersby, but they were not brothers at all, they were men who walked walked walked, having met each other by chance, Abel and Babel, and then Abel, Babel and Cabel.[13]

From such an unassuming opening paragraph Weiss then opens the door upon a startling world which he describes as a "Fragment": "a surreal but certainly not unreal waxworks."[14] The central image of a heavily trafficked bridge spanning a wide river becomes the focal point for the narrators' conversations. Although none of them can recall when it was built or ever having seen it before, it stimulates them to speak of fantasies, half-remembered incidents, vague personal experiences, and hypothetical possibilities concerning people, city life, buildings, garbage dumps, automobiles, and anything else which happens to occur to them.

In contrast to *Coachman's Body,* here the reader's attention is split into three perspectives which are equally important and illuminating. Weiss's intention remained basically the same: he was trying to objectify and explore his experience, rendering reality in its full complexity and in all its confusing detail. As one critic aptly described Weiss's approach, "the three perspectives are like as many nets cast into a sea of reality . . . a sample of reality made more real by its division into three temperaments."[15] It was also a strategy of self-effacement for Weiss, whereby the writer tried to remove himself from the scene entirely in order to present it through others' eyes.

Simply to recount the narrative threads or the host of unrelated phenomena which flesh out this surreal *Panoptikum* would lead to little real appreciation of Weiss's accomplishment. For this reason many critics have addressed themselves to other aspects, such as the author's possible search for personal freedom, or the psychological dissection of Weiss's personality, or even the analysis of his boyhood milieu in order to explain his later turn towards socialist thinking. From a philosophical standpoint, however, it is necessary to answer first a few questions about the activity of writing as Weiss's method of symbolically making contact with the world.

In the sense in which Kenneth Burke speaks of literature as a "strategy designed to encompass a situation," we ought to regard Weiss's two novels as attempts to make contact with a world which the writer regarded as radically different from his perception of it. Just as Weiss's narrator in *Coachman's Body* feels the impulse to write of his experience in order to organize it, so too did Weiss begin to apprehend the postwar world by documenting its many details faithfully and without apparent bias. He took a similar course years later when he explored the possibilities of documentary drama for explaining complicated political situations. Thus it is important to note that here in the 1950s Weiss already sensed that his activity as a writer could lead him outward, away from interiority and into closer touch with society.

An important parallel to this situation is the case of Arthur Adamov who also moved from absurdity to political writing for the same reason—to externalize his awareness. In Adamov's case, insight came in the form of a "dream" of a postage stamp from Belgium which bore the image of the Belgian lion. In *Professor Taranne,* Adamov for the first time named an actual place, a place existing in the real world—Belgium. As Adamov remarked: "This looks like a trifle, but it was, nevertheless, the first time that I emerged from the no man's land of poetry and dared to call things by their name."[16] While Adamov moved from fiction through the real object of a postage stamp to ideological realities, Weiss moved from confusing personal experience *through his literary art* to the same point of contact with reality.[17] In fact, by writing these early novels from a radical narrative perspective, Weiss was actually creating a game with his reader in hopes of "trapping" him into identifying with his own viewpoint. In this way, the two novels became the basis for a closely shared experience between author and reader.

In these two prose experiments, Weiss perceived the apparent lack of pattern in objects and events surrounding him. Bewilderment and alienation were his responses to the phenomena he recorded in *Coachman's Body; Three Wayfarers* created an even more chaotic situation for the reader on account of the three separate narrators. In both novels events are presented in all of their confusing simultaneity rather than as parts of an intelligible pattern. Derivative of Kafka, Henry Miller, or surrealism though they may be, the novels are far more important as reflections of the author's immediate impulse to render experience strictly according to his dominant and evanescent mood at the time of writing.

This conclusion is supported by two essays which Weiss wrote and published at the same time as *Three Wayfarers*. In his 1963 essay on avant-garde films, Weiss mentions one film by Germaine Dulac, and a portion of his criticism on this early absurdist work bears quoting at length. It clarifies Weiss's stance toward the visual imagery he used in *Three Wayfarers*, which plays so large a part in his literary development at this time:

> Such a complex theme can only be ambiguously rendered on film. There is no resolution to the plot. *There emerges only the impulse to narrat.* We blink here as in a dream. These indistinct thoughts, filled with the raw images of experience, are part of myself, having a more powerful effect on me than all the logical turns of plot which a more traditional film could ever produce. After seeing this film I've completely forgotten what everything led to, I can't even distinguish one character from another any longer; I find myself in unfamiliar surroundings, and it doesn't interest me at all what anyone has said—in fact, I'm completely indifferent as to how the so-called plot turned out or what was said. But yet I've become part of it all—the activity of my own moods and fantasies has been stimulated, I've been thrown directly up against the experience itself, and been brought face-to-face with its ultimate insolubility.[18]

These statements reflect the attitude of a man suddenly confronting a world familiar, perhaps, to others (and this is part of its terror) but unfamiliar to himself. Although he is able to observe that world in all its baffling complexity, reality yields no clear pattern. It permits only a journalistic catalogue of its many unrelated components and welcomes only a literary posture of exploration.

The shadow-ground of experience where the self encounters the other, the no-man's-land lying between perception and fact—these concerns form the narrative topic of both novels. The writer begins to extend feelers into the world which he had previously avoided and feared. Weiss's activity as a writer was helping him make this contact with society because language, however limited, will in any case reflect the writer's intention to move outward and to communicate. It is the beginning of this movement on Weiss's part which is important to our study.[19]

Weiss's understanding of the world during the period of the early novels emerges less as an "understanding" than as an artistic exploration. He must continue to investigate and to make contact with the outer world, just as his three-in-one wayfarers, Abel-Babel-Cabel, must persist in their own search at the novel's conclusion: "And I crept down the road and ran breathlessly along the path on the riverbank, here, where streets have now been built, bridges and underpinnings for wharves, here where we are walking, walking, walking."[20] Like the fragments of conversation recorded in *Coachman's Body*, this novel is not a conventional story which moves from a beginning, through a middle, finally reaching an end. It is merely a segment snatched from life. Both

Coachman's Body and *Three Wayfarers* demonstrate the flux of experience; as Weiss described it, they are like newspapers torn up into sheets for toilet paper. The problem for the narrator, and for Peter Weiss, is to find a continuous thread of experience. It is a linguistic exercise to a certain extent, but it is founded in Weiss's everyday experience, his own peculiar imaginative fantasy, and in his desire to communicate.

The Tower

In 1946 and 1947 the literary outlets for both younger and older German authors were extremely limited because of the shortage of funds for the publishing industry and the cautious political stance of editors and contributors in a fast-changing society. Alfred Andersch's literary magazine, *Der Ruf,* provided one focal point for many writers, most of them exiles and all of them in some way deformed by the recent German experience. As Peter Demetz describes the immediate postwar literary scene in his book, *Postwar German Literature,* "good intentions were more numerous than new manuscripts, and what publications there were . . . followed literary tradition instead of breaking new ground." The poems and prose of the postwar period, he continues, "contained the belated classicism of the 'inner emigration' and the inevitable folksong stanzas on cities in ruins, but only a few . . . suggested potential changes of poetic idiom."[21]

Within a few years, however, the genre of the lyrical radio play began to command the energies of writers because the broadcasting industry—under postwar funding programs from foreign sources—was financially much stronger than the publishing industry. Friedrich Dürrenmatt, Max Frisch, Martin Walser and others were some of the many German authors who were well paid for their radio plays during the late forties and early fifties. The genre of the *Hörspiel,* in contrast to the revivals of foreign plays which dominated the stage, soon achieved great popularity among German-speaking audiences. It was within this context that Peter Weiss's first drama, *The Tower,* was written for radio in 1948.

The play is a poetic parable which describes the life and death of the circus artist Pablo. As a child he had been mysteriously dropped off at the tower's doorstep, "left on the threshold, just like a dirty bundle,"[22] and had been raised by the Director and the Manageress who ran the tower's circus act, famous for the virtuosity of its performers. Pablo had been trained by the Director as an acrobat, performing a ball-balancing routine in the show along with Carlo the weightlifter, a Magician, Nelly the lion tamer's assistant, and a deformed Dwarf in the freak show. Eventually Pablo escaped from the mysterious tower where everyone lived and rehearsed: he was encouraged by the Magician, who then treacherously sounded the alarm. The lion with whom Pablo escaped was shot in the melee, and for many years thereafter nothing was ever heard of

Pablo. The play begins with Pablo's return to the tower as he seeks to rejoin the circus, this time as an escape artist. He secretly hopes to demonstrate his independence of the tower, believing that only in this way can he be truly free from the influences he once suffered there, and be able to embark on his own life.

Weiss left no doubt in his listeners' minds that his play was to be taken allegorically. In a prologue to the broadcast, he explained the play's allegorical structure and pointed out its references to themes of existential freedom, dependency upon the past, and the psychological makeup of personality. Thus Pablo's return to the tower of his childhood, Weiss declared, "is like forcing his way into his inner self. Only when he tries to break deep into the tower once again and confront his past face-to-face, can he perhaps free himself."[23] The social configuration of the tower's inhabitants reflects the structure of Pablo's personality and family influences. The Director and Manageress represent his parents, "two old people; . . . they'd still want to capture me with their weaknesses . . . with their lonelinesses"; Nelly, the Lion Tamer's beautiful assistant who was killed in the circus ring, is the "ghost of his love"; the Magician represents "all death wishes" and "is the strongest force in the tower"; the lion who was killed in Pablo's escape was the "headstrong" side of his personality, and he is now replaced by "the Dwarf, crooked and misshapen." By returning to this symbolical home, Pablo "wants to defy the power of the tower" because "he was not really free. The tower still lives inside of him with a stifling heaviness." He enters disguised under the pseudonym of Niente: "By this he means that he is nothing. When he first freed himself from the tower he found himself, he found his own name."

In its psychological analysis of a young man recognizing his dependency upon his past and trying to break free of parental influences, the play is directly related to Weiss's need to seek out and explore the roots of his personal situation in 1946–47. Weiss states this explicitly in his autobiography when he describes his separation from his parents as a defeat, "not the defeat of the emigrant in the face of the difficulties of living in exile, but the defeat of one who does not dare to free himself from dependence."[24]

His dependence upon his parents as a young man and their perpetual opposition to his artistic inclinations are recurring themes throughout all of his autobiographical writings. His mother was more sympathetic towards his attempts at painting and writing than his father. She had been an actress with the great Max Reinhardt prior to World War I, a career which she abandoned when she married. His father had been a soldier who later turned successfully to textile manufacturing. Although both Weiss's parents were cultured and well read, and although Weiss was exposed in the family homes to the latest and most significant writers of the early twentieth century, nevertheless he received strong pressure from his parents to enter some type of commercial profession.

Weiss resented this pressure and felt that his authoritarian and middle-class Jewish upbringing provided no encouragement for his personal artistic development. He described his childhood as a period of "yawning emptiness . . . like the dull ache of an ulcer."[25] As the political pressure upon Jews intensified in the early 1930s, and Weiss's family was forced to emigrate, the economic survival of the family's business became a central concern for them all, and Weiss began more and more to assist his father in his work. He spent long hours preparing contracts, handling correspondence, and making translations of technical material. But in his spare time, especially in London, Weiss would visit the coffee houses and meet other writers and painters, and he would devote much of his weekend time to his own painting. He lived a "schizoid" life, particularly in Britain during these years. As the family business declined there and they were forced to emigrate, this time to Czechoslovakia, Weiss felt even more of a need to pursue his own personal artistic development. When he arrived in Prague, he immediately began to study painting under the famous Willi Novak, who secured for Weiss a scholarship and his parents' support for enrolling in the Prague Academy. Weiss commented in his autobiography, "I could not make my parents realize that for me painting and writing were work. Their accusations from outside had steeped me in profound listlessness. Every day I began my work with a feeling of absolute uselessness."[26]

Weiss did many fine paintings during the year and a half he was in Prague, and won the Academy's highest prize as a visual artist. He referred to this period as the first time in his life that he could wholeheartedly commit himself to artistic work, and he spent his summers trekking through the Alps and seeking out other writers there wherever he went. His painting work was extremely productive, and it was at this time (1938–39) that he made contact with Hermann Hesse, whom he had long admired. Fortunately for Weiss, the two men got along very well together—Hesse even secured for him a commission to illustrate two of his books—and Weiss lengthened his stay in Switzerland until the winter, thus avoiding the occupation of Czechoslovakia by the German forces. Practically all of his early paintings which he had left in Prague were destroyed by his mother when his parents fled the country to take up residence in Sweden. And when Weiss rejoined them in Göteborg in early 1940, it was extremely difficult for him to reside once again under the parental roof. It was soon after this, in 1940, that Weiss rented a studio in Stockholm to paint in a climate of artistic freedom, although he still "commuted" to his father's factory each week in order to earn money and survive, since he was unable to sell his paintings and support himself.

What is most significant about *The Tower* is the fact that by 1948 when he finished it, Weiss recognized that the possiblity of freedom from his parental upbringing and social class was only an illusion. His hero dies strangled in the attempt to release himself from the tower's bonds; the past is part of him and cannot be excised. "Powers of an unsuspected strength have kept him helplessly bound," declares the Magician figure as Pablo performs his act. "Now finally he seems to have realized the uselessness of his efforts." In death, however, Pablo gasps, "Nothing here can touch me anymore . . . I'm free." Out of the absolute silence which ensues when all the characters' voices have been stilled at last, an anonymous voice-over announces, "The rope dangles down from him now like an umbilical cord."

This was Weiss's first literary attempt between the autobiographical period of 1945–47 and *Coachman's Body* in 1952. When we compare this play with the later novel in terms of their attitudes towards the outer world and towards the author's past, it seems clear that Weiss first felt it necessary in *The Tower* to accept the painful memories of his childhood as part of himself; and that only later—by the time of *Coachman's Body*—could he begin to objectify that experience in a realistic way, pessimistic though it might be.

The most striking aspect of *The Tower*'s theme is the skill with which Weiss avoided any simplistic rejection of his past. Pablo is continually forced to admit his own share of responsibility for his upbringing—a factor of sensitivity and guilt which complicates the dramatic action of the allegory to a great extent. The parental expectations which Weiss denounced in his autobiography became encapsulated in *The Tower* in the image of the ball-balancing act.[27] Pablo refuses to perform publicly any longer, "always the audience's favorite. Beautiful in your white knitted tights with your powdered face and your long black hair," as the death-wish Magician taunts him. "But I'm not Pablo any more! I'm not going to balance on that ball any more!" Pablo screams.

The power of this early play lies in its subtle manner of forcing Pablo/Weiss to recognize his childhood role-playing. "I'll rip you out of me!" he threatens. But the Voices turn all his accusations back upon himself: "Just what do you want from us anyway? We have our own life here. You're the one who sees only distortions! You can't criticize us!" Pablo must admit the truth of this: "It's true . . . my real bonds were everywhere. Everything I touched—bondage. Every word, every feeling is still sealed up tight, here inside this tower." For Weiss in 1948, childhood exile was only another reflection of the existential exile he had always experienced.

These are not the thoughts of a man trying "to fight the introspective middle-class *bohemien* in himself" as some critics have maintained.[28] Instead they seem to be a young writer's attempt to grapple with that middle-class experience by integrating it with his current situation through relentless self-analysis, by a making present of the past in the manner of a realist unafraid of what his investigation may turn up. It is highly significant that early in his career Weiss demonstrated this ability to approach his material—whether deeply personal as in *The Tower* or detached and fictional as in *Coachman's Body*—with an all-inclusive, objective, and exploratory frame of mind. *The Tower* displays Weiss's absolute fairness to every aspect of his subject; he rejects nothing in his search for understanding.

The Insurance

Between 1952 and 1963 when Weiss finished his autobiography, he made three experimental films and wrote three dramas, and he produced three translations of Strindberg. With *Vanishing-Point, The Tower,* and *Coachman's Body* behind him, he began work in 1952 upon something which he termed a "surrealistic visionary" play, *The Insurance.* He intended to create "a multi-media production in which film footage of different scenes would accompany actual stage performance." The result would be "smaller onstage action blended together with pictures of the larger social scene; bringing the outer world into the theatre space; expanding the dramatic action by the use of film; stage action, documentary footage of riots and natural catastrophes."[29]

This is a very important yet little-known play in the canon of Weiss's work. The drama was not performed until 1966 when it received a studio production at the University of Göteborg. The reason for this probably lies in the technical complexity of its multi-media design. Weiss pointed out that the play was experimental and, along with other works which remained unpublished and unperformed at this time, it grew directly out of his film studies of the early fifties. Weiss's concept of combining film and stage action recalls the early constructivist and epic style productions which followed World War I, theatrical styles which would heavily influence his major plays 10 years later. Most critics have classified *The Insurance* as imitative of the German theatrical heritage of the Weimar period, although it does prefigure the mid-sixties German concern with theater of the absurd by almost a decade.

The play offers its own particularly modern viewpoint towards surrealist and expressionist themes, and this is only natural. Post-World War I troubles have not disappeared but have become more complex and acute in our time, and modern treatments of such ideas—particularly those by Weiss—always bear their own unmistakably contemporary stamp.[30] *The Insurance* makes good use of pantomime, vaudeville, and Artaudian elements, and thus it must be regarded as less imitative than experimental in its design. In addition its social issues are pertinent to modern society. As Weiss remarked in his autobiography about the legacy of the Weimar years when he first discovered writers like Tzara, Huelsenbeck, and Kayser: "Everything that had been attacked during that decade still existed today."[31] His return to earlier German theatrical ideas in the play was not just a technical experiment (this was to be his first stage drama) but also a move which had contemporary purchase and good future potential.

Because of its subject of rebellion, this play has something in common with *The Tower.* In this case, however, the treatment is satirical and political rather than analytical and introspective. In *The Insurance,* Weiss shows the breaking down of middle-class family, society, and industry by the forces of historical change, portrayed in their general destructive aspects of animality and sexuality. His target is bourgeois society, the social class from whose influence he had long been trying to free himself, and which he loathed as "this entirely twisted, guilt-laden, doomed and damned bourgeoisie."[32] The basic conceit of the drama involves society's attempt to "insure" itself against every possible historical accident, and the playwright's hilarious demonstration of the absurdity of such a middle-class idea.

Weiss begins the play at a bourgeois dinner party where the influential members of the community (police chief, bank directors, corporate executives) consider the possibility of taking out insurance policies to cover any eventuality, thus preserving the status quo. After one of the drunken guests suffers an accident during a striptease, the entire party moves to the local hospital where the insane Dr. Kübel performs surgery on the victim, and then throws everyone into confinement as subjects for experiments. Kübel returns home through a deafening tornado and abuses his wife, who has been patiently awaiting his return from the office. He is abused in turn by his son Leo, a muscular, brainless sexual athlete who seduces married women and who eventually comes to lead revolutionary mobs rampaging through the city. After several rapidly alternating scenes in which Weiss shows the breakdown of domestic relationships because of Leo's sexual liaisons and the collapse of the political-economic system as a result of the mass kidnapping, the scene shifts again to the hospital where the "guests" are being fed, clothed, tortured, and abused by pathological warders.

Weiss establishes numerous connections between the hospital staff and Leo, thus clarifying their function as destructive forces of revolution in a very general way. Meanwhile the police chief has been vacationing with his mistress at a seaside resort. Although he is curious about the disappearance of the city notables, he remains unbothered by this fact—as well as by the calamitous revolution and various natural catastrophes which have also occurred. When he decides to get a haircut, however, he emerges from the barbershop missing his hat, moustache, clothes, and curly black hair. Change and revolution have caught up with him too, Weiss implies. No one recognizes him any longer, his mistress abandons him, and the gendarmes jail him for creating a nuisance. Despite his protests he no longer resembles the photo of their leader upon the wall. He has completely lost his identity, and can only look on as an outsider when Leo leads the rioting mobs past the jailhouse to shouts of "Freedom! Down with tyranny! *Vive la révolution!*"[33]

In its reliance upon type figures and situations, its political target of industrialists and financiers, its blatant disregard of probability, and its grotesque satire, the play obviously shares much with avant-garde plays of the early twentieth century. In Weiss's search for artistic models during his period of political exile, he had discovered the work of artists like Gertrude Stein, Kayser, Jarry, Toller and Oskar Schlemmer. He felt that "the pictures and the sculpture, the plays, dances, films, fiction, and music were not isolated but embodied values which one could continue to develop."[34] What he admired most about these artists was their radicalism in revolting against social order, against normality and western European notions of progress: they were "saboteurs," he felt, "destroyers of the home." They courageously held up "direct reality" to the faces of the bourgeoisie and for this they had been persecuted and their works banned.

Because of the "reality content" of their work, Weiss felt their words had survived the wreck of the social order which they had attacked. Thus these artists had proven themselves historically more viable, and their ideas had contemporary purchase. "They didn't propose solutions," Weiss observed, "but they always stood at the beginning of a process. They tried to grow and keep exploring. And the more conformist the world became, the more this unrespectable, rebellious art came to be a living reality. We too need such strong artistic statements once again—in our self-satisfied, complacent, and sleepy condition!"[35]

Derivative as Weiss's play may be, the drama displays numerous modern features and signals Weiss's later development as a major playwright. One of these features is the drama's relentless attitude towards its subject. The tone established by the callousness and morbidity of its characters' activities is unrelieved throughout. This is probably the major source of the drama's interest; the intensity of the visual imagery is conditioned not so much by psychological perspectives (as in expressionist and surrealist plays) as it is by the grotesque sociopolitical standpoint from which the satire is delivered.

Another important feature of the staging is the way in which Weiss reverses our expectations and reveals the grotesque side of events with a sudden twist. Familiar situations are instantly transformed into threatening and unfamiliar ones by the unexpected eruption of violence. The hospital orderly Grudek, for example, suddenly lunges at Dr. Kübel's assistant and rapes her inside a coal bin, while miners unconcernedly eat their lunch and look on. Dr. Kübel's operating room with its impressive array of medical hardware and professional staff suddenly becomes a hideous experimental laboratory which recalls the terror of Caligari or of Auschwitz, and which prefigures the psychotic megalomania in Dürrenmatt's *The Physicists*. In addition, the perfectly ordinary experience of a police chief visiting a barbershop turns into a nightmare of lost identity, revolution, and natural catastrophes.

In addition to this scenic dynamism, Weiss's handling of characters is vivid, strong, and confident; his approach is neatly designed to attack bourgeois society and to deny any possibility for improvement. Social leaders are portrayed as gross, bestial parasites. At the dinner party, reminiscent of the terrifying caricatures of Georg Grosz, the guests fornicate with each other and slaver over the meal, and a drooling hound sits at the table, presiding over all the activities as the guest of honor. The wife of the police chief later tries to copulate with Leo in her own bedroom, surrounded by her sleeping children and husband. Unlike many expressionist works, there is no optimistic note sounded in *The Insurance;* there are no social reformers nor idealistic poets. No one is allowed to express anything more than despair, decadence, violence, and bestiality. It is this intense Artaudian vision which marks the play as peculiarly modern, and the drama's incisive social criticism is a feature which will recur in Weiss's later plays of the sixties.

The play's demands upon actors is another noteworthy feature. "From the beginning," said Weiss in a 1966 interview with Paul Gray, "everything I have done has been extremely visual—even my novels—and this is essential to the staging of my plays. I have chosen my media so that they were visual, and sometimes I have forced them to be so."[36] *The Insurance* reflects this concern in its use of pantomime. Sometimes Weiss uses it to compress the plot, such as in scenes 3 and 5 when Kübel performs journeys through lightning, wind, and rainstorms. Occasionally pantomime provides comic relief, as in scene 2 when the hospital staff perform a vaudeville routine to set up operating equipment in the surgical room. Erna's wordless, sexually perverse dance with the dog which closes the first scene provides the occasion for Leo's mysterious entrance, and establishes the erotic-grotesque tone of the drama through gesture and tableau. Some of Weiss's later pantomimic techniques, therefore, can be found here in embryo.

A final point of contact between *The Insurance* and the contemporary theater is the way in which Weiss's developing existentialist ideas controlled the dramatic issues. Here as in *Marat/Sade* and *Trotsky,* revolution is regarded more as a philosophical phenomenon than as a political one. Although Weiss would later formulate more precise observations upon the subject of terrorism, and even sympathize with radicals like Marat and Trotsky, in *The Insurance* he makes no distinction between "revolution" and "copulation." Leo, the revolutionary leader, bays at the moon and howls at neighborhood dogs in heat as though he were a dog himself. He has no other ambition—as his father repeatedly reminds him—than to seduce the nasty wives of public officials and businessmen. Weiss plays off the breakdown of marital relationships against the breakdown of bourgeois society in general. Violence assumes major proportions here and politics becomes simply another human urge towards oppression, cruelty, sadism, and destruction—ideas which will recur in all the later plays.

Because of Leo's self-indulgent anarchy Weiss suggests that revolution is the most evident manifestation of ordinary processes of historical change. "Big things are happening today," Leo tells his mother as he unconcernedly devours a disgusting breakfast, "changes. Overturnings. . . . The hour of freedom has struck . . . *Vive la révolution!*" This is much more Ionesco than Brecht because Weiss is speaking existentially. For Weiss, social upheaval in the modern world has more than just a political face. Revolution and historical change also manifest themselves through the brutalization of the ruling class by their own instruments of power, through Leo's glands, the police chief's moustache, or

Kübel's state-supported medical atrocities. He shows historical development to be beyond everyone's control—except perhaps for Leo who seems to reap enormous personal advantage from it. The movement of history, Weiss seems to say, is absurd, cruel, and grotesque; after World War II there can be no insurance against human barbarism and political catastrophe.

Eleven Years of Research

A seven-year period of study and experiment followed *The Insurance*. The visual media occupied much of Weiss's attention during this time. His paintings and experimental films continued to receive exhibitions in Stockholm, and he was slowly earning the dubious distinction of a "restless immigrant . . . an ambitious mediocrity in all three media—novels, paintings, films."[37] He continued to translate articles for publishers and he designed textile patterns for his father's business in order to support himself. He was working in isolation, and he would publish nothing until the end of the fifties. His major activity was the study of the development of the European avant-garde between the wars: the growth of absurdist writing by Ionesco, Beckett, and Henry Miller, and the dramatic works of Strindberg, Artaud, and Brecht.

Weiss learned much from this experimental period about dramatic technique. He was especially impressed by the cinema on account of his background as a graphic artist and his enjoyment of films as a young boy. As he traced the development of camera technique in avant-garde filmmakers like Méliès, Edwin Porter, and Durand, he came to admire the way in which they broke down static narration and provided different perspectives by "the trucking camera shot, the closeup, the montage . . . methods by which the spectator's viewpoint could be immediately shifted, in which the exterior and interior scenes could be juxtaposed and their different *tempi* combined."[38]

Weiss was also impressed by the avant-garde filmmakers' attitudes towards society. Weiss remarked upon their social role as artistic outcasts, and he admired their attack upon the social order of the middle class in their art. He discovered that "everyday, familiar objects were separated from their usual contexts and used to produce surprising conflicts." This was the basis of Brecht's alienation effect, of course, and throughout Weiss's essay on these filmmakers he referred to various techniques of shocking the spectator into new awareness by suddenly establishing surprising connections between objects and incidents.[39]

Unlike earlier experimenters with the *V-Effekt*, though, Weiss avoided emphasis upon shock value, feeling that they had paid too much attention to breaking down existing values without providing constructive alternatives. He felt they had created an art of destruction instead of communication. He learned that his own playwriting technique could borrow many effects which the avant-garde had developed, but only if they were augmented by a deeper sensitivity to the contemporary problems of Western industrialized society:

There was Antonin Artaud the forerunner of today's absurdists: Ionesco, Adamov, Beckett. He wanted a theatre of cruelty, and by this he meant a theatre in which the audience would be exposed to psychic shock. The film *La Coquille et le Clergyman,* however, used something of Artaud's visionary dramatic form, something borrowed from these unruly modifications, these ecstatic incidents which had themselves been borrowed from the Chinese and Balinese drama—but the film used them with a lyrical-aesthetic tone which was foreign to Artaud. He had wanted a ruthless, hard style, had tried to bring the spectator into a state of panic with his unrestrained situations. But Germaine Dulac produced a more hermetic work—and it is certainly intriguing through its basic lyricism, in which something of a dark Oedipus drama is suggested by means of hallucinatory images.[40]

This concern for lyricism signals one of Weiss's most important discoveries, and sets his work apart from many other political-historical playwrights of the modern period. Lyricism appealed to a young writer who had less a political program to deliver than a deep-seated awareness of personal loneliness and historical upheaval. These factors still had not surfaced in his work. He had been "caught" between the two romantic poles of *Taboo* and the *Thief of Baghdad* for many years. He had hesitantly been directing his attention outwards through the novels in order to find some points of contact in an alien postwar society. Through his autobiographies he had tried to discover the key to his problems in his own past and parental upbringing. He had examined this past experience, and in *The Insurance* he had attacked it viciously. He had found nothing redemptive in bourgeois society, and in the drama he argued for its absolute destruction (the desire for a "social cleansing" which would soon be reflected in the play about Marat). By the end of the fifties, however, as this statement on Germaine Dulac demonstrates, Weiss began to feel that there was more to be said about social problems and historical change than was possible through simple opposition and satire or didactic moralizing.

These developing ideas were also strengthened by Weiss's contact with the plays of Strindberg, a dramatist in whose work he recognized "an existence full of menace, persecution, and murky phenomena. . . . He gave me courage and strength, just as cruel fairy tales had done for me earlier, and it was better to recognize disaster when it confronted you than to grope in the dark."[41] Strindberg had been a social realist, Weiss felt, as well as a social critic and a rebel. He thought this was Strindberg's most important characteristic, and he titled his essay on the man "Against the Laws of Normality."

Strindberg's insanity, Weiss felt, was a form of realism par excellence in the face of a world which "was too narrow, and thus he was actually a pioneer and everything he wrote or did should cause a startling re-awakening" of human consciousness today. Weiss was surprised to discover just how much Strindberg had influenced the course of Western drama; he believed that "we stand today at the beginning of a new age of Strindberg. . . . We can see what followed him—surrealism, Beckett, Adamov, Ionesco, Henry Miller."[42] During this time Weiss began work on translations of Strindberg's plays, three of which were finally published by Suhrkamp in 1963: *Miss Julie, The Father,* and *A Dream Play*.

Strindberg also gave Weiss an answer to the problem of historical optimism versus existential despair. Strindberg had found political revolution too narrow; instead he had espoused an existential rebellion bordering on anarchy. "He never became a fighter for the people," Weiss remarked, "but he recognized and identified the new industrial society with its unfortunate, materialistically enslaved men. He held fast to his anarchy because only here could he think with absolute freedom and self awareness." Strindberg's highest accomplishment, Weiss felt, lay in his ability to create and to write honestly despite his isolation, his insanity, and the opposition he encountered during his career.

This idea of remaining true to one's inner convictions through difficult periods of loneliness and personal suffering would continue to fascinate Weiss as late as 1971. He would see it in Marat isolated in his bath, in Trotsky pursued in Mexico, in Che Guevara, Hölderlin, and others who had endured social rejection and yet remained convinced of the soundness of their views. In his 1962 essay on Strindberg, Weiss saw it reflected in his famous declaration: "By my writing I shall uncover a synthesis of natural science, poetry, and madness. I shall throw off the mask which I have scarcely accepted and give my seditious thought free rein, I shall think, think, think without cowardice, without reservation."[43]

Night with Guests

Many of these ideas on alienation, dramatic lyricism, and the dark aspects of Strindbergian thought found their way into the short *Moritat, Night with Guests,* which Weiss first staged in the studio of Berlin's Schiller Theater in November of 1963. Having written no plays since *The Insurance* 10 years previously, he now found inspiration in the Punch-and-Judy plays of circus shows. Weiss was fascinated mostly by their lusty, vigorous world where even the most barbarous acts could be frankly presented and cheerfully accepted.

> There was no intrigue and no human souls were depicted, the problems were plowed under by slapsticks and stabs with a knife. Everything happened blow-by-blow. . . . And they were all unkillable, they were all only crackable wood, they'd stand right up again and grin with their chipped faces. The Punch-and-Judy stage stood in the fairgrounds every year, near the tootling carousel, amidst the shouts of the barkers, the splendid pictures of *Moritat* scenes, the Magicians and the Freaks who peopled the fairway. It was one of the many things which turned the whole spectacle into a theatrical stage which I'm bringing to life again: The puppet-booth.[44]

The simplicity of the Punch-and-Judy show, as many serious writers have realized, is an extremely disarming theatrical technique. Almost transparent and universal as a medium, the puppet booth permits a writer to introduce a wide range of material, even the most violent, and the broad coarseness of the presentation ensures that the writer will be able to score his moral point with effortless humor. Thus it afforded Weiss a good opportunity for discussing themes of absurdity and violence within a very entertaining framework. The theatrical circus context permitted him a free hand with the staging, and the colorful, vigorous tone.

For his production in 1963 Weiss began by borrowing from popular circus and Kabuki traditions:

> From the Punch-and-Judy play we took the coarse farcical tone, the broad effects, the loud shouts—often falsely intoned—and the violence and morbidity beneath the surface jollity.
>
> From the Kabuki stage came the acrobatic virtuosity in the enactment the antinaturalism, and the strange vocal tricks in the delivery. . . .
>
> The bright colors bordering on garishness, the masked faces of the actors . . . the starkly simple decor which used only the most essential stage elements . . . helped to bring the two theatrical traditions together.[45]

Using stylized Kabuki gestures and broad choreographed movement, a cast of five men and a woman enacted a simple folktale of robbery and murder. What strikes one immediately about the play is the simplicity of means, the dramatic economy which Weiss employed: a short, one-hour climactic script delivered in uncomplicated doggerel, type characters with only the barest motivation, and an uncomplicated plot which begins in medias res and swiftly builds to a terrifyingly violent peak. Of all Weiss's plays, *Night with Guests* is certainly his most unilinear script—a feature which has led many literary critics to brand the play as inane and frivolous.[46] It is a style piece, however, a director's and actor's piece just as the Kabuki theater celebrates the performer's potency and skill in a frankly theatrical context. Weiss's play follows directly from the experimental material he had been admiring and criticizing during the fifties; and the Strindbergian darkness of its theme and mood can support the most extreme performance styles with little difficulty.

The play also indicates the degree of playwriting skill which Weiss had achieved by 1963. Pared down to only the most essential elements, the script contains nothing which is gratuitous. A man lives in a remote farmhouse with his wife and two children. A robber threatens to kill them all unless he is given gold; and in the ensuing struggle the children babble in mindless doggerel while the parents and the robber are killed. Upon opening the chest of gold, the children discover that it is filled only with turnips. This simple plot was fleshed out with carnival decor, singsong and intoned delivery styles, and the melodramatic gestures of the performers.

Night with Guests marks the end of Weiss's years of anonymity and artistic exploration. By the time it went into production, Weiss was already working on the forthcoming *Marat/Sade*. He had finally discovered a satisfactory medium and he had learned to control its tools with precision. He was sensitive to the literary and social currents in recent European history, and he was able to see his own place within that tradition with a greater clarity and self-confidence than ever before. His criticism had helped to codify these thoughts for him, and his dramatic models—Strindberg, Beckett, Brecht, Artaud—now signalled the direction he was to take.[47]

He had learned much from living in obscurity and devoting himself to disciplined experimentation; and the total artistic control he was now exercising over *Marat/Sade* was perhaps stronger than anything he had experienced before. Between November when *Night with Guests* had its premiere and the following April when *Marat/Sade* opened, the 44-year-old playwright had little time for anything but close collaboration with the director, with Gunilla Palmstierna-Weiss the designer, and with the acting ensemble in Berlin.

The intensity of this work on *Marat/Sade* is difficult to appreciate today in light of the play's widespread acceptance. But in fact Peter Weiss was at the major turning point of his career. Due to his lack of any real success as a filmmaker and painter during the fifties, it was now only the avenue of playwriting which was opening itself to him. Gunilla Palmstierna-Weiss felt that he would never have pursued a dramatic career had a similar opportunity presented itself to him in the fields of painting and cinematography. Additionally, the production conditions of *Marat/Sade* were unbelievably difficult for them both. Suhrkamp Verlag, Weiss's prestigious publisher, had compelled the Schiller Theater to accept the new Charenton script for production, and the theater's management greatly resented the financial and artistic risk it was thereby forced to assume. The author, though somewhat successful, was not at all an established playwright. The director, Konrad Swinarski, was a young Polish communist. The designer was a woman. For all these reasons, therefore, the theater allotted only four days to rehearsals on the set, as opposed to the standard practice of three weeks. Both Peter Weiss and his wife were ready to leave Berlin the very next day following the opening, expecting the worst from the critics.

Despite these circumstances, Weiss threw himself into the rehearsal process, believing absolutely in the artistic soundness of his play. From all accounts, therefore, he was working surely and successfully, carefully controlling the theatrical means by which his personal feelings on the subject of the writer's social importance might receive widespread public attention.

Committed Writing and *Marat/Sade*

Weiss's Ambivalence towards Political Activism

Between 1962 and 1968 Weiss explored the limits of his political influence as a playwright. He abandoned graphic arts and film studies, wrote almost entirely for the stage during this time, and relied exclusively upon political-historical material in his dramas. Between *Marat/Sade* (1964) and *Mockinpott* (1968), he developed his political views by measuring his historical understanding against different political ideologies.

Although he would not entirely commit himself to any particular party, Weiss wished to focus upon sociopolitical problems in order to move away from strictly personal concerns in his work. He set aside his painting, therefore, because he felt it was "too static" as a medium for grappling with the fast-changing political conditions of the postwar world. Initially he hoped to find a more activist approach to social change by rejecting the political indecisiveness and passivity of his earlier years. He sensed that his proper role as a writer in the postwar world was connected to his 40 years' experience as a social and political exile. As a result, the general course of his work during these next years brought that personal/political experience upon the stage for analysis. Weiss searched for an answer to the question of whether that experience could have been different, could somehow have been changed by a more intelligent approach to the problems in which he had found himself.

When Weiss examined his political sympathies in 1963, he realized that his outlook was still undecided and that a certain amount of self-analysis would be the necessary first step. In this respect there seems little doubt that the dialectical conflict between Sade and Marat reflected a self-conflict within Weiss's own personality. The choice between political activism and historical skepticism, between theorizing about change and implementing it, had troubled him during his years of exile and during the experimental period of the fifties.

It also seems clear that Sade's role in the play as a man who "flinched . . . from the violent methods of the progressives and, like the modern advocate of a third approach, fell between two stools"[1] was the personal stance of the playwright. Though Weiss had felt for many years a need to attack the values of Western capitalism, and of the bourgeoisie in particular, he had been unable to espouse revolutionary causes, and this inability disturbed him. "I don't dare offer any other political society because I don't believe in them as they are now," he told an interviewer in 1965. He admitted that this "third standpoint" as a political fence sitter was dissatisfying because he wanted to avoid writing about the "personal rubbish" of his private concerns, and instead "to write with the point of trying to influence or to change society."

The playwright was beginning to extend political feelers into the world around him and he was doing this in a state of acute indecision. Revolution, politics, and his inability as a writer to influence social reforms were important to him in 1963. A strong awareness of historical absurdity, however, still conditioned his outlook. He admitted that "my solutions very often are not clear because the world I live in is not clear. It's mad and it's too difficult for me to understand." The only sensible alternative was to be honest about his ambivalence, and thus Weiss finally described his intention behind the Charenton play as the desire to "give my doubt, that I show my situation of doubtfulness."[2]

The Growth of Weiss's Political Thought

The roots of Peter Weiss's ambivalence towards revolution can be traced to the early 1940s when he was pursuing a career as a painter amidst the political upheavals of World War II. He was reluctant to adopt a political stance because his artistic work seemed far more important in that it helped him to form a sense of his own identity: "I had not come into contact with radical circles," he commented in *Vanishing-Point*. "What I had experienced by way of rebellion had not been directed against the bourgeoisie but only against the narrowness that restricted my personal freedom . . . it was in art that I found the only weapons to attack or defend myself."

His autobiography also records the grim conclusions he formed about his own personality and the motivations of political and military groups: "I might have been on the other side," he admitted. "All I saw clearly was that I could be on the side of the persecutors and the executioners. *I had it in me to take part in an execution.*"[3] He had been disgusted by the holocaust of World War II and he wished to concentrate instead upon his own creative tasks:

> I had simply not learned enough. I wondered what it was like to plunge the knife into a living body and to hear the crunch of bones, or to have a knife thrust into your own ribs or your own throat; I tried to imagine how it felt when the blood burst out of your throat or when your abdomen was a mutilated steaming mess, or what the split second was like when the bullet struck your head. . . . I saw them creeping up on one another, the brave ones, friend and foe, the cannon-fodder of shifting ideals, how they murdered one another, how they found allies to attack others whom they then joined in order to fall upon new adversaries. . . . I did not want to belong to any race, ideal, city, or language, and I wanted to see strength in my detachment alone.[4]

A second explanation for his political ambivalence was his skeptical attitude towards aligning himself with the working class. He first began to shed his bourgeois class influences by gaining employment immediately after the war as a farm laborer, a temporary identity largely motivated by financial necessity, similar to "bookish tramps" like Henry Miller, George Orwell, and Jean Genet. This first direct contact with the proletariat was disturbing for Weiss. He approached his working-class milieu intellectually and he grew more contemptuous than enlightened by the extent of the problems he encountered. He despised the stolidity of the Swedish working man, "this benightedness, this reluctance to face changes, this primeval situation prior to enlightenment and culture."[5]

His autobiography also records his repulsion by the depraved and destructive tendencies of common laborers with whom he shared living conditions in Sweden's lumber region:

> They could not understand . . . why I should sit writing in a notebook and sometimes sketched. They would have despised me if I had not gone out with them in the mornings into the forest and emerged from it again in the evening. . . . When for a short while they got drunk everything that was latent and dissatisfied in them came out and they lumbered about and shouted, started fights and lashed out, only to sink finally into imbecile stupor.[6]

Weiss produced a series of drawings and sketches about this milieu, and used some of his experiences as material for his autobiography. But for the most part, the tawdriness and depravity which he recognized there in human nature made a strong impression upon him. He had learned lessons from his proletarian experiences which he would never forget.

A third and final influence upon Weiss's political thinking prior to *Marat/Sade* was his contact with the work of Franz Kafka and Henry Miller. In one of his autobiography's numerous self-pitying passages he compared himself with the victimized figure of Joseph K. in Kafka's novel *The Trial*. Weiss felt that as a refugee he had been crushed beneath a strange undeserved burden of guilt like Kafka's hero. "While reading *The Trial* I began to listen for the trial in which I myself was convicted." "Sentenced" to years of exile and intellectual isolation, Weiss accused himself of having blindly accepted the "verdict" of an imaginary "authority" which had condemned him, and he looked in vain for an escape. "All I discovered was the impossibility and lack of an outlet, although I was apparently completely free."[7]

He realized that the "wall" which had blocked his development as an artist and as a person was both social and personal, and that self-liberation was necessary:

> Kafka was always in front of that wall which finally destroyed him, he was constantly running up against *this wall which was, after all, no broader than himself*. This wall was composed of the traditional laws and I needed to move only one step to the side in order to stand in front of an open space. But to be capable of this simple step I had first to abandon the chimera under which I was struggling.[8]

Henry Miller's *Tropic of Cancer* pointed the way for Weiss in 1947 because it offered him a model of self-liberation. "The world where I stood alone with Kafka received its death-blow," Weiss explained. "It was still near, it still existed, but it was a sepulchral vault in which I ran my head against a wall. Kafka had never dared to revise the verdict of the judges; he had exalted their superior force and constantly abased himself before it." Kafka never considered outright rebellion against society, Weiss realized. Kafka had been incapable of the mid-twentieth-century existentialist declaration of freedom, "*Je me révolte, donc je suis.*" As Weiss recognized, "whenever [Kafka] was on the verge of seeing through it he sank to his knees and apologized." Kafka's mistake was to have surrendered his inner convictions to the social demand for conformity.

Henry Miller, however, had refused to abase himself before the authoritarian walls of the society which had condemned him to social ostracism and banned his writings. Miller had dared to push forward and experience life "in a more intense, a more brutal and feverish way." Weiss was amazed that Kafka's problems, and his own, "had all been surmounted by a device which seemed extremely simple, but which could only be attained when the decision to surrender oneself up completely to this world and to give up every possibility of retreat was carried through." Crime, anti-idealism, sexual excess, and social revolt in Miller's novel provided Weiss with an idea of freedom which stimulated his pent-up energies, and which would help to form the groundwork of *Marat/Sade:*

> Here the dazzlingly bright world of daylight prevailed where body struck against body; here they snapped their fingers at the idea of community, and guilt and respect were so much dead wood. The hierarchies of offices, the all-embracing laws were smashed, and free life began in a fertile chaos. Everything was tangible and possible and sex, which in Kafka lay dimly in the background, assumed a tropical luxuriance.[9]

These were the major directions in Peter Weiss's thinking at the time he came to write *Marat/Sade*. The play's concern with the issue of radical socialism versus individualism indicates that Weiss was trying to discover the limits of his influence within the political arena. He wanted to create a dialectic between individualism and social activism, a public dialogue wherein the writer's personal concerns, fears, and existentially disturbing observations would also be regarded as the social and political concerns of Western audiences. The point of contact between Peter Weiss's interests and those of his audience was the issue of social reform. Specifically, it was the writer's possible influence as a force for change which Weiss intended to investigate in his play on Marat.

Weiss also needed to discover whether or not there could be any viable political response to the misery he had known in his own and in others' experience, and to the fundamental cruelty and destructiveness which he had observed in human nature. For if there were no counterforce to the "meatgrinder of history" as Dürrenmatt, Frisch, Ionesco and others maintained, then Artaud would be right. Unreason would carry the day, and Weiss would have progressed no further in his thinking than he had in 1947 when he first described the hopeless imprisonment of family and society in *The Tower*. He wanted his new play to be more than just an exercise in self-expression or a restatement of absurdist themes. "In the theatre," he declared in 1963, "something must be communicated, placed into question, or presented in a new light, the audience should discover something and this demands clarity and immediacy."[10]

History and the Revolutionary Hero

The trend towards political subjects in all dramatic genres during the sixties is unmistakable and the number of German writers who explored the dramatic possibilities of political material in their plays was extremely large. The most famous examples were Rolf Hochhuth's *The Deputy* (1963) and *Soldiers* (1967), Heinar Kipphardt's *In the Matter of J. Robert Oppenheimer* (1964) and *Joel Brandt* (1965), as well as Weiss's *Marat/Sade* (1964), *The Investigation* (1965), *Lusitanian Bogeyman* (1967) and *Vietnam Discourse* (1968).[11]

Within the context of all the historical plays which appeared during the decade it is important to remember that *Marat/Sade* was probably the most peculiar and innovative of them all, in addition to being the most widely known and commercially successful. Its multilayered play-within-play design allowed Weiss to mix successfully a great deal of political-historical material on various levels according to the context established. This dramatic framework challenged audiences to participate imaginatively in the performance by deciding for themselves what was most "real": Marat's assassination (the historical event), the Charenton madhouse enactment of that event (Charenton as a reflection of the larger society), or the relevancy of the issues to twentieth-century problems. The distinctions between political theory, historical analysis, and contemporary applications thus became relatively flexible in the play; and this fact accounts for the widespread controversy about directorial interpretations of the play and about the author's own changing opinions of the drama's meaning as the years passed. It probably also accounts for the play's widespread popularity.

Looking back upon the drama at this point, though, more than two decades later, we can observe that whatever meanings the play may hold or have held for author, audiences, or critics, its subject is certainly the development of history and it focuses upon how or by whom that historical process can be influenced. In light of Weiss's two later historical plays which traced the careers of Trotsky and Hölderlin, we should specify *Marat/Sade*'s dramatic action more clearly as *the writer's influence upon historical change*.

Weiss analyzes this problem by centering upon the rapidly changing nature of historical events in revolutionary France. In doing so, he seems to have relied upon a somewhat positivistic interpretation of historical change. As Weiss

Figure 1. *Marat/Sade*
Clive Reville as Marat, Ian Richardson as the Herald, and
Susan Williamson as Simonne. Royal Shakespeare
Company, London, 1965, directed by Peter Brook.
(*Photo courtesy of the Royal Shakespeare Company*)

told Ernst Schumacher in 1965, "When I take up an historical theme, I'm interested above all in the evolution of the present."[12] In *Marat/Sade* he traces the influence of different historical factors which led into revolutionary struggles of the modern period. Every historian, of course, is obliged to regard past events from a contemporary standpoint. In fact the contemporaneity of history or "historical relevancy" is one concept forming the cornerstone of modern historical positivism as it is found in such historians as Barth, Butterfield, or Toynbee. In the case of *Marat/Sade* Weiss used his contemporary perspective upon the past in order to pronounce an ethical judgment upon his protagonist, just as Brecht did in *Galileo*. In the Charenton play the history of revolutionary France seems to develop according to autonomous laws which defy the ambition of social reformers like Marat. Weiss shows this character in defeat; he was unable to guide historical developments intelligently, and he disrupted those developments by his ineffectual revolutionary theories.

Weiss was less concerned, however, with exploring these developments in revolutionary France than he was with examining the personality of Jean-Paul Marat. He was seeking clues which would explain the nature of revolutionary leadership in *any* historical period, particularly the modern period. It is obvious, that is, that the French Revolution failed to create a viable government, just as the Russian Revolution had failed in 1917. The important question for Weiss as a postwar writer was the question of commitment—the dilemma of the writer *engagé* who seeks to influence social changes through his art, but who cannot align himself with parties. It was for this reason that Weiss originally refused to settle upon any political pronouncement in the drama's conclusion. Instead he allowed both his writer-heroes, Marat and Sade, to deliver presentationally to the audience a single observation which summarized their respective viewpoints.[13]

When we examine these concluding statements, we find little that can be called political in them. Neither character stressed an ideological point. Each of them forcibly presents an attitude, a philosophical posture towards social change, and allows the audience to form their own conclusions. Hence the Marquis de Sade:

> The point? Some light on our eternal doubt
> I have twisted and turned them every way
> and find no ending to our play . . .
> So for me the last word cannot ever be spoken
> I am left with a question that is always open.

This is immediately countered by Marat's statement:

> The important thing
> is to pull yourself up by your own hair
> to turn yourself inside out
> and see the whole world with fresh eyes.[14]

What Marat affirms here is not a political policy, but an encouragement to take action, however misguided or unclear, when the occasion demands. The writer *engagé,* that is, must often act upon impulse. Marat's words also contain the implication that political action is the starting point for personal self-growth and liberation. Sade's statement, however, leads to solipsism wherein the audience may "create your varying theses / and keep them on your mantelpieces." While Sade relies upon reasonable *arguments* in the play, Marat continually opts for unreasoned *action* in response to need. The choice then becomes one between inactivity and action, or reason and lunacy. In performance Marat's attitude should receive greater emphasis because it is the more dynamic response. Despite Sade's arguments against violence, we recognize that nothing will destroy the absurd faith of reformers like Marat who will always respond to social need with action.

Marat is not the only character who recognizes this "historical necessity" for revolution, but he is the only character who chooses to act in full knowledge of the effects he is producing. Other key figures in the play are motivated by less realistic concerns, except for Jacques Roux, whose radicalism Weiss ridicules in order to stress Marat's absurd faith. Sade, for example, joined the revolution because he "saw in the revolution a chance / for tremendous outburst of revenge / an orgy greater than all my dreams." Corday was motivated by naive idealism and sexual curiosity: "She was tired of her isolation / and stirred up by the new age / and gathered up in the great tide." The Parisian *sans-culottes* were aroused by the persuasiveness of demagogic leaders or by the prospect of orgiastic self-indulgence, and as the Singers demonstrate, their loyalties were completely unpredictable. Others were motivated by sheer self-interest: the bankers, attorneys, generals who reaped financial advantage from conditions of social upheaval. Marat, however, is the only character who is shown acting not only idealistically, but also with full knowledge of his limitations, and with the visionary understanding that his cause would be betrayed after his death.

This is not to say that Weiss painted an entirely favorable portrait of Marat. In scene 26, for example, "The Faces of Marat," Weiss criticizes the personal background of his hero in order to sketch in Marat's rebellious obstinacy as a child and as a young intellectual. Throughout the play Sade repeatedly connects the situation of Marat scratching himself in his bloody bathwater to his feverish urge to whip up the people. Weiss did not shrink from relating pathological excesses to political ones. He created a fictitious structure— the play-within-play structure of Sade's madhouse drama—by means of which Marat could be made to realize the sources and impact of his actions, and the eventual failure of his cause.

This realization, however, does not prevent Marat from acting out of faith, and this is the important point which few Western productions have made. Marat's decision to act, in fact, is made to seem even more incredible, more absurd, more impulsive and unjustifiable as a result of Sade's withering opposition, and for this reason Marat's choice seems heroic. "I don't watch unmoved," he shouts angrily in scene 12, "I intervene / and say that this and this are wrong / and I work to alter them and improve them."

Weiss wanted to stress this need to take action—a need which he personally felt very strongly in 1963—despite the certainty that abuses could never be entirely eliminated. Indeed, in the final moments of the play Marat openly admits that there can be no end to the reformer's work. "When I investigated a wrong," he laments in scene 28, "it grew branches / and every branch grew twigs / wherever I turned I found corruption." This does not dissuade him, however. Although he is momentarily despondent, he quickly recovers and pushes on with his work: "Simonne / Simonne / Fetch Bas / so that I can dictate my call." Unlike any other character in the drama, Marat continues to work for what he believes up to the very end. The play's final tableau, recreating the famous portrait by David, aptly summarizes Weiss's view of Marat's career: the writer who courageously pursued his unpopular beliefs, pen in hand, up to the moment of his death.

The heroic dimensions of Weiss's Marat are extremely important for understanding the Charenton play and the dramas which followed. The ability of great men to hold unpopular views, to remain faithful to their inner convictions despite persecution and social ostracism, is an idea which inspired his later dramas on Trotsky and Hölderlin. All these men were heroic martyrs. Each of these plays pivots upon the crucial point of the necessity for change, which men in every historical period have chosen either to ignore or to assist. The critic Otto Best has remarked concerning *Marat/Sade* that "a basic characteristic of human existence is brought to light, that of the unbridgeable gulf between the natural, bio-psychological activities of men, and the demand for an idea which is objectively and conceptually recognizable by its very necessity."[15] That such characters as Roux and Marat should recognize revolution to be an "historical necessity" is a point which few critics have sufficiently stressed. Yet this idea is also echoed in the plays on Trotsky and Hölderlin, men who failed to effect successful reforms but whose instincts and efforts pointed the way for revolutionaries of the modern period.

In discussing the question of the playwright's sympathy for his revolutionary hero in *Marat/Sade,* one cannot help but compare Weiss's play with the nineteenth-century German drama on the French Revolution by Büchner, *Danton's Death.* Like Peter Weiss, Büchner was also inspired by the conditions in France about 1789, but for a different reason. What was merely an intellectual concern for Weiss was a political reality for Büchner who, like numerous other young German intellectuals of the period, identified with the Jacobins. It is curious to note that although Weiss has never publicly commented upon Büchner's drama, he later adopted the same dramatic focal point upon the revolution in his play *Hölderlin* that Büchner chose for *Danton's Death*—the betrayal of Jacobin ideals during the Reign of Terror.

In *Marat/Sade* he certainly emphasizes the violent excesses of the Parisian mobs, but he does not celebrate the personalities as Büchner did. Instead, he places most of his stress upon the movement of history in the situation, particularly upon the emergence of the strongman Napoleon. While Büchner devoted a substantial number of scenes to the personal situations of the victims of the terror, including their families, Weiss emphasized ironically the dismal political conditions which followed the period of the Republic. Weiss's portrait of history was thus dialectic-centered rather than personality-centered. His vivid staging of the drama's penultimate scene, degradingly entitled "Interruptus," combines song, dance, and grotesque pantomime as the Herald quickly flips over the historical dates printed on cards hanging from his staff, as with salacious pantomime he mocks the dying revolutionary's expectations of future social reforms.

The problematical relationship between the writer and his troubled society and the tactics which post-World War II intellectuals must employ in order to effect social change were questions which Peter Weiss could not answer in *Marat/Sade*. Yet he was able to clarify the issue in great detail; and to a large extent, the drama's major achievement was to have expressed the dilemma of the modern writer's problems so fully.[16]

The *Marat/Sade* Controversy

The conflict between Sade and Marat is irreconcilable. As the Marxist critic Hans Mayer pointed out, "Writing *can* bring about material change just as Marat did—but without producing universal emancipation, nor the personal emancipation of the writer himself."[17] Weiss recognized this in 1963, but what was more important for him was understanding just what an artist *might* accomplish from political involvement. As Weiss remarked in 1972: "Writing is my work. I'm trying to make the best of it and . . . trying to clarify my own political sympathies in doing so."[18]

By examining the failures and successes in Marat's career, Weiss was discovering factors which could constitute sound revolutionary leadership. In *Marat/Sade* he could offer no positive, complete picture of a socially effective writer, but he underscored the importance of acting impulsively, of being wary of idealism, and of being careful not to mix one's own pathology with political objectives.

His analysis of the writer *engagé* yielded only an ambiguous conclusion. Marat should be praised for having recognized the necessity for revolution, and for having acted vigorously despite the many difficulties he encountered. "From our vantage point today," Weiss remarked, "we must bear in mind that Marat was one of those in the process of building the socialist image." At the same time, however, Marat had made fatal mistakes. Marat came "perilously near to the idea of dictatorship," Weiss observed. "Much in his ideas of change by forceful means was still undigested or overreached itself."[19]

It was difficult for Weiss to remain in this ambivalent condition because he felt a strong need to take action despite his doubts. He was no longer satisfied with political fence-sitting. To refuse to take a stand was unrealistic and self-indulgent. He now began to feel that artistic independence was highly questionable in the arena of political struggles. His own aesthetic objectivity had been too complacent, he complained. It was like "an escape hatch through which I could flee into the no-man's-land of sheer imagination."[20] Weiss wanted to have a direct impact upon society after 1964, and he felt this could only be achieved through political writing. "Of course the ideal would be for an artist to show the situation in which we live so strongly that, if people . . . saw it on the stage they would go home and say: 'Well we have to change this. It's not possible. We can't live any longer like this.'"[21]

Marat/Sade had clarified his political thoughts, however. He had begun the drama in "a condition of uncertainty" and had initially desired only to "express doubt" in writing it. He never pushed skepticism towards political action to the point of total absurdity, despite the rhetorical power which he gave to Sade's role. Instead Weiss stressed the importance of taking some action, however ineffectual, to remedy social abuses. Because of this he was able to restore to Marat some stature as a revolutionary hero. In existentialist terms, Marat was depicted as "acting ironically," desperately hoping for success despite the fear that all political action might amount to nothing in the end.

Another consideration which occupied Weiss's thoughts at this time was the value of propaganda, especially in regard to his future work as a committed writer. Was not all writing propaganda of some sort? And have not men such as Marat, or Marx, or Trotsky been able to derive tangible political results from writing and theorizing? Although Marat was perhaps a bad example of effective leadership, as Weiss would conclude in the years following, his influence had been enormous. Marat had been "the possibility whose impossibility the play violently demonstrates in the hope that it may yet be possible."[22]

In short, the experience of *Marat/Sade* encouraged Weiss to explore more possibilities for social impact through literature by using modern historical examples. In the post-World War II period, he felt, ideological theory and practice seemed to be better integrated and results seemed to be more positive.

Weiss's postproduction interpretation of *Marat/Sade* changed drastically as a result of such considerations. Between 1963 and 1965 there were no fewer than seven versions of the script, and his opinions on the drama's meaning were also affected by different productions of the play. He first began to insist upon a socialist interpretation of the drama as the play became widely produced and discussed. In December 1965 after seeing a socialist production in Rostock, Weiss was impressed by the way the director, Hans Perten, had clarified the dialectical features. "From the very beginning," Weiss noted, "Marat was portrayed as a positive hero . . . Sade as a decadent, lifeless libertine." That such an interpretation should arise in a socialist environment was only natural,

Weiss knew. The East German production, however, merited his special praise because he felt that he could "accept Perten's black-and-white interpretation as a response to so many Western productions wherein Sade was shown as the victor and Marat the mistaken madman."

Weiss also became increasingly disappointed by the way in which Western productions were failing to stress the importance of Marat as a socialist hero. The original Berlin staging seemed "only a preparation . . . scarcely a production." At the Aldwych in London it seemed to him that "the group of Charenton inmates were too grotesquely portrayed," while in Bergman's Swedish version, character psychology had taken full focus. In Rostock, however, Perten had turned the madhouse into a concentration camp. Weiss admired the impression that show created of "objectivity and sharp focus." The chorus had been handled as a politically unified group, and Weiss couldn't help feeling that "if Swinarski [the Berlin director] were to do the play again, he would de-emphasize the spectacular stage effects and stress instead the intellectual debate between Sade and Marat."[23]

Weiss was greatly mistaken in these beliefs. For one thing, his interpretation of Marat as the unequivocal "moral victor" of the piece is not supported by the text. In the East German production Weiss admired, Marat's lines about the necessity for bloodbaths were cut. Furthermore, in order for the patients to portray the positive (socialist) masses, their insanity was hardly suggested; Perten characterized them as political prisoners. The bloody riot and chaos of the original drama's conclusion were also eliminated. As Ernst Wendt remarked about this Rostock version: "That revolution should end in bloody senselessness was something which . . . the East German government could not allow."[24]

Nor did the drama lend itself to the sort of political interpretation upon which Weiss was now insisting. The play's greatest strength lay in its ambiguous conclusion, its articulation of the unresolvable, almost tragic paradox in which the political writer is always trapped. In order to produce this effect a vigorous performance style is required; the madhouse environment *needs* to share focus with the rational political arguments. Swinarski had recognized this, and his close collaboration with Weiss in 1964 had helped to transform the script into a powerful theatrical event. Peter Brook had gone even further with the script's possibilities and had brought the drama to international prominence by stressing its "Artaudian" implications.

Although Weiss had formerly admired Artaud during the fifties when avant-garde art had occupied his attention, he felt that the "theatre of cruelty" was too subjective and diffuse an approach, and therefore unsuitable for handling subjects of a political nature. This is what most bothered him about Western productions of *Marat/Sade*. He thought Brook's production had "assaulted" the spectator to such an extent that the grotesque, Artaud-inspired cruelty blurred the political message.[25]

Figure 2. *Marat/Sade*
The National Assembly. Volkstheater Rostock, 1964,
directed by Hans Perten.
(*Photo by Hildegard Levermann-Westerholz*)

Figure 3. *Marat/Sade*
The Chorus of Patients in the final scene. Volkstheater Rostock, 1964, directed by
Hans Perten.
(Photo by Hildegard Levermann-Westerholz)

Brook had established a strong connection between Artaud's ideas and modern political upheavals. He defined this connection as a deep sense of existential dislocation, and he correctly perceived the drama's strong absurdist thrust which the playwright later sought to de-emphasize.[26] Brook rejected historical optimism outright and insisted that today "the theatre of doubting, of unease, of trouble, of alarm seems truer than the theatre with a nobler aim."[27] Disturbance and cruelty, he believed, can bring the spectator to life in the playhouse and force him to make a judgment: "That whole wave of dark plays," he said later in 1972, "came out of a sense, perhaps, of this being the only area where an affirmation was possible, even if the response was through disturbance." His staging of Weiss's play in London and in New York offered "something that most spectators could relate to very directly, violence and madness."[28]

Weiss remained adamant, though, in press interviews dealing with Brook's production. He insisted that the spectacle should never take precedence over the dialectic. Weiss charged that Artaudian concepts had been a directorial imposition upon the script: "Peter Brook *was* thinking about Artaud before he produced *Marat/Sade,* and thus he used Artaudian techniques." This had given the production a stylistic emphasis instead of an intellectual thrust, and had blurred the drama's meaning for critics and audiences. "If there are very strong elements onstage, they shouldn't be acted either in a sadistic or a masochistic way, because either one makes it impossible to analyze the situation."[29]

Caught up in the sudden glare of international publicity in 1964–65, after so many years of literary and artistic obscurity, Weiss often felt compelled to explain his own position towards the Sade-Marat controversy in extreme terms such as these—particularly with regard to the play's ending. At one point in 1965, for example, he declared:

> Though the West Berlin production was good for its purity of form, and though the London production was spectacular for gruesome presentation, the Rostock production offered an analytical style in which the political message of the play was held in the foreground. . . . Any production of my play in which Marat does not emerge as the winner will be mistaken.[30]

Though certain Western critics have used this statement to stress Weiss's purported communist sympathies, Gunilla Palmstierna-Weiss remarked that the comment was only made impulsively, out of deference to Weiss's close friendship and association with Hans Perten in Rostock. Consequently he never publicly retracted this statement, even though he continued to revise the ending several times, in seven different versions which he developed with the collaboration of his wife.

Weiss's Ambivalence and the Dramaturgy

Marat/Sade was inspired by Weiss's unsettling feelings about the value of political engagement for writers. He knew that literature had only an indirect influence upon society, yet he also knew that many intellectuals had performed significant theoretical work as a result of their involvement with social causes. The connection between literary and political influence, therefore, was both certain and unclear, and Weiss explored this relationship in his play.

Weiss also realized that political efficacy was conditioned by existential possibility, that fundamental limitations of human nature always inhibit attempts at social reform. Weiss presented strong arguments, therefore, for writers to focus upon the problems of human nature rather than upon political strategies. The choice was to write about politics or to try to liberate what Sade called "these cells of the inner self." Weiss felt sympathy for both sides of the argument and *Marat/Sade* reflected this in its unsettling conclusion. As Sade points out, the play's purpose was simply a clarification of the writer's paradoxical situation: "Some light on our eternal doubt."

The dialectical nature of the dramatic action was the most visible reflection of Weiss's desire to portray his writer-heroes as men in "eternal doubt." Weiss created roles which could be played on any one—and sometimes all— of three symbolic levels. On one level the actors portray mental patients whose psychological disorders require graphic representation in performance. On a second level, the actors are also characters in Sade's psychodrama, and their individual afflictions are connected to the stage roles they are called upon to play. The difficulty which the patients have in distinguishing between these two roles creates tension which suddenly explodes in unpredictable outbursts, making it extremely difficult for the spectator to decide whether the patient or the character is delivering the comment. Finally there is a third level of playing which is that of the twentieth-century performer behind the dramatic mask: the play's contemporary applications are always visible beneath Weiss/Sade's play-within-play structure.

Each aspect of the revolution, therefore, is dialectically criticized from three perspectives—1789, 1808, and 1964—and this enables Weiss to introduce sudden turns and sharp surprises into the dramatic action with relative ease.[31] The critical interplay between the various levels of enactment becomes so intense that many times we are unsure just which timeframe is operative at any given moment. We must regard all the action from an ironic standpoint, critically assessing the issues which are highlighted by the play's theatricality. One critic–director has found great theatrical advantages in this:

> This two-dimensional aspect of the role [patient–actor and historical character] afforded me a technical means for demonstrating more clearly and dramatically the weakness of Marat's pretensions and his ruthless ideology. It permits one to arouse clearly a measure of distrust for the ideals passionately defended by a man who feels totally beleaguered and betrayed by

the world around him. Though this double characterization deprives the figure of Marat of some of its heroic luster it has the advantage of investing the figure with a pathetic quality of great dramatic power which is, nonetheless, unsentimental.[32]

In this way the dramaturgy focuses upon the writer's situation by shifting back and forth across the historical action, continually producing new viewpoints and new insights.

This dialectical development of the ideas (the "persecution" of Marat) is connected to the narrative of the play's historical subject (the "assassination" of Marat). Corday's murder is the structural thread of the drama; it is interrupted at three points, however, in order for Weiss to discuss the implications of the event for the French people, for the fictitious character of Marat, and for the audience's historical understanding. Weiss reveals the subsurface of history, therefore, by constantly juxtaposing historical action against interruptions from the madhouse environment. Such interplay creates a certain amount of confusion in performance, a feature which the critic Max Spalter calls a "hypnoid ambience" which serves to unify the play. Marat's rational historical understanding is continually in conflict with the subrational madhouse perspectives, and the writer is thus shown to exist in a condition of uncertainty towards the value of his work. The intellectual ideas, Spalter comments, "merge with the overwhelmingly surreal atmosphere rather than detaching themselves as ideas to be coolly considered."[33]

Very little is "cooly considered" in *Marat/Sade* because of the madhouse context of the event. The play bristles with intensity at every turn in the action: the relentless arguments between Sade and Marat, the "unforeseen" interruptions by berserk patients, the grotesque mimes and choral songs, the ever-pervasive censorship of Coulmier. As Sade declares in scene 12, "No small emotions please . . . only the most extreme actions matter." The question of the value of the writer's work is debated from two rigid positions: one is that of Sade, the skeptical writer who refuses to assist revolutionary change and who pursues individualistic concerns in his work; the other is that of Marat who tries to influence events by his writing despite the knowledge that his efforts might fail. The writer's struggle, therefore, takes place in an extreme situation, over issues which are intense, ideals and objectives which are absolute. Weiss, the historical characters, and the audience are trapped in a dialectical argument between one position which denies meaning and another which affirms it.

Within this melange of continuously shifting attitudes and perspectives, Weiss introduced themes of crucial philosophical significance. The modern theater has rarely produced stage characters with such tremendous vitality as Weiss's Marquis de Sade, who presides over the madhouse event and sheds important light upon some of the most fundamental problems of modern society: the paradox of living with absurdity, the pathological bases of political extremism, the tangled processes of historical development. The critical intellect is hard at work at every turn in the action because the playwright leads both his writer-heroes to the ultimate in each of their arguments. In the case of Sade: "All your revolution remains / only a prison mutiny / to be put down / by corrupted fellow prisoners." And in the case of Marat: "The important thing / is to pull yourself up by your own hair / to turn yourself inside out / and see the whole world with fresh eyes."

After *Marat/Sade,* Weiss felt a strong compulsion to continue with political writing because it offered him the best solution to his problem of personal commitment. As he declared to an interviewer late in 1966: "Even if I had the most brilliant theatrical idea, I would never turn it into a play—never, never—if I could not also make it express a message. . . . I cannot and do not want to find refuge in some imaginary artistic no-man's-land."[34] He recognized the truth of Sade's viewpoint that humanity is unperfectable and incapable of becoming truly free, and that political reforms cannot succeed in any absolute way. But he also sensed that Marat's faith in the perfectability of society was absolutely necessary as a counterforce to nihilism. Weiss had spent too many years in exile, politically inactive and "independent"; hence he suspected the literary cynicism which many Western writers expressed towards political activism. Pablo Neruda, one of Weiss's favorite writers, described this attitude as self-indulgence: the "independent" writer today is "a victim of individualist pride, which entrenches itself in skepticism so as not to espouse the cause of human suffering."[35] Like Neruda, Weiss too believed there were times when it was necessary to take action when limited political goals could be attained by politically conscious artists.

In order to underscore the importance of this observation, Weiss pointed out that Western intellectuals should recognize Marat's contribution to "the evolution of revolutionary thought."[36] With these words we perceive the scope of the historical research Weiss would undertake in the years following. The "evolution of revolutionary thought" between Marat's time and the present would lead Peter Weiss through the stormy years of Germany's nineteenth century, into the early years of this century with the Russian Revolution, and on into the post-World War II period with national liberation movements in underdeveloped nations. "I find the most stimulating dramatic ideas," Weiss remarked in 1966, "in the conflicts which are going on now in the whole world." The plays he wished to write would surely be politically pertinent, he observed. They would treat the evolution of history in a broad sense, "regarding the whole world situation today, in a political way and in a psychological way too."

Weiss wanted to be a contemporary writer *engagé* whose field was history and whose dramas were politically pointed. He believed that modern writers needed to analyze many lines of political and historical thought, and to discover many ways of influencing social change through their artistic commitment to political causes. This is one belief which he held throughout his career, restating it emphatically in interviews as late as 1981. As he expressed the idea in the mid-sixties: "What is essential today is the search to find our way through this mass of contradictory currents. Somehow we must discover a path which leads out of this, and we must know where to go."[37]

3

Art and Political Experience, 1965–1968

Points of Style: *Marat/Sade* and *The Investigation*

"I think if one emigrates once, one is always an emigrant. . . . Not belonging to any special place makes one a citizen of the whole world. Everything that is happening in the world now is in a way happening to myself."[1] Weiss made this statement early in 1965 when he had just begun work on *The Investigation*. Immediately following the premier of *Marat/Sade* Weiss had travelled to Frankfurt where the Auschwitz trials were underway. His remarks about "not belonging anywhere" suggest that he wished to integrate his past experience with the play he was now writing. He had found in his experience as an exile a point of contact with other victims of political upheaval and persecution in the postwar world.

His recent work on *Marat/Sade* had shown him several ways of drawing parallels between past events and contemporary conditions, and this was getting to be exciting business: "I think that when I investigate historical material I'm more concerned than anything with making it immediate, relating it to the present, and perhaps even revising it." In *Marat/Sade* he had shown how the problems of revolutionary intellectuals in France related to problems faced by post-World War II writers. When considering the condition of the Jews under Fascism, Weiss found what he called another "extremely clear historical process" at work again; but he knew from the outset that in dealing with material so recent and so explosive, he would have to develop methods very different from those he had used in *Marat/Sade*.

One of the major problems Weiss faced in writing about Auschwitz was that the subject seemed to pertain only to National Socialism, to recent German history. Weiss wanted to generalize the material, though, for broader applications. He was "interested in the human situation of oppressed people. I could as well identify myself with the situation of the Negroes in South Africa. . . . In our world there are people who are aggressors and there are others who flee or try to."[2] So he began the Auschwitz drama by trying to remove the play's subject from its historical matrix in order to illuminate its universal aspects.

This question of distancing the material in order to achieve universality is crucial to understanding Weiss's achievement in *The Investigation*. Weiss was aware of the international acclaim which Hochhuth's play *The Deputy* had received in 1963. This drama had provoked a storm of controversy on account of its ad hominem attack on Pius XII and its portrayal of the apparent indifference of the Roman See towards the extermination of the Jews. In Hochhuth's play these personal and political viewpoints were never clearly distinguished and the drama succeeded mainly in whipping up emotion instead of producing understanding.

Rather than providing an historical portrait of Pius's dilemma, Hochhuth aroused indignation at the crimes committed against the Jews. The dramatist's personal bias towards the issues is responsible for the play's emotional effect, and betrays Hochhuth's inability to move beyond the mere facts of his subject into a more problematical, more philosophical treatment of the issues. Dramatically speaking, Hochhuth had allowed his characters to *reenact* the events of the early 1940s, thus presenting issues and events simultaneously. Weiss, however, chose to cast his play in the form of an oratorio, a dramatic narrative, in which characters *related* their experiences within the theatrical context of the war crimes trials. This enabled Weiss to separate issues from events, to capitalize upon the advantage of imaginative perspective which the playwright holds over the historian.

In order to achieve this distance, Weiss planned to develop techniques for language and staging which were vastly different from those he had used in *Marat/Sade*. In the Charenton play he had sharpened his poetic skills through the variety of verse forms he had employed. Language had distinguished characters and their sociopolitical attitudes, had marked off the separate stages in the development of the dialectic, and had achieved different emphases through music and rhythmic choral techniques. Weiss had used the ironic *Knittelvers* form for the Herald in order to reinforce the character's formal function when introducing scenes, and to sharpen the character's satirical comments. In the choral passages Weiss relied upon vigorous, rhythmic patterns often recalling military marches. Such rhythms were frequently modulated by accelerating the tempo (as in the final song celebrating Napoleon's victories); by suddenly diminishing or increasing volume (as in "We want a revolution NOW"); or by suddenly fracturing the regular march tempo with frantic outbursts, strangely intoned words and phrases, or haunting repetitions. Weiss had introduced powerful rhetorical free verse for the dialectical passages between Marat and Sade, and for the scene in the National Assembly. Coulmier, the bourgeois apologist, had spoken in almost conversational style, although Weiss added occasional rhymed couplets when a political comment needed to be stressed. To Corday Weiss gave a stuttering, non-rhythmic, labored speech pattern, except for her duet with Duperret—the only place in the drama where the beautifully fragile, lyric waltz form softened strident passages and retarded the scenic rhythm.

From *Marat/Sade* Weiss had also learned how to combine numerous theatrical styles within a single event. Many critics had hailed the play as an example of "total theater" in which a visually spectacular type of staging had illuminated and highlighted complex problems of modern society. Weiss's background as a painter and cinematographer and his collaboration with Gunilla Palmstierna had helped him to visualize certain production concepts of staging scenes; he enjoyed what he called "the possibility of having both the visual aspect of life and the word."[3] By late 1965, therefore, he had come to appreciate the impact which stage performance had upon spectators, an impact different from that of painting or film. He was convinced that theatrical images could not only contain as much information as these other media, but could also deliver that information more forcibly through puppetry, mime, music, song, dance: "The theater can renew itself, can say everything about our time that film can, and be even more alive than film."[4]

Weiss remarked to Ernst Schumacher that the vast resources of the modern stage had impressed him tremendously as a result of *Marat/Sade*'s success, but that he wished to tighten his control over the spectacle elements in *The Investigation*. He had grown wary of what directors would do with his script, and he wanted now to create something entirely different in *The Investigation:*

> Most of all there is hardly anything that happens onstage, the scene is very static, composed of large unmoving groups, Chorus and Counter-Chorus and main Speakers, and there is nothing there which gives a director any possibility for bringing special effects into play. The drama is built only upon language, with very little stage action, characters enter and speak to one another, and that is all there is.[5]

Weiss wanted the weight of the material itself to speak from the stage. The impact of the new play must rely upon its content more than upon imaginative enactment or its technical methods for presenting Auschwitz onstage. "It's not imaginary," he said, "it is built on reality, but the form of the whole play, of course, is a work of art . . . it's not meant to be a realistic court atmosphere but instead it resembles antique tragedy." Thus the note of guilt which the dramatic material contained was diffused into Western society as a whole. This helped remove the material from a strictly German setting and placed it "onto another level from the real trial atmosphere."[6]

One idea Weiss carried over from *Marat/Sade* was the organizing principle for the bulky historical material. In the Charenton drama, the architectural principle was association; Weiss had related all the events to Sade as the author of the play-within-a-play. Because of this the action focussed on Sade's condition—the writer's dilemma—rather than upon the narrative features of the revolution. "I don't really understand what is meant by a plot," Weiss declared. "For me there are only events upon the stage, and these don't necessarily have to have a plot, but they can constitute a condition."[7] *The Investigation* would be organized around the central condition of modern political oppression in order "to show the possibilities of human beings, either to let themselves be suppressed and exterminated . . . or on the other side, the possibility of the accused to slowly develop this mentality of mass murderers."[8]

Experimental Dramaturgy and *The Investigation*

The scenic flexibility which a loose associative format permitted was something Weiss felt to be essential for the new play. Different viewpoints upon the implications of Auschwitz would have to merge smoothly because he did not want theatricality to draw attention. Descriptions of the camps needed to flow on continuously, without interruptions for dialogue, set changes, or choral commentary. From the beginning Weiss envisioned the play as only minimally dramatic, as an oratorio. Statements would be presented as songs: "The Song of the Death of Lili Tofler," or "The Song of Cyclon B," or "The Song of the Fire Ovens."

Weiss took his inspiration from the *Divina Commedia* as he planned the drama's form. He developed the action in three stages: "Inferno," "Purgatorio," and "Paradiso." In the first act Weiss's criminals would not be shown in punishments (unlike Dante's sinners) because Weiss felt that "the tyrants, the exploiters, the gold-diggers of our time will be seen . . . still planning, still fortifying their possessions, still defending them with their corruption and brutality." Act 2, "Purgatorio," would express "a state of doubt" towards the reasons behind the Jews' acceptance of their fate in Auschwitz: their obedience of the official relocation orders, their educational and cultural training as Germans, their unwillingness to resist. The third act, "Paradiso," would then explore the lack of hope for victims of persecution who do not take responsibility for their oppression. As Weiss explained the emphasis here, "He who suffers will never get a reward for it. . . . The suppressed, the persecuted, the slaves, have only one chance, to struggle for a change of their living conditions. . . . This has to be done here and now, while you are still alive."[9] There are 11 major scenes or "cantos" in the play, each of which contains three units. Each phase of the action—the three acts—thus develops in threes.

In his handling of characters Weiss wished to portray the dehumanization of the victims by stressing their anonymity. "The figures onstage speak free from any apparent emotion," he explained to Ernst Schumacher. "They deliver their statements, which are taken from record, as simple facts to be communicated in the trial." Through this contrast between an unemotional delivery style and "the heavy emotional weight" of the testimony, the audience "should naturally be astounded." He wanted "one voice to be raised out of that mass, and to let that voice symbolize what happened to millions." He refrained from giving the witnesses names; they would be designated only by registration numbers, their anonymity standing in sharp contrast to the publicized names of the camp officials. Even the words "Jew" and "Auschwitz" would be absent from

Figure 4. *The Investigation*
Kurt Wetzel as the Judge and Dieter Unruh as the Prisoner. Volkstheater Rostock, 1965, directed by Hans Perten.
(Photo by Hildegard Levermann-Westerholz)

the script. Emphasis was to be placed upon "making a picture of the present-day in which the past could be seen as alive and still at work."[10]

Weiss also relied upon language to add a mythical atmosphere to the drama. He knew that the myths and symbols used by the Nazi propagandists had helped to project a national image of Wagnerian grandeur within which the politicians could "act out" mythic roles in everyday life. Hitler, for instance, posing as Siegfried in armor astride a horse in the forest, or the flamboyant Goebbels in a diabolical black cape and thigh-length leather boots, were two obvious manifestations of a deeply mythical, occult, mystical aura which pervaded Nazi Germany. Regarding the concentration camps, Weiss wished to stress their nightmarish and surrealistic features by presenting them as scenes from a cosmic drama. Through language he created a sense "of antique tragedy . . . with the chorus, the leading voice, and so on." The play thus became somewhat dreamlike. Characters seemed caught up in some fatalistic limbo reminiscent of Beckett or the nightmares of surrealist writers. "There is an unending coming and going of anonymous victims," Weiss pointed out. "You can barely hear what they say, and sometimes you're too tired and frustrated to understand, but it's going on all the time. You listen if you want to, and if you don't you can shut your ears. The play should be about four-and-a-half hours long . . . part of the play's essential quality is its enormous length— it is unbearable. It should be unbearable."[11]

Political Problems and *The Investigation*

Weiss's attempt to relate the experience of the Jews under Nazism to the oppressed conditions in postwar Third World nations became more than just an exercise in pointing up the relevancy of his historical subject. He also wanted the play to be politically incisive, and his confusion between contemporary history and political history is evident in a statement he made to Walter Wager: "It is capitalism, indeed the whole Western way of life, that is on trial. . . . A large part of it deals with the role of German big industry in exterminating the Jews. I want to brand capitalism which even benefited from the experiments in the gas chambers."[12]

One receives the impression that at this time Weiss was forcing a political issue from the trial transcripts. Regarding Nazism as the logical (rather than coincidental) result of the capitalist system was shabby intellectualizing for this writer. Yet in the context of his personal experience as a Jewish exile, as well as his distaste for the Cold War "Americanization" of western Europe, and in light of his changing political outlook after *Marat/Sade*, it is easy to see why he wished to draw anticapitalistic conclusions from his research. With material so close to home, Weiss wanted to do more than just report atrocities—he also wanted to shock audiences into doing something about them.

Figure 5. *The Investigation*
A Chorus of Prisoners. Volkstheater Rostock, 1965, directed
by Hans Perten.
(*Photo by Hildegard Levermann-Westerholz*)

These personal motivations were reflected in a short story which Weiss wrote in May of 1965, entitled "My Place," which describes his visit to Auschwitz and his impressions of the experience. Weiss was struck by the contrast between the peaceful condition of the site as a postwar tourist attraction and the grim history of the site as he had known it during the forties. "The living man who comes here," Weiss says, "from another world, has nothing but his knowledge of figures, written reports, statements from witnesses; it lies heavy upon him. . . . Then he knows that it has not ended yet."[13]

Here Weiss describes the difficulties facing any postwar writer who tries to deal with the implications of the Nazi experience; the artist feels helpless yet he must somehow come to grips with those implications through his art. Speaking of his own feelings Weiss says that "he arrived twenty years too late." The situation compelled him, for political and personal reasons, to write of it years later. He could not ignore Auschwitz because he felt that all the places where he had lived as an emigrant, "all those cities became blurs, and only one place, where I spent only one day, remains constant." That place was Auschwitz, he continues, "a place for which I was destined but which I managed to avoid."[14]

Over 20 years later, therefore, Weiss needed to examine the role which he might have played during the years of war and exile.

> Part of Auschwitz is in that for me . . . a very heavy thing has happened to you which you say you can't understand. When you see the ruins of the gas chambers, they're just heavy blocks of iron or concrete or steel, with weeds already grown on them. You almost can't see them but they're bits of our reality. . . . I worked with just words, the words of the victims' evidence, to make these things up for us, so that we could investigate them.[15]

Although Peter Weiss felt that he had been "destined" for Auschwitz, he had escaped, and this led him to ask why so many others, including his childhood friends, had not. It was absurd, he felt, that millions should have accepted their fates. "And most of them did," he remarked, "in a very passive way. That's a great tragedy, that they didn't find *any* possibility of fighting against the sort of pressure that was put." The reason, he hesitatingly concluded, was that they were good Germans in addition to their being Jews; he felt that perhaps most of them had been nationalists who had dutifully obeyed the official relocation orders. As he awkwardly explained: "I point it out as a suggestion that there are some of them who could even become, would even have the possibility of sitting on the side of the accused because there were German Jews who were nationalists."[16]

This idea became more than a "suggestion," however, when the play was finished. By the time Weiss had reworked the material and given it his own individual stamp, his attack on the victims had assumed major proportions:

> Many of those who were destined
> to play the part of prisoners

> had grown up with the same ideas
> the same way of looking at things
> as those
> who found themselves acting as guards
> they were all equally dedicated
> to the same nation
> to its prosperity
> and its rewards
> and if they had not been designated
> prisoners
> they could equally well have been guards.[17]

Witness #3, Weiss's strongest character in the drama, speaks these words and dominates the important fourth scene. Weiss allows the statements to stand unopposed, and then develops the character's statements in order to level additional accusations against Western society in general: "The order that prevailed there was an order whose basic nature we were familiar with," the Witness continues. The concentration camp was "the logical and ultimate consequence" of capitalistic expansion, a place

> where the oppressor
> could expand his authority
> to a degree never known before
> and the oppressed
> was forced to yield up
> the fertilizing dust
> of his bones.

Weiss wished to stress the ideological significance of the evidence in order to show that similar tendencies were operative in the postwar period. He called Nazism "a system that implicated in its guilt many others who never appeared in court."[18] In the three scenes entitled "Song of the Death of Lili Tofler," Weiss tries to explore this point. He uses the testimony of a former director of one of the factories attached to the camp, and attacks the forced labor operations through the words of the prosecutor. The defense counsel protests that such questions are "entirely irrelevant to the stated purpose of these proceedings," but Weiss has the prosecutor badger the witness and uncover the incriminating evidence. "Let us once more bring to mind," declares the prosecutor:

> That the successors to those same concerns
> have ended up today in magnificent condition
> and that they are now in the midst of
> as they say
> a new phase of expansion.

Figure 6. *The Investigation*
Karin Seybert as the Prisoner. Volkstheater Rostock, 1965, directed by Hans Perten.
(Photo by Hildegard Levermann-Westerholz)

Critics and audiences bought very little of such anticapitalistic extrapola-
tions from the evidence. Walter Jens accused Weiss of deliberate, irresponsible
distortion: "The more resolutely Weiss ties up and packages the material, the
more he interprets and adds."[19] Peter Demetz took Weiss to task for shoddy intellectualizing: "Old fashioned concepts of capitalist exploitation certainly do
not suffice to explain the origin of the German or any other camp system."[20]
Ernst Wendt, in his review of the original production, accused Weiss of
exploiting the material for its sheer sensationalism: "He has no inhibitions
about . . . using the fate of Lili Tofler as a peg on which to hang statements
about the advantage accruing to industry."[21] Weiss's attempts to use the documents in order to attack Western society thus met with widespread criticism,
particularly from Jewish quarters.[22]

In addition to Weiss's falsification of the evidence and his shaky political
moralizing, the play also suffers from its author's poor handling of the dramatic
focus. Just who or what was being placed on trial was never entirely clear.
Many audiences had come expecting to see another *Marat/Sade,* but they were
greeted with an accusing finger which held them all responsible for Fascism.
Weiss had removed the material too far from its German matrix; as a metaphor
for Western society, Auschwitz did not function as well as the metaphor of the
asylum had done in the Charenton play. Weiss stood on unpopular and dangerous ground when he refused to indict the war criminals directly and instead in-
dicted the political-economic system which had produced them. The play provided hard evidence in the dialogue, documentary realism in the photographic
projections, ethical substance in the issues, and great pathos; but the definite
courtroom judgment which all of this seemed to demand was not forthcoming.
The criminals seemed exonerated because they were the product of a system,
and the condemnation of that system implicated in its guilt the spectators, the
criminals, and even the victims themselves. The drama, although widely produced in 1965 and 1966, was generally greeted as a disappointing successor to
Marat/Sade. It proved more important as a tragic oratorio on the horrors of
Nazism than as a significant critique of Western capitalism.

This point about the difficulty of recounting the Auschwitz horrors onstage
is especially important. The guilt which Weiss's drama implies has only general applications to society, and thus numerous atrocities which it chronicles
can be variously interpreted and even exploited. By staging horror in detail a
director can guide the production towards the audience's sadistic tastes. As
Tom Driver commented upon the marketability of holocaust subjects during the
sixties, "A sort of merchandising of guilt is going on. Some people are buying
and others are trying to sell. The theatre manager makes a profit either way."[23]
On the other hand, the sense of incomprehensibility which arises from such
grisly reportage can lend the play an overwhelming coloration of absurdity.
Demetz, in fact, went so far as to accuse Weiss of taking "the invisible dignity
of dying away from the dead" by his insistence upon the interchangeability of
victim and aggressor roles.[24]

Theodore Adorno, the influential German social philosopher and critic, spoke about this problem in 1965 within the context of Auschwitz, asking "whether any art now has a right to exist; whether intellectual regression is not inherent in the concept of committed literature because of the regression of society." He concluded that artists must "not surrender to cynicism" and he warned against artists like Weiss who cannot make up their minds about assigning guilt:

> The so-called artistic representation of the sheer physical pain of people beaten to the ground by rifle butts contains, however remotely, the power to elicit enjoyment out of it. The moral of this art, not to forget for a single instant, slithers into the abyss of its opposite. . . . In such a homely existential atmosphere, the distinction between executioners and victims becomes blurred; both, after all, are equally suspended above the possibility of nothingness, which of course is generally not quite so uncomfortable.[25]

Weiss strongly believed that the people involved—victims and aggressors—were basically no different from ourselves. "I think it is a human psychological thing," he said, "which develops under special circumstances where the ordinary values disappear, so the negative values will grow in special people." And he stressed the international manifestation of this point: "You find it, I think, in most armies. In what has happened in the French war in Algeria and in Vietnam, and even in Vietnam now [1966]. . . . You find it everywhere."[26]

In conclusion, we should keep in mind that this insistence upon the play's universal applications does not fully describe the potential of the work, because it has also been performed successfully in a style directed unmistakably at the contemporary realities of West Germany. In fact, Weiss's opinions about the play's reliance upon ancient ritual drama and his insistence upon austerity in the staging were radically reversed in 1980 when a storm of controversy erupted in West Berlin over a new conception of *The Investigation*. The young director, Thomas Schulte-Michaels, created a sleazy nightclub setting for the play in which sections of the cross-examination were staged as TV quiz shows, gutter press interviews, and pornographic encounters. Actors were costumed in garish drag, drinking and smoking while fluidly moving in and out between multiple roles as victims and aggressors. Critics from a wide range of backgrounds created such a storm about the scandalous production which seemed to vilify Jews, Nazis, members of the government of the Federal Republic, and others that Weiss himself had to come out in support of the director to prevent the play from being censored and cancelled. "I think that the polarization that has come about is very good," Weiss commented. "I sincerely hope that the actors and the whole ensemble will have the strength and courage to hold out. They have my solidarity. Cancel it! Certainly not!"[27]

Weiss and Radical Politics

Weiss's growing interest in the affairs of the underdeveloped nations marks an important stage in his political writing. His next two dramas dealt with revolutions in Africa and southeast Asia, and many of his essays during the next five years dealt with events and personalities connected with national liberation movements: Che Guevara, the Arab states, African nationalism. In speaking of Weiss's political commitment during the mid-sixties, it is important to recognize that his sympathies lay with Third World nations rather than with the socialist superpowers, Russia and China. Weiss grew increasingly critical of Russian policies during the mid-sixties because he felt that the Cold War, the growing capitalism in the bureaucratized Soviet state, as well as its Stalinist legacy, was an unfortunate setback for socialist progress and leftist artists.

Weiss was finding it difficult to define his political allegiances during these years because he was very independent as an artist. He was a product of the western European bourgeoisie and he knew that he could never entirely shake off the influence of this upbringing. He continued living and working in Stockholm except for two brief trips to Cuba and southeast Asia; but he was unable to identify with Russia or with any of the eastern European satellite countries.[28] Thus he was forced to work in isolation, removed from any direct contact with revolutionary struggles. He was writing from neutral Sweden, mainly for bourgeois audiences about political revolutions in parts of the world he had never even seen. Nevertheless, he felt that this work might bring him into solidarity with revolutionary causes and thus satisfy his need to see himself as a writer whose work was socially significant.

Weiss could only become politically involved through his art. This helps to exlain some of the heavy-handed diatribe in his agit-prop dramas on Angola and Vietnam, and it also helps us to understand his eventual return to a position of political independence at the close of the decade. He believed that political oppression occurred everywhere—Cuba, the Mideast, eastern Europe, Africa, Vietnam—and that the writer *engagé* always had to work independently, forming perspectives in terms of a total world picture. In this way, he believed, artists could assist in correcting social abuses, and thus they performed a useful social function. Between 1966 and 1968 Weiss tried to play an active role in influencing such changes by writing two dramas dealing with international problems.

Documentary Drama: *Song of the Lusitanian Bogeyman*
and *Vietnam Discourse*

Song of the Lusitanian Bogeyman and *Vietnam Discourse* were political dramas with a strong propagandistic thrust. Between the time of *The Investigation* (1965) and *Mockinpott* (1968), Weiss was concerned with the fact that the course of modern history was taking its direction from revolutionary struggles occurring at mid-century. The guiding force of these movements was socialist ideology. Early in 1965 Weiss published an essay on the problems of the modern writer *engagé,* "Ten Working Points of an Author in a Divided World," in which his political sympathies were clearly expressed. "The evolution of revolutionary socialism," he declared there, "seems to me the best political program. . . . Only in a socialist society can I see a possibility for solving our present problems."[29] The documentary dramas he was writing at mid-decade were helping him to define his allegiances more clearly: he was exploring through his art the central question of how he as a playwright could assist the forces of social change in the postwar world.

More than just didactic ideological pieces, however, Weiss's next two plays were specifically designed as models for a "documentary theater" which he hoped could adequately deal with the most pressing problems of modern history. The aesthetic blueprint for this type of drama was his 1968 essay, "The Material and the Models: Notes towards a Definition of Documentary Theater."[30] Although confusing and contradictory in certain sections, the essay is a good distillation of the ideas which grew out of this period of political playwriting because it was completed after *Bogeyman* and *Vietnam Discourse.* In its attempt to discover a workable combination of art and politics, the essay demonstrates that Weiss's commitment to socialism at this time was not an overriding consideration in determining the content of his plays. In fact the essay raises the question of whether the playwright's aesthetic interests were becoming more important to him than his political concerns.

To be sure, Weiss makes a strong case for a documentary-style theater which would be politically sensitive. He speaks in the essay of the political weight of the genre, calling it variously "a political forum first of all," "a tribunal," "an instrument for forming political opinion," or "a theater of reportage . . . which is aimed against those groups who are interested in a policy of obscurantism and opacity." He also regards documentary drama as a theater which "takes sides" and which presents such subjects as colonial exploitation or genocide as "one-sided crimes" where "black-and-white strokes are justified."

At the same time, however, Weiss holds no illusions regarding the drama's political leverage. "It can never measure up," he admits, "to the dynamic expression of opinion which is generated in public action." Despite the genre's ideological bias, he hopes it could lead "to attention, consciousness, reflection." In its focus upon contemporary politics, documentary drama can exist on the one side as "a reaction against the contemporary situation" of political helplessness in Western society; and as "a montage of snippets of reality" culled from all areas of the mass media, it could also be "a demand for explanation." Ultimately, however, he regards its political function as investigative. He admits that his ideas on documentary plays derived from "the days of the

'Proletcult' movement, 'Agitprop,' the experiments of Piscator and the didactic plays of Brecht."

Throughout the essay Weiss remains cautious about insisting upon the propagandistic weight of documentary theater. Despite the genre's political thrust, that is, Weiss knows it could never be entirely spontaneous in the sense of "an authentic political event" but must always remain aesthetic, imitative in the sense of "a reflection of life." This stress upon the philosophical and aesthetic weight of his plays, in contrast to whatever political statements they may contain, shows his documentary style to be a hybrid form. The artistic merit of the presentation should become the playwright's ultimate criterion. "Even when it attempts to free itself," he says "from the framework which defines it as an art form, when it dispenses with aesthetic considerations and does not try to be a finished product; when it merely takes up positions, giving the impression of bursting into existence at the moment and to act without preparation—the result is still a form of artistic expression, and it must be a form of artistic expression to have any validity."

Despite Weiss's socialist bias which runs through this essay, there is a great deal in it which is not propagandistic in any sense of the word. One gains this feeling from the persistent stress upon historical analysis which Weiss displays. He speaks of "aesthetic distance" in the documentary collage which will provide detailed coverage of material. Characters, for example, should be placed "in an historical context. At the same time as their actions are presented, the development of which these actions are the result is traced, and attention drawn to other possible consequences." Such a drama might become philosophically and historically informative rather than narrowly political. Moreover, Weiss insists that the play "should not lead to confusion" by skimming over complex problems, "but must draw attention to the many facets of events."

Another noteworthy feature of the essay is the way in which Weiss regards his political dramas as exercises in self-understanding. The problem of absurdity, for example, which had surfaced repeatedly in his work, could be avoided because documentary drama would offer concrete suggestions to its audience. He declares that documentary theater is "opposed to that drama whose main theme is its own anger and despair." Weiss wants to approach problems in a spirit of rationalistic inquiry because "reality, however opaque it might appear, can be explained in every detail."[31]

This is surely a far cry from his earlier rejection of historical meaning when, after *Marat/Sade,* he declared that the world was too complex and confused for him to understand, and that he held no political solutions up his sleeve. That he had now changed his mind and reversed his position seems clear. With the new plays on Portugal and the United States, Weiss felt there should be no doubt of their pertinency, and of their importance to a writer who wished to understand his society by "explaining it in every detail."

This idea of contacting society through committed writing recurs frequently in the essay. The world which Weiss had shunned for so long, which he had gradually approached through his literary work for the past 20 years, would now be described in concrete political terms.[32] In this way he and his audiences might come to feel themselves "in solidarity" with others' lives and problems all over the globe; documentary drama might even lead to changes in nations where change was desperately needed. He also expresses the naive hope that documentary theater might supplant the major news media as a source of information and insight, and be socially useful by amplifying the political consciousness of its audience.

Writing Documentary Plays

There were three principles which Weiss believed could guide a writer in creating this kind of play. The first of these was to present events by juxtaposing different viewpoints and factual materials,

> reports and parts of reports, divided rhythmically into carefully timed sections. Short moments, consisting of just one fact, one exclamation, relieve longer, more complicated sections. A quotation is followed by the enactment of a situation. By quick-cutting the situation is switched to another, contrasting with it. The scenario consists of antithetic pieces, of sequences of similar examples, of contrasting forms, of changing values. Variations on a theme. . . . Interruptions. Dissonances.

Variety thus becomes the keynote, a principle dictated by the complexity of information available on modern historical upheavals and fast-changing political situations. This was a technique which Weiss had developed earlier with the two novels *Coachman's Body* and *Three Wayfarers,* although in those two novels Weiss attempted to demonstrate the absurdity of human experience. Now, however, history is to be grasped by directly confronting its many details which are "divided rhythmically," depending upon where the writer chooses to place emphasis. Broad coverage is mainly achieved by this simple method of controlling the length of a scene. An important fact or incident may be treated at length if it is periodically relieved by "short moments" of commentary, or counterpointed by "exclamations" and "dissonances."

The structure of *Bogeyman* best displays this first principle at work. Like *The Investigation,* the play is episodic in structure, each scene treating a single aspect of the total situation. In *Bogeyman,* however, there are far fewer episodes (11 as opposed to 33 in *The Investigation*), and in many of them the internal rhythm is extremely complex. In scene 2, for example, Weiss chronicles the arrival of the first Portuguese under Diego Cao, and he describes the white slaving operations. Three actors deliver the pronouncements of the Portuguese, while the other four perform either as natives miming the situation or as a chorus of slaves. As the colonizers speak of "a harmony / between the

Exotic / and the Occident" and "kinship of soul with soul," the chorus repeats the ironic refrain: "In the Overseas Provinces / which have belonged to us / for 500 years."[33] The chorus splits into semichoruses who answer the statements about Portuguese "benevolent civilizing" with an Angolan chant. This emphasizes the gulf between the two cultures and their painful historical encounter:

> CHORUS: The earth it rips open it tears open it heaves open
> 2: Let the men feel the pains of the woman in labor
> CHORUS: The earth it rips open it tears open it heaves open
> 2: Let the men feel the pains of giving birth
> CHORUS: The earth it rips open it tears open it heaves open
> 2: Let the men feel the bloody giving of birth
> CHORUS: The earth it rips open it tears open it heaves open
> 2: Let mankind be in labor and the fruit burst forth.

Actor #5, a Portuguese government spokesman, steps forward to conclude the scene with an official statement: "From the study of history we will plainly learn . . . why this African continent is labelled Dark." The historical development of colonization in Angola is neatly summarized by this contrast established between a "bloody birth" and the militant Christian values of the western Europeans.

So long as the playwright carefully selects the topics of his discussion and limits their number, he can achieve focus and maintain the continuity of the narrative line without becoming bogged down in a wealth of detail, and he can also achieve variety by the quick-cutting technique. For these reasons, *Bogeyman* displays a more complex internal structure than *The Investigation.*

Weiss's second principle takes up the important question of performance style, which also assists in organizing the issues broadly and economically. Weiss declares, "In a quotation, the typical is emphasized. Personalities are caricatured, situations dramatically simplified." Although this seems to be warmed-over Brecht or Piscator agit-prop (and Weiss admits that the Brechtian demonstration was his inspiration), Weiss goes a step further by stressing the imaginative, almost demonic qualities of the presentation. "Reports, comments, abstracts are turned into songs. Choirs and mime are introduced. . . . Parody, masks, scenic effects. Musical accompaniment, sound effects."

In the original production of *Bogeyman* Portuguese villains waltzed across the stage wearing grotesque animal headdresses, and presentational statements to the audience often took the form of a macabre chorus line of pitiful victims. When the figure of the Bogeyman toppled to the stage floor in the finale, littering the front rows of the audience with dust and debris, its supporting structure which remained erect onstage resembled the shape of the guillotine. To a certain extent, therefore, Peter and Gunilla Palmstierna-Weiss were moving away from the scenic austerity of *The Investigation;* they were now trying to find more dense visual outlets for Weiss's rich dramatic imagination.

Figure 7. *Song of the Lusitanian Bogeyman*
Acting ensemble with the Bogey. Volkstheater Rostock, 1968, directed by Hans Perten.
(Photo by Hildegard Levermann-Westerholz)

The plays on Portugal and Vietnam taught Weiss important lessons about style, particularly with the handling of the acting ensemble. In fact, Weiss's work on this production in the Stockholm version was one of the first European experiments with group-developed theater pieces. Brecht's own work in East Berlin, of course, had convinced Weiss of the value of developing scripts in collaboration with the actors; and Peter Brook's Vietnam play, *US,* was another political group experiment from the sixties. Weiss was also very impressed at this time with the work of America's Bread and Puppet Theater and with The Living Theatre. In Stockholm, Weiss was able to continue the kind of ensemble work on *Bogeyman* which Ingmar Bergman had initiated in his own stage productions there, working with younger actors in the experimental approaches at Stockholm's Scala Studio. Many productions of Weiss's plays on the continent, of course, did not permit him to work closely with actors in this manner. So it was continued work with this group in Stockholm—even as late as 1982 with his adaptation of Kafka's *The New Trial*—which enabled Weiss to develop scripts with strong performance qualities; and to assume much more artistic control, as director, with the interpretation of his plays in production.

The Angolan and Vietnamese plays, of course, employed mass heroes, and in handling the choruses for these pieces Weiss developed new techniques for integrating pantomime (there is much use of mime against spoken narration), for experimenting with indigenous musical instruments, and for employing elements of the southeast Asian shadow play for alienation effects. Portuguese administrative decrees are satirized in *Bogeyman*'s fifth scene, and shadow-play parodies the conflict between government officials and native workers. Two actors mime a situation whose dialogue is spoken by two others holding a curtain:

> 3: Show your money
> 7: Haven't any more money
>   What was left from my pay
>   went for the train trip
> 3: Knocking about without money
>   That's punishable
> 7: Wanted to work at home
>   with my wife
>   with my children
> 3: There's no permission stamp for taking residence
>   in this district
>   That's punishable. . . .
>   Since you're staying around
>   without a permanent residence
>   and since you haven't any work
>   and no money
>   you'll now be taken to a camp.

Figure 8. *Song of the Lusitanian Bogeyman*
Christian Stövesand and Gerd Michael as Colonial
Administrators, and Erhard Treffkorn as an Angolan native.
Volkstheater Rostock, 1968, directed by Hans Perten.
(*Photo by Hildegard Levermann-Westerholz*)

In his handling of personalities Weiss was guided by techniques of simplification, especially by the use of typical statements which enabled him to work economically. For instance, Weiss divided *Bogeyman*'s characters into three easily recognizable sociopolitical groups. Four Portuguese oppressors, played only by men, formed one level; a group of three speakers, two men and a woman, performed as African leaders making cynical comments; and a third group, also men and women, formed the Angolan chorus. Weiss remarked that ideally the play should be performed with an all-black cast. Weiss reinforced these groupings with appropriate language for each: oppressors spoke in rhythmic prose, as used in *The Investigation;* African leaders always spoke in ironic *Knittelvers;* and the chorus used free rhythmic lyrics based upon African rhythms.

Bogeyman did not meet with much commerical success, possibly because the play's theatricality seemed inappropriate to its subject. Critics complained that Weiss had apparently exploited the Angolan situation in order to score another theatrical coup, just as he had used the war crimes testimony to attack Western capitalism in *The Investigation*. Weiss attended the rehearsals and worked with an impressive production team in the *Bogeyman* production. Paul Dessau composed the music and Hans Perten (from Easy Germany; he had directed the version of *Murat/Sade* which Weiss most enjoyed) developed innovative pantomimic and choreographic approaches to the script. But all of this seemed an unsuccessful attempt by Western artist-intellectuals to portray political realities which were far removed from these artists' immediate experience.

It may help to understand the importance of this play's failure by comparing *Bogeyman* to Jean Genet's play *The Blacks:* another anticolonial drama, which was written in 1957, first produced in 1959 (thus within the context of French social upheaval over the Algerian and Indochinese situations); and one which still remains vital and undated in its treatment of colonial oppression. Genet consciously admits the theatricality of his dramatic methods in *The Blacks,* and uses that admission to stress the lack of understanding between the black and white races. As Gabriel Marcel described this approach: "Everything which has contributed to the honor and dignity of the Western Christian world is here rejected. And this rejection is not just stated but *spat out, spewed forth.*"[34] The responses intended by Weiss's play seem tame in comparison because his actors, while purporting to represent Angolan natives, must speak and move and argue the issues in a theatrical style which is familiar to Western audiences, but which remains unconnected to the dramatic issues. Performers must voice the dialectical arguments and political ideals of Weiss himself, while Genet's blacks use these very same arguments ironically—as blacks—to insult and ridicule their white audience. As one critic has described the dramatic purchase of Genet's method: "The shock of this confrontation is not acted, it happens. Seen from this angle, the performance is no longer mimetic, but actual. Furthermore, the feeling of enmity created by this clash is not purely

Figure 9. *Song of the Lusitanian Bogeyman*
The Bogey with dancing Colonial Administrators, Christian
Stövesand and Ursula Figelius. Volkstheater Rostock, 1968,
directed by Hans Perten.
(*Photo by Hildegard Levermann-Westerholz*)

theatrical, but is the product of political, social, and economic realities *which pass unsublimated into the theatre building.*"[35]

In addition to the questionable suitability of Weiss's dramatic means, the dramatist also encountered serious problems with oversimplification of the political issues, particularly in *Vietnam Discourse,* which was completed that same year. With the language, for example, he could easily develop stylized verse patterns as cultural indicators (native chants accompanied by indigenous native musical instruments, administrative colonial jargon and the like), but he also faced the problem of documenting the public statements of political figures — statements which were often familiar to spectators from news reports. In this regard, Weiss felt no obligation to quote his sources verbatim, and he freely paraphrased the spoken record in order to make his political points unmistakable. The following purported "conversation" between Kennedy and Diem is a case in point:

> 9: Mr. President
>   My people and I
>   know how much
>   we already owe
>   to the United States
>   Now however only
>   total mobilisation
>   can bring us victory
>   over the Viet Cong
>
> 10: Deeply alarmed
>   and shocked
>   by the onslaught
>   on your country
>   we are sending
>   at once
>   everything you need.[36]

Such distortions were understandably overlooked by eastern European audiences who were in general more appreciative of Weiss's anti-American stance than many Western critics. Weiss's cavalier treatment of political realities, however, did amount in many cases to deliberate distortion. Western critics were skeptical, if not outright disgusted, at the way in which Weiss manipulated the facts. Ernst Schumacher, for example, who has consistently supported Weiss's attempts to explore political drama, hailed the 1968 Rostock production of *Vietnam Discourse* as "political theatre in the best sense." At the same time, though, he felt compelled to point out: "This is a method of heightening the theatrical impact, but the impression of factuality produced by Weiss's statements is greatly diminished."[37] The opposite extreme is typified by the comment of Bernd Jürgen who insisted on distinguishing between poetic license and downright lies: "Realistic may signify, according to one of Brecht's

Figure 10.   *Vietnam Discourse*
              Arrival of the American Administrators. Volkstheater
              Rostock, 1968, directed by Hans Perten.
              (*Photo by Hildegard Levermann-Westerholz*)

statements, what the 'social causal complex' reveals; but the text of *Discourse* goes beyond the clumsy utilization of concrete facts. . . . What it provides as information is scanty, if not falsified."[38]

This discussion is not meant to imply that the Vietnam and Angolan dramas were totally valueless as dramatic experiments. Weiss learned much from his handling of choruses, exploring several possibilities which would later serve him in good stead when he designed the choral sections of *Hölderlin.* In *Bogeyman,* for example, he used a three-person chorus at one point as a character in the dramatic situation of a confidante speaking to political prisoners. Another noteworthy choral technique appeared in scene 2 of *Bogeyman.* There Weiss situated one character between two semi-choruses in order to show how individuals are caught between two ideological groups of colonizers and revolutionaries, each of which attempts to win them over to their camp. As the individual tries to perform his daily tasks, one group encourages him from the sidelines to work and produce harder while the other faction urges strikes and noncooperation.

In *Vietnam Discourse* Weiss introduced another innovative choral technique. He handled his character groupings and their movements in precise choreographical patterns. At Gunilla Palmstierna's suggestion, the performers were costumed either in black (for Vietnamese) or in white (for colonialists and other foreigners). The stage floor was "sectored" into the four points of the compass in order to stress the influence of geographical factors upon the development of Vietnamese history. The frequent mass movement of the ensemble illustrated how the population density changed as a result of treaties, migrations, and invasions. Stage directions in the Vietnam play, therefore, are more extensive than in any of Weiss's other dramas. Consider the following example of only one blocking movement representing a Chinese invasion:

> 1, 2, 4 are armed in W. Commencement of strong march rhythm. 1, 2, 4 as peasant soldiers, 11 as commander move from W. in direction SW. 12, 13, 14, 15 as warriors move from W. in direction NE. The groups of inhabitants 3, 5, 6, 7, 8 form a ring in center. 9 as emperor, 10 as commander of Vietnam remain back on the dais in W. The groups of warriors plant their flags of nationality in SW and NE.

The third architectural principle of Weiss's documentary drama concerns the narrative development of the event. Weiss insisted upon producing a fast-paced presentation which he hoped might capture the sense of events actually bursting forth onstage. The drama, he declared, should have an immediacy to it, as though "reporting from the battlefield." Incidents should seem like "raw material, compact or in a loose stream." Every appearance of fiction, all sense of an artificially created stage world should be avoided in favor of "cross-cutting" or "interruption of the story." New issues would "break into the story, causing uncertainty, sometimes creating a shock effect." The aim is to provide a sense of "genuine experience," or "experience that is verifiable." The drama-

Figure 11. *Vietnam Discourse*
The Vietnamese peasant army. Volkstheater Rostock, 1968, directed by Hans Perten.
(Photo by Hildegard Levermann-Westerholz)

Figure 12. *Vietnam Discourse*
An early Chinese invasion. Volkstheater Rostock, 1968, directed by Hans Perten.
(Photo by Hildegard Levermann-Westerholz)

tic action should not unfold as history but as history in the making. The play-wright thus produces "a presentation of the violence in the clash of forces" rather than an explanation of causality; and "dissolving the structure" is all-im-portant for achieving spontaneity. Although the writer must plan the event care-fully, the play should seem "not a calculated rhythm" but instead "raw mate-rial."

It is difficult to see how this notion could ever be successfully realized in stage terms, and perhaps Weiss was not speaking in "absolute" terms, but only in suggestive ones. As we have already noted, Weiss displays confusion be-tween authenticity per se and the illusion of authenticity which is an artistic product. It would take a very clever playwright indeed to produce a documen-tary 100 percent "authentic"; and many critics sensed behind Weiss's documen-tary mask a posture just as calculated as that of a writer with direct propagan-distic intentions. Weiss maintained that a documentary play must "be a form of artistic expression to have any validity," but his attempts to "dissolve the struc-ture" and improvise in order to capture a sense of immediacy did not meet with much approbation from critics or audiences.

The Failure of Documentary Theater

The political revue form with its loose structure, spontaneity, and quick-cutting of material always requires a large amount of political consciousness on the part of its audience in order to function at its best. Both of Weiss's documen-tary plays lacked this political underpinning in Europe, which may help to ex-plain their failure at the box office. The performance style, of course, was another problem, as we have noted already. Weiss had intended that both plays should be a sort of "carnival" experiment which would explore the possibilities of popular theatre forms and mass heroes for worker audiences.[39] He was thinking of his role as a socially concerned writer in attempting to define and to reach his audiences in this way. His goal of authenticity and political spon-taneity, however, was not achieved. With Paul Dessau's music, intricate choreography, and grotesque spectacular costuming (especially in *Bogeyman*), these dramas confused their audiences. They raised the question of whether their author was more concerned with the "culinary riches of the modern stage"[40] than with the political abuses the plays assailed.

Weiss did not attempt to write any more documentary-style plays. Perhaps he recognized from their critical reception and their poor box office that they could not give his writing the immediacy and contemporary impact which in-itially he had desired. In the Angolan and Vietnamese dramas he had written about political conditions with which he had no personal contact and about which he possessed only an intellectual—though very thorough—understand-ing. He had therefore abandoned the combination of the personal with the polit-ical which had inspired *Marat/Sade*.

These documentary plays and the essay which resulted from them did teach him important techniques. They also helped him to clear away naive ideas he had been harboring about understanding history simply through its political manifestations. Weiss remarked about this latter point that he felt he had come very close to grasping historical development through a journalistic approach in the two plays. He commented to Henning Rischbieter in 1967 that "the plot has been replaced by the historical process."[41]

This accent upon history instead of upon politics is especially illuminating. The final version of *Mockinpott*, already underway in 1967 before *Vietnam Discourse* had opened, signalled a turn away from propaganda by a total absence in the script of any documentary materials or specific political references. *Mockinpott* was a philosophical parable, abstract and schematic in its presentation of the conflict between society and the individual. Besides this play, which occupied most of his energies between 1968 and 1969, he would also begin the play on Leon Trotsky. In this drama he would seriously criticize Russian socialism from an historical standpoint which avoided specific political references entirely. By late 1967, therefore, Peter Weiss's "propagandistic" phase was drawing to a close and he was beginning to focus upon historical analysis in his work once again.

Puppets and Politics: *How Mr. Mockinpott Was Cured of His Sufferings*

Two months after the opening of *Vietnam Discourse,* Weiss's farcical parable about the sufferings of Mr. Mockinpott opened at the Hannover Landestheater, directed by Horst Zankl. Although the play was new to audiences and critics, Weiss had begun it in 1963 and he had been reworking the script during the interim. No published information is available on the development of the final script, and Weiss remained unusually silent about the play's themes and development over a five-year period. The drama has had very few productions outside of Germany since 1968, and Weiss himself described is as "another stylistic experiment" dating from the period before *Marat/Sade.*

On one level the drama seems fairly consistent with Weiss's major prose and dramatic writings because of the familiar conflict it postulates between self and society. The hero, Mockinpott, develops political consciousness through a brutal confrontation between his personal desires and the extraordinary demands of his society. Mockinpott's growth thus parallels Weiss's own development from personal concerns in his art to public and political activities as a result of his socioeconomic circumstances.

Mockinpott also reflects several of Weiss's pre-1964 concerns with theatrical experimentation. Kafka-esque themes of absurdity and the grotesque (as in the early prose novels and *The Insurance*), the senseless violence and brutality underlying everyday experience (Strindberg, *Night with Guests*), and the staging devices of mime, puppetry, epic theater—all these are present in *Mockinpott* and connect the play with the stage techniques discussed in chapter 1.

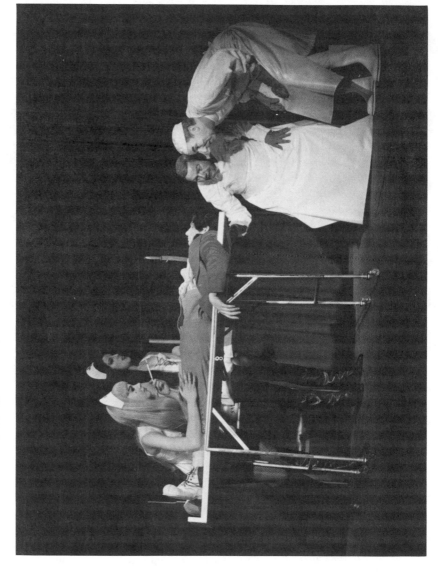

Figure 13. *How Mr. Mockinpott Was Cured of His Sufferings*
Mockinpott undergoes diagnostic surgery. Landestheater Hannover, 1968, directed by
Horst Zankl.
(Photo by Kurt Julius)

The play is a farce which uses Punch-and-Judy, boulevard satire, and circus clown conventions in order to trace the development of political consciousness in a typical middle-class individual of modern society. It is extremely schematic with its use of character types, stock situations, and staging devices to illustrate the simple point that "men must help themselves and reject existing social forms" in order to find happiness. In 11 episodic, burlesque scenes Mr. Mockinpott goes on a quest for the different typological representatives of government and society in order to find an explanation for his political oppression. He tries to discover the underlying rationale for all the conventional societal rules which have conditioned his life. His search leads to an increasing radicalization of his outlook, and he finally concludes that the norms and regulations of bourgeois existence are unjustifiable. They are coverups for a total absence of social responsibility, facades for the tyrannical policies of those in power. As a result, Mockinpott decides he will no longer conform, and he declares in the end that he is done "with the swindle now for good."[42]

One cannot help noticing in *Mockinpott* certain Brechtian derivations. Like the story of Galy Gay in Brecht's 1926 anti-imperialist *Mann Ist Mann,* Weiss begins his drama with a "kernel scene" which outlines the issues and which then plunges the central character into the conflict. Just as Galy Gay is conscripted by British soldiers whle on his way to buy a fish, so too Weiss's Mockinpott is arrested and jailed for no apparent reason while going to buy a newspaper. Mockinpott is sure there is some mistake and that everything will soon return to normal because "my wife with the kettle on the boil for tea / is waiting as always at home for me." The play demonstrates exactly the opposite. The world will never be the same for Mockinpott after his initial confrontation with political reality. Just as Brecht demonstrates that a man can be changed as easily as the parts of a machine, Weiss focuses upon the steps by which a man can be changed and radicalized. In both plays the central characters undergo total personality changes and arrive at new functional identities in the end.

Mockinpott requires no imperialist war in India to inspire him in his development, and this is an important point of departure from Brecht's play; Mockinpott's course is paved with the ordinary social problems of everyday bourgeois life. Because of Weiss's reliance upon puppetlike characters and popular conventions for staging and scene structure, he dispenses with realism in his handling of situations and personalities. The thesis always remains clearly in the foreground—perhaps too clearly—and thus the play must be seen as consistent with the traditional form of the "learning play" as it was developed in Germany by practitioners of the epic theater writing for popular audiences.

Although several of Brecht's plays were written as parable dramas, the carnival puppet show inspiration for *Mockinpott* clearly distinguishes Weiss's play from any other recent dramatic model. The play begins, for example, with Mockinpott's imprisonment and his confrontation with the figures of Jailer,

Figure 14.   *How Mr. Mockinpott Was Cured of His Sufferings*
Mockinpott and Pudding. Landestheater Hannover, 1968, directed by Horst Zankl.
(Photo by Kurt Julius)

Magistrate, and Lawyer. As Mockinpott fumbles clownishly with a large chain anchoring his foot to the floor, the officials fleece him and throw him out. Justice is reduced to a question of economics. Booted out in utter poverty, Mockinpott then encounters his companion figure for the rest of the play, Jack Pudding (the traditional German comic antihero). Pudding cares little for Mockinpott's desire to investigate the extraordinary occurrences and wonders why he's "not content to sit at home with [his] wife / or lead an orderly working life." Stuffing himself with food and wine, he advises Mockinpott to forget his grievances because, he says, "it's much more comfortable I've found / to sit up here than on the ground." Pudding accompanies the hero through various situations in order to help with Mockinpott's program of self-improvement and enlightenment.

After several burlesque encounters with typical social authority figures (politicians, employers, and the like), Mockinpott has no other choice but to take the matter to Dear God. Pudding assures him that "for the suffering man He always lives next door / so let's go and ask him what's the score." Pulling at a fat cigar, Dear God announces that He's pleased to see "such seriousness and such a genuine thirst / for knowledge unlike those who put their pudding first." But He reminds the pair of clowns that "it's difficult enough to run this business," and He admits that He really doesn't know "how far my firm at any minute / with all that's been invested in it / is functioning in all its parts." The social irresponsibility of capitalist industry is thus associated with the action of Divine Providence.

At this point Mockinpott blurts out in rage:

> If it's you who's responsible for the whole show
> My job and my marriage and police and all my dough . . .
> then I must say it puts me in a rage
> for I find myself put down at every stage
> I once thought that sufferings had their reward
> in heaven but I see now my good Lord
> that injustices when they befall
> the likes of us mean nothing to you at all
> but I can tell you and I hope I'm understood
> I've done with the swindle now for good.

Shaking his head, Dear God exits from Weiss's circus stage "like a broken man. His cigar hangs crookedly out the corner of his mouth." In a final scene of pantomime, Pudding stuffs himself while Mockinpott painfully learns to tie his boots on the proper feet. He then dances excitedly around the stage while Pudding snores in a thick stupor; and in a vignette lifted from Brecht's *Good Woman of Setzuan,* two angels descend on a trapeze to deliver the final lines: "May others learn from his sufferings / Miserere Miserere / and judge whether they were necessary."

The Clown as a Modern Hero

In a preface to the published version of *Mockinpott* Weiss mentioned that his thoughts about the 1963 drama *Night with Guests* "concerning popular theater, the carnival fair booth, and circus technique also apply to this play."[43] Weiss had been inspired by Punch and Judy at that time; what had appealed to him was the anonymous character of puppet show violence where serious problems could be "alienated" for critical appraisal. Audiences identify quickly and harmlessly with puppets and clowns, and a moralistic conclusion to puppet shows is usually a regular feature of the event. In *Mockinpott* the audience learns along with the central figure, parable-fashion, that love, science, representative government, industry, and religion can offer only sham solutions to problems. Real solutions can only arrive when Mockinpott, like Marat, learns to tie his own boots and pull himself up by his hair. Although the mechanics of the puppet show and the simplicity of the moral seem easily understandable, Weiss's play failed in production. Perhaps the best way to understand this is to begin with a few structural comparisons between *Marat/Sade* and this farcical parable.

Like that earlier play, *Mockinpott* used a dialectical structure on the character plane: Sade and Marat, Pudding and Mockinpott. Each character is the antithesis of the other: Sade's skepticism grapples with Marat's absurd faith, and Mockinpott's curiosity stands at odds with Pudding's indifference. In theory, such contradictory positions can be made to yield good dramatic conflict. When translating such ideas into stage terms, however, the writer must control the reductionist elements in order to keep the dramatic structure from becoming too schematized.

Marat/Sade had avoided oversimplification of the issues mainly because of the writer's personal inability to resolve the conflict. The play's unsettling conclusion produced an ambiguous response from the spectators (as the variety of critical interpretations on the drama illustrates). In *Mockinpott*, Weiss's mask was perhaps too transparent; his political sympathies were visible on every side. Thus the parable became lopsided, speaking more to believers than to skeptics. Henning Rischbieter criticized the original production on this basis, arguing that the role of Jack Pudding needed to be played up more in order to balance the emphasis placed on Mockinpott.[44]

The script seems to bear this out. It reads like a commedia-style scenario with its numerous *lazzi* for the performers. Thus it requires a director and an ensemble with comic abilities in order to gain as much dramatic mileage as possible from the all too simply phrased dialogue. Horst Zankl may have given insufficient production emphasis to Pudding's role. On the other hand, any director might well have asked himself why he should be obliged to correct this shortcoming; should he have to make the play a clown show instead of a political parable? generate spectator interest in a drama which needed more to flesh out its thin statements? Probably the greatest weakness in the script is the absence of any analysis by the dramatist; Weiss demonstrates effects alone, and he completely avoids dialectical discussion.

The dramatic reasons for striking a fair balance between the positions in a dialectical structure are evident from the success of *Marat/Sade*. What made Marat more than simply the mouthpiece of radical socialism was the fact that Marat had shared his opponent's skepticism to the point of deep psychological disturbance. The sequence entitled "The Faces of Marat" where the revolutionary leader is forced to examine his personal background, demonstrate how revolutionary ideals could arise from private pathological motives instead of from sound philosophical analysis. Conversely, it is Sade's envy of Marat's capacity for action despite setbacks which makes of him more than just the decadent cynical libertine of literary history. In this type of structure, the absolute weight of conviction in each position is necessarily weakened, but a dynamic tension is generated which propels the action forward without losing clarity.

Ultimately what is lacking in *Mockinpott* is just this sort of dynamism. The play needs balanced criticism, a certain sharing of viewpoints between the opposing parties. This is always more dramatically effective onstage. It is all too easy to point an accusing finger at type figures when dealing with complex problems; and yet this is just what *Mockinpott* set out to accomplish. Weiss had demonstrated in *Marat/Sade* that the reasons for failures in society can be found within the individual; and this observation cannot be successfully demonstrated within the limitations of such a unidimensional character as Mockinpott. To insist in defense that the play is intentionally simplified, that it is a parable, seems an evasion of the more important issue as to why the play failed at the box office. Theater does not usually tolerate simple statements. Mockinpott moved schematically from one political point to another as a thesis figure, and he elicited very little audience identification in the process. He only succeeded in making clear certain political ideas which need no such great theatrical effort or stage time to explain.

To question the polarization of theme and character in *Mockinpott* is not to demand that Weiss produce another *Marat/Sade*. If *Mockinpott* were to have any effect on contemporary audiences, it would have had to reflect more realistically the concerns of Western bourgeois spectators. The simple fact is that the "mass man" which Weiss successfully brought onstage in *The Investigation*, and even for brief moments in the documentary dramas, was nowhere to be seen in *Mockinpott*. By contrast we might call to mind similar puppetlike representatives of ordinary people: such figures as Chaplin's Tramp, Marceau's Bip, Strehler's Arlecchino, or even Handke's Kaspar (who had first appeared on the same Hannover stage as Weiss's Mockinpott only eight weeks before).

These comic characters are always more effective when their simplicity is used to highlight universal human problems instead of immediate political concerns. The pathos they elicit from spectators stems from their failings as ordinary human beings trying to cope with ordinary human problems rather than with complex points of ideology. Nor are they suitable for demonstrating any significant "growth in understanding" in the types they symbolize. As Robert Corrigan has observed: "A type character is one who needs no explaining and whose future is predictable no matter what his situation might be. Such a character is . . . a creature of habit, and he brings a great energy to the theatre. He has the characteristics essential for farce."[45] Farce does not ordinarily tolerate direct political statements unless they come from the pen of a great comic genius. Nor can its characters demonstrate the complex dimensions of contemporary political problems.

Weiss's thesis that "man must learn to help himself" is certainly universal enough; it is capable of eliciting a sympathetic response from most spectators with common sense. As Corrigan points out, though, it is also a *predictable* response, one that amuses us instead of surprising us. The danger here is that a response which is *too* predictable can become a crashing bore onstage unless something else is added to keep the scenario afloat. With the genius of pantomime Marceau can hold interest upon Bip. With the assistance of Goldoni's or Gozzi's portraiture of nineteenth-century Venice, Strehler can do the same for Arlecchino. Because of an unparalleled facility with language, Handke can astound audiences with the everyday discoveries of Kaspar. Mockinpott, while sharing many surface similarities to all these, clearly cannot function in the same way for two hours of stage time.

Weiss Retreats from Propaganda

Ultimately what betrayed Weiss in *Mockinpott* was the very same partisanship and narrowness of perspective which had worked against his other dramas on Portugal and the United States. He learned an important lesson from his years of political involvement, however. After *Marat/Sade* Weiss had been searching for dramatic heroes who could hold the attention of contemporary audiences, and simultaneously illuminate the socioeconomic facets in the playwright's analysis. In *The Investigation* Weiss used characters drawn from recent history because he felt that the relevance of their concerns to modern problems was unmistakable. The chorus of the Auschwitz play had been anonymous, and it had given voice to the accusations of millions of Jewish victims.[46] Weiss used mass heroes again in *Bogeyman* and *Vietnam Discourse* in order to present liberation movements in the Third World.

These attempts were not always commercially successful, however, and experimentation with the parable format in *Mockinpott* was the least successful of all.[47] Weiss's "common man" had devolved into a cardboard type, too abstract and ineffectual. It was at this point, after the failure of *Mockinpott,* that Weiss abandoned work with mass heroes and returned to the strategy of using a single major protagonist. In his next two plays he would try to unite in a single character both the typical individual filled with self-doubt and groping for perspective and the great historical agent capable of influencing the course of history. Trotsky and Hölderlin would contain within themselves the important questions which Weiss was asking about the role of the concerned leftist intellectual in modern society.

These later portraits of revolutionary leaders indicate more than just a shift in the dramatist's technique; they also suggest an important shift in his thoughts upon the subject of revolutionary change. Socialist optimism, for example, yields to personal disillusionment in *Hölderlin,* and to martyrdom in *Trotsky;* and this raises the question of where the writer himself stands with regard to the issue of progressive historical change through rational methods. Can political conditions be improved simply by building up enough mass resistance to topple the bogeyman of Western capitalism? And is the social phenomenon of mass resistance a positive virtue in all situations, a satisfactory remedy for social oppression?

These were problems Weiss had grappled with in his drama on the French Revolution. At what point, that is, had a "social cleansing" of the oppressing classes devolved into the nightmare of revolutionary terror? Seven years later in 1969, Weiss was asking why the Russian Revolution had also failed. Judging by Weiss's interest in the Third World after 1965, one might argue that the playwright only believed in the possibility of revolution in underdeveloped nations instead of in the industrialized West. Even here, though, Peter Weiss was aware that Third World nations encountered serious problems with national liberation. In his criticism between 1966 and 1970, he complained about artistic censorship in the Iron Curtain nations, Israeli dependence upon the West instead of upon socialist bloc countries, and the bloody power struggles which greeted emancipation in many African states.

Thus Weiss's political consciousness had reached the point after 1968 where he wanted to undertake a more philosophical approach to the question of modern revolution and the intellectual's social role. Important moral questions needed to be examined, and Weiss's plays on Trotsky and Hölderlin would deal with this kind of ethical analysis of revolutionary motives and expectations. As Herbert Blau commented about the handling of revolutionary themes in the theater of the sixties:

> Nobody can but cheer when plutocracy and false privilege are overthrown and freedom is achieved. Yet, if we must be moral realists, we should see that some of these revolutions lack, because of the speed with which values are transformed and rejected in our age, the articulated moral fervor of our own [American Revolution]. The anarchy begins in some cases after freedom has been granted by controlled historical process; then the power struggle begins. The chains off, there is a swift clamor for economic parity and industrial development. It is all understandable, desire moving as fast as the times. But though these revolutions have their spokesmen and their heroes, and I do not mean to deny them ideals, they do not seem to speak with the natural religion of a Jefferson or even the egalitarian outrage of a Tom Paine. Some are plain tyrannies, some barbarous, some pervasions of their democratic intent. And a Jean Genet seems to know more about them than U Thant.[48]

Marat/Sade testifies to Weiss's "moral realism" on the issue of violent revolution; after the failure of *Mockinpott* in 1968 Weiss turned away from political simplification and grew skeptical of political idealism. He wanted instead to deal with the *ethics* of socialism in order to understand why it had failed in the twentieth century.

Thus Weiss's search for a dramatic hero parallels his own search for political sympathies and his social function as a committed writer.[49] By turning to heroic portraiture and by expanding the political features of his choruses in *Trotsky* and *Hölderlin,* Weiss hoped to achieve both dramatic purchase and political focus. More than a summary of a hero's career, Weiss's plays could thus show these men as they developed their forms of commitment, and how the times changed around them. Both the individual and the historical process would be in the foreground of the plays he would soon come to write.

4

The Revolutionary Intellectual, 1969–1971

Weiss's Experience in Vietnam

Between May and June of 1968 Weiss travelled to North Vietnam as a guest of the People's Revolutionary Government. For several months prior to this Weiss had been active in Stockholm as a member of Bertrand Russell's War Crimes Committee, and this journey was an outgrowth of that militant antiwar work. Vietnam was his first contact with a revolutionary society-in-the-making, and the experience had an important impact upon his writing. The journal and the notes which he kept during his stay in Hanoi reflect the strong political character of his thoughts at the end of the decade.

The trip was educational for the 51-year-old writer. He was impressed by the Vietnamese, who were engulfed in a national struggle for their independence (which Weiss compared to his own search for personal freedom as a young man),[1] and the enormously complicated task of building a revolutionary society was brought home to him in vivid detail. Weiss had known wartime situations, of course, and he had been keeping abreast of political developments in the Third World nations. Face to face with the North Vietnamese, however, he could only wonder how it was possible that "a third generation can accept the war as a natural condition, a concept which in its totality overshadows the catastrophe of World War Two."[2]

Weiss tried to confront the terrible dislocation of Vietnam in 1968 by once again affirming his commitment to the socialist cause. He wanted his art to become "a weapon"; its importance should lie in its "social, pedagogical weight."[3] Self-indulgent artistic independence had no place in a wartime atmosphere, he insisted. The "rubbish literature" and the "brutalizing films" of America deserved to be scrapped and replaced by politically committed art. He railed against the "moral bankruptcy of modernism which can offer only subjective visions, skepticism, and rejection of the outer world, and which becomes either sentimental or elitist and specialized in its foreign relations."[4]

It is easy to uncover Weiss's political sympathies in his journal. He was highly impressed by the treatment and respect he received in North Vietnam.

In fact, before they would return to Europe, all the members of Russell's committee would be furnished with a "complete" report on the scope of United States aggression in southeast Asia: statistics on the number of civilian casualties, timetables showing the military escalation against the North, tonnage of ordnance dropped on nonmilitary targets. All this material would find its way into his *Notizen* (*Notes*), which Suhrkamp published later that same year. Weiss's *Notes,* however, would also include his personal reflections on the nature of the conflict, reflections which mainly arose from several interviews he conducted with an American prisoner.

His conversations with this man, an Air Force major and fighter-bomber pilot, provide the most engaging section of Weiss's *Notes.* The interview seemed to highlight for Weiss the unique achievements of the Third World in contrast to the bankruptcy of ideals in the industrialized West. Weiss was appalled by the pilot, whom he regarded as a typical product of American culture; he was certain the major was insane, "not in command of his senses." The man trembled like a crazy puppet as he spoke, "an empty man in whom nothing was functioning properly." He had committed fearful atrocities upon innocent civilians without any remorse, and Weiss regarded him as "the representative of a system which ignores questions . . . which recognizes no ideals." He was "a picture of total rootlessness," a man "bereft of ideals" and one who "never questioned his life . . . a murderer and a powerseeker."

These observations added nothing new to the thoughts he had advanced in *Vietnam Discourse* the previous year. The enthusiasm for Third World revolution which he had expressed in that play, however, was intensified because of Weiss's exposure to wartime conditions in Hanoi. This was necessary for him in 1968 because he was still troubled by political indecision. For one thing, his commitment to socialism had drawn some bitter rebukes from important critics in communist countries. Weiss had not been welcomed by socialist intellectuals although he had hoped for such recognition in order to validate his committed stance as a playwright. Except for *Vietnam Discourse,* his plays had been regarded with suspicion by eastern European audiences. In 1966, for example, the highly respected East German author Hans Magnus Enzensberger had ridiculed Weiss's commitment. It was merely an act, Enzensberger said, "of patting yourself on the shoulder, of seriously believing that you're taking a risk." The class struggle for Weiss was only "just material for exotic drama, and solidarity only an intellectual ornament."[5]

Another political thorn for Weiss at this time was his growing skepticism towards the foreign policies of Russia and China. He regarded the power struggle between these two superpowers as fruitless and divisive. This attitude began to surface at the time of his return from Hanoi and Cambodia in 1968. In a letter to Lew Ginsberg in Moscow, Weiss spoke with contempt of the way in which "Soviet historians reduced the vital, colorful history of the Russian Revolution to a monotonous, dull narrative" about Lenin and Stalin, and how "the young socialist generation can better understand" the importance of Trotsky's theories on national liberation movements.

He was convinced that the course of future history would be determined not by what he called the "death culture" of America and the industrialized West, nor by the "social disaster" of modern Russia,[6] but instead by the developing countries of the Third World. Estranged from political camps in both western and eastern Europe, Weiss felt that he should exert influence as a writer by highlighting national liberation struggles in the postwar period. This was one reason for choosing Leon Trotsky as the subject of his next play. He said that he wished "to restore the proper historical proportions" to modern socialist thought by a play which would celebrate the forbidden subject of Trotskyism. He said this kind of "research into the true facts [was] more important than fashionable party politics and backbiting."[7]

Trotskyism and the Third World

The connection between Weiss's interest in the underdeveloped nations and his drama on Trotsky lies in Trotsky's theories on "permanent revolution." As a militant program, Trotskyism urged worldwide agitation, one attitude for which Trotsky was ultimately denounced and later assassinated by Stalin's agents. Weiss felt that the recent "class history" of growing liberation movements in every part of the world testified to the correctness of Trotsky's views, and that there was much in his theories which was valuable for contemporary leftist intellectuals.

Weiss also commented upon the fact that the Soviet experiment had misfired after the death of Lenin. Although Trotsky had been forced to work in exile after Stalin took control, Trotsky had managed to defend and preserve many of Marx's theories which he believed Stalin had perverted. China had mistakenly chosen the same path as Russia, Weiss believed, by allowing a strong dictatorial leader to shape its repressive domestic policies. The new play which Weiss was preparing argued strongly against aggressive militarism and against the "personality cult" of a Party chairman; and thus it advanced views which were different from Soviet or Chinese-style socialism. *Trotsky in Exile,* Weiss insisted, would criticize Stalinist repression and censorship; the drama would honor Lenin "by celebrating his fundamental belief in the necessity for open discussion."[8]

In addition to rectifying historical misunderstandings about Trotsky's importance, Weiss was also seeking practical guidelines for contemporary political problems:

> What concerns us here and what still remains unclear, is the question of how Trotsky's theoretical alternatives have been confirmed in the post-Stalinist world; which of his theories are still viable today after successful revolutions in Vietnam, in China, Korea, and Cuba,

after the onset of national liberation struggles in Africa and Latin America; what new forms have since been tested and, under certain conditions, have now been found to be absolutely necessary.[9]

Although the world of Trotsky and Lenin was certainly a part of past history, Weiss felt that by analyzing this period he might make a significant contribution as an artist to the socialist cause. His recent participation on Lord Russell's committee had placed him in close contact with other European leftist intellectuals—Sartre among them—an experience which provided him with an opportunity for working practically on behalf of political goals. Much the same could be said of his Vietnam journey because it focused his thinking on revolutionary development and encouraged him to seek out alternatives to the Russian or Chinese-style programs.

In summary, Weiss's firsthand contact in Vietnam with a revolutionary society, a society which was being "victimized" by aggressive Western powers, strengthened his faith in the future of the Third World. It also fortified his determination to attack Western neocolonialism in his writing. On the other hand, Weiss held few illusions about the role which the communist superpowers could play in Third World development. His criticism of Soviet repression in Czechoslovakia displayed contempt for Stalinist attitudes which were still operative in the postwar world. His decision to continue to live in neutral Sweden reflected his wish to maintain his artistic independence, despite his recent espousal of radical politics in the documentary plays. From all appearances, therefore, Weiss was beginning work on *Trotsky* with more political dexterity and objectivity than he had commanded since *Marat/Sade*. His commitment to socialism had gradually led him back to a position of artistic independence.

Leon Trotsky and Artistic Censorship

"To hell with Trotsky—give us Lenin!" the radical students in the audience shouted at the Düsseldorf premiere. The play was Weiss's offering in celebration of the centennial of Lenin's birth. "It honors Lenin," Weiss declared, "by the fact that it shows those who fought beside him, those with whom he disagreed, those with whom he made progress and produced the greatest social revolution of our century."[10]

It was important that a reassessment of Trotsky and his ideas be made, 30 years after his death. Stalin had denounced Trotsky and his followers as counterrevolutionary deviationists. His attitude was adopted by the post-Stalin party members and had been exported to the satellite countries during the 1950s and 1960s. Trotsky had been held responsible for subversive acts of counterrevolutionaries during the 1930s and he had been publicly denounced in the 1936 Moscow trials—the culmination of Stalin's purges of all suspected enemies of the revolution. Since then, nothing had appeared in Russia in the least favorable towards the man who stood beside Lenin for 22 years, who had built the Red Army, and whose writings in exile had inspired Mao, Che Guevara, Castro, and Tariq Ali.

Weiss was also impressed by Trotsky's exile, a man cast out of his homeland who had continued his work while living under constant persecution. Like Strindberg, Henry Miller and others, Trotsky had espoused unpopular views despite social criticism. His independent spirit arose in part from the fact that he had spent so many years in exile before 1917; he really did not join the Party until the eve of the October Revolution. Hence he never developed that sense of party organization which was Lenin's greatest strength; and after Lenin's death in the early 1920s, Trotsky withdrew from active involvement in Party affairs and turned to writing about socialist theory.

Weiss felt that Trotsky's independence helped him arrive at accurate perspectives upon the future of socialism, perspectives which came into focus during the post-World War II period. The international features of Trotskyism and its cornerstone of "permanent revolution" were examples of this. Stalin had tightened his dictatorial control over politics within the Soviet Union; Trotsky, however, had urged the party to extend its activities outside of Russia in order to promote revolution worldwide. In 1935, Trotsky asked,

> Is it possible for an isolated Soviet state to maintain itself for an indeterminate period of time in an imperialist environment, within the constricting circle of fascist counter-revolutions? The answer of Marxism is: No. The answer of the internal condition of the U.S.S.R. is: No! . . . Outside of the world revolution there is no salvation.[11]

Weiss felt that by his insistence upon extending revolutionary work beyond the borders of Russia, Trotsky had recognized the germs of historical development which would shape the political struggles of the modern period.

Weiss affirmed these accomplishments in his drama: "It is a play which should be done in revolutionary countries; only there can one appreciate its arguments."[12] Weiss felt it had been a great mistake for the Soviet Union to reject a worldwide revolutionary program in 1926. Instead Stalin had consolidated the nation into a conservative bureaucratic state. This had been a radical departure from classical Marxism because Stalin had built up a dictatorial regime. Trotsky, though, had urged a strengthening of the Comintern in order to promote Communism in *every* country.

Weiss admired Trotsky's courage in defying the Soviet Party line and in accepting his banishment. Weiss had always been fascinated by intellectual "deviates" because he felt such people usually rebelled against social norms which repressed creative thought. Weiss also believed that Trotsky had argued for a strong role for artists within revolutionary societies. He felt that Trotsky had wanted to leave the ideological door open for a variety of approaches in *many* lands, instead of forcing intellectuals to adhere to the tastes of a dictator or to the censorship of the Party.

Figure 15. *Trotsky in Exile*
The First Party Congress. Landestheater Hannover, 1970, directed by Harry Buckwitz.
(Photo by Kurt Julius)

Trotsky had in fact written with fire and conviction as the apostle of revolution, but he had also written—after his exile in 1928—as the critic of a revolution gone wrong. He had not only been the champion of the dictatorship of the proletariat but also the censor of a totalitarian bureaucracy established in its name. Weiss admired this. Trotsky's liberal views had certainly caused extreme polarization within the Party ranks in 1929 when the split surfaced, but Weiss felt that Trotskyism had been the correct alternative.

Weiss's own situation as a leftist intellectual had much to do with Trotsky's situation and beliefs. Weiss too needed to discover his role in advancing the socialist cause, especially through writing. His views on art and politics, he felt, were similar to Trotsky's. He thought it essential that revolutionary development have the cultural underpinning of independent artists and intellectuals. As he remarked years earlier, in 1965, "My work can only be fruitful . . . if it broadens the openness of eastern European societies, and if it leads to the development there of more free and non-dogmatic statements of opinion."[13] Writers must play important roles within the movement, but under present day conditions of "socialist realism," and in light of the repressive attacks against intellectuals during the postwar period, creative experiments of socialist artists were discouraged and often censored. By choosing to celebrate Trotsky's career Weiss was writing with his own self-image in mind. He was discovering solutions to his own problems while at the same time he was working on a project of current interest.

The Drama as Biography

Weiss's play begins in 1928 with Trotsky's banishment from Soviet Russia. As his family and friends are rounded up by Red Army soldiers, Trotsky gathers his books and papers and issues final orders: "Always ready to move on. Orders disturbed, restored. Materials China, India, South America. Liberation movements in the colonies. Struggles of the blacks in the United States . . . send on the newspapers as fast as you can."[14] The play's first scene thus establishes the keynote of banishment and exile which is central to Weiss's conception of his hero. In scene 2 the drama moves back in time and recounts the events which led up to Trotsky's situation in 1928. We see him in 1901 exiled to the penal colony of Verkholensk, fretting at his inactivity and making halfhearted plans for future revolution. "We shall not be silenced," Weiss's hero declares. "History. This terrible machine. It grinds slowly, agonizingly. Drinks our blood. . . . We must summon up our strength. Push. Move it on. Anything but wait." The next scene shows Trotsky with Lenin in London a year later. There he hears Lenin's plans for party unity within the Russian social democratic movement. "Give us an organization of professional revolutionaries," Lenin declares, "and we shall turn Russia upside-down."

Scene 4 moves forward another year to show the two leaders forming their party in Brussels at the first Party Congress. Moderates, Zionists, and other splinter groups are ruthlessly expelled and a terrorist program is adopted. In scene 5, 1915, Father Gapon leads striking workers in their famous march on the Winter Palace. The crowd is slaughtered by the Tsar's soldiers, Trotsky defies the Imperial justices, and is once again sentenced to exile. A year later, in the next scene, Trotsky has escaped and has joined Lenin in Zurich where the two radicals encounter avant-garde dadaists: Tristan Tzara, Hugo Ball, Huelsenbeck, Janco, Jennings, and Anna Blume. This scene argues the issue of individual art versus political propaganda which earlier had formed the core of *Marat/Sade;* but here Weiss restates the problem in terms of the importance of avant-garde art within a revolutionary society. "We'll go down in history too, just like you," Tzara explains to Trotsky. "You say bourgeois values must be destroyed, we don't want to keep any of them . . . that's our program too."

Here Weiss reveals Trotsky as a man open to the ideas of others, something of a compromiser, in fact. "To that extent you are right," Trotsky admits. "These shocks and upsets. . . . They must produce a new form of art." Lenin is opposed to this, however: "Art has no right to absolute freedom. Art must take sides." After the dadaists depart, Lenin confides to Trotsky that art really has no place in a revolutionary environment. "Music affects the nerves," Lenin complains. The only way to deal with artists is to "beat them on the head, that's what one must do."

Weiss concludes the first act with two scenes dealing with the revolutionary events on October 25 and 26, 1917, in Moscow. A seemingly interminable series of messengers arrive and announce each phase of the battle. In the final moments, after the Bolshevik victory, Lenin delivers his first speech to the assembled radicals. This speech, though, fades out at the very end and reveals a similar Congress of Party members 12 years later: the occasion of Trotsky's banishment. The conclusion of act 1 simultaneously shows Lenin frozen at his desk in 1917 and Red Army soldiers hustling Trotsky offstage in 1929.

The second act is considerably shorter than the first, and it seems to move more quickly. It traces Trotsky's exile panoramically across Europe and into Mexico, and stresses the international features of Trotsky's theories. In scene 10 Trotsky is on the Sea of Marmara reminiscing about Lenin's death. He ruefully recalls how Lenin had agreed with him on international revolution. "Didn't Lenin always stress our final dependence on international revolution? The revolution can't be contained within a single country. It's part of a general overall development."

The scene then dissolves to reveal Lenin's death in 1921, an occasion when Trotsky had failed to argue his beliefs when he had the chance. What had blinded him, he asks himself? "Beside you I could work," he tells the imaginary figure of Lenin. "I watched the new generation, I could talk to them . . . defend them. But when you died, all that remained was the struggle for power. I couldn't join in that." Weiss closes the scene with Stalin's funeral oration over Lenin's coffin, thus emphasizing how Trotsky had tragically forfeited the reins of power to a dictator who would eventually destroy him and his family, and betray the revolution.

The next five scenes follow quickly, as Trotsky falls farther away from political power. Scene 12 in Grenoble (1935) shows the revolutionary leader fielding questions from foreign students, most of them from Third World nations. Scene 13 takes the form of a nightmare presenting the terrible Moscow trials in 1936. In scene 14 Trotsky and his associates are hiding behind furniture after a machine gun attack on Trotsky's Mexican villa. André Breton, Diego Rivera, and Harold Robins accompany the hero and speak of Trotsky's absurd faith in the future of socialism. "I can't stop believing in reason," Trotsky tells them. "Socialism, in spite of the crimes committed in its name, can change. It can be improved, can be given new life." Weiss shows Trotsky as defiant, even at the nadir of his career, a stoic revolutionary strong in his own convictions. "Failures and disappointments can't stop me from seeing beyond the present defeat," he declares. "If death were to take me today, I could say I had worked for the exploited and colonized masses in the permanent struggle for liberation. For the need of culture and science to develop freely. For an art that allows unrestricted expression to man's urge for renewal."

Thus Weiss's hero speaks out in the end for freedom of artistic expression, denial of repressive Stalinist tendencies, and for the importance of art in a revolutionary society. In the play's final scene, barely a few minutes long, Trotsky works on some papers at his desk while the murderer approaches. The characters freeze in tableau with the hatchet poised above Trotsky's head as the curtain falls.

Dramaturgical Emphasis on the Writer's Situation

From a chronological standpoint the material on the Russian Revolution would seem to lend itself to an epic type of staging whereby the major incidents in the 39-year career of the central character could be episodically presented. Weiss had something very different in mind, however. He chose an expressionistic style in order to present Russian history through the eyes of the title character; all the stage action unfolds as a dream in the hero's mind as he sits writing in his study in Coyoacan, Mexico. This enables Weiss to present the material from a highly subjective yet "cool" and distanced critical standpoint, and to emphasize the nature of historical development as continual change and movement. Weiss wanted to portray "the great flux of historical events as they are reflected through the fantasies of the main character."[15]

The design concept by Gunilla Palmstierna-Weiss reflected this intention. On a bare stage backed only by a cyclorama and defined mainly by selective

Figure 16. *Trotsky in Exile*
Trotsky (Richard Münch) at his writing desk. Landestheater
Hannover, 1970, directed by Harry Buckwitz.
(*Photo by Kurt Julius*)

lighting, a cast of 24 men and 6 women performed the 62 speaking roles (there were also nonspeaking supernumeraries). The stage directions stipulate "a room that could be anywhere, with a writing-desk covered with papers and books, a camp bed, trunks and packing cases and a few widely spaced chairs." This basic scene remained unchanged throughout the performance in order that all the activities during Trotsky's exile—meetings, disputations, revolutionary struggles—could flow against an image of retirement, isolation, and intellectual detachment.

The play thus resembled a collage of flashbacks of the central character, a projection of his memories. The wide open stage and the selective lighting plan allowed Weiss to easily introduce or dissolve large and small groups and individuals at a moment's notice. Somewhat in the style of the Living Theatre, performers created the scene by donning period costume pieces or by carrying a few properties onstage as they appeared from the surrounding darkness. A few items—packing cases, trunks, chairs—sufficed for the necessary furniture. The sole unifying element thus became the figure of Trotsky at his writing table.

In addition to this experimental production concept, the play displayed other original features. Weiss had previously defined geographical elements or political attitudes in his documentary dramas by sketching in his characters typologically and by choreographing their movements, as in *Vietnam Discourse.* In *Trotsky,* though, the roles were more conventionally enacted despite the doubling and tripling of parts by the performers and the static, almost formal and chorale-like grouping of the characters onstage. More than ideological mouthpieces or typical representatives of social classes, the historical figures in *Trotsky* were individuals, characterized in greater depth and detail than those in the recent documentary plays or in *Mockinpott.*[16]

In addition to experimenting with dramatic portraiture, Weiss handled the setting in a politically provocative manner. As in *Marat/Sade,* historical events were enacted against a critical background—in the earlier play a background of lunacy, while here in *Trotsky* one of reason and detachment. Instead of a drama written by a scandalous antisocial extremist, these stage activities were the recollection of a world-recognized public hero, the dynamic leader of the Russian Revolution. This aspect of the play's credibility was reinforced by the directing approach of Harry Buckwitz in Düsseldorf, who worked closely with Weiss and Gunilla Palmstierna-Weiss during the seven-month production period. The actors were coached to develop a type of uniformly emotionless diction (similar to Weiss's work on *The Investigation*) which would allow the "dialectical development" of the play's theme to emerge uncluttered by stage spectacle. In a director's note contained in the program for the Düsseldorf premiere, Buckwitz described this method as a "linear and conversational diction according to which all the play's characters might seem in synchronization with the features of Trotsky himself . . . a synthesis of dramatic representation and demonstration."

Weiss was trying to show the "inside" of historical events—their impact upon the central hero—without sacrificing objectivity in the process. He wanted to reveal the personality and thoughts of Trotsky while still maintaining a focus on the sociopolitical arena in which he moved. The performance resembled an hallucination in Trotsky's mind, and thus it stressed the centrality of Trotsky the writer's understanding of historical development. Although the dream-vision production concept could be dangerously confusing and the wealth of material was substantial, Weiss believed that it was possible to stage the play uncut if a good director were in charge. "The play should be done just as it's written," he insisted, "taking a lot of time with it, working very basically and systematically, and clarifying its political statements with ensemble playing."[17] The fluidity of roles, the changing timeframes accomplished through flashbacks, the ideological arguments—all the action revolved around the figure of the writer, analyzing the situation from a detached standpoint onstage. "The beginning," Weiss said, "is explained by the end, which shows Trotsky in retirement and isolation, just before his death."[18]

This attention to the personal side of his historical characters was radically different from the types of stage roles Weiss had created for the documentary plays. Weiss was able to deepen his treatment of the dramatic issues by introducing his Russian characters to situations which called for personal reflection. In scene 9, for example, events crash forward and seal the future of the revolution in October of 1917, and Weiss provides a short interlude between Trotsky and Lenin to clarify the role of the historical agent in bringing about historical change. "Do you think," Lenin asks, "that without us the October revolution could ever have taken place?" "Sometimes I think so, sometimes not," Trotsky replies. "We have the overall vision. See the immediate possibilities. Put into concrete form what was present in the raw." In scene 11, the bewildering flux of events and the mind's inability to cope is revealed by Lenin's fictitious deathbed admission of his personal failures. "It's true. I try to steer," he complains to Trotsky, "but the wheels won't respond. The vehicle swerves about in all directions. I can't control it any more." In Weiss's play, the revolutionary intellectual's failures are often more important and more inspiring than his successes.

Weiss was able to portray his hero's sufferings in the play, and this humanized the portrait of Trotsky to some extent; for example, self-doubts continually riddle Trotsky's thoughts as he sees his relatives butchered by Stalin: "Was it right to put my work first, before everything: family, friendship, love? To see myself just as part of an historical process?" Self-doubts about his lack of influence during his banishment also gnaw at him: "Move you on. Nearly ten years in exile . . . what can we do from here to set the wheels of history in motion?" Robert Payne, one of Lenin's biographers, has commented upon this feature in the lives of modern revolutionary figures: "The mind of the conspirator in exile, cut off from news about the revolutionary movements in his

Figure 17. *Trotsky in Exile*
Richard Münch as Trotsky and Kurt Beck as Lenin. Landestheater Hannover, 1970,
directed by Harry Buckwitz.
(Photo by Kurt Julius)

own country, feeds on illusions of power. It is a desperate life, never more desperate than when all the evidence points to the disastrous defeat of his dreams. There is no middle ground for the conspirator; he must either see himself as the arbiter of destinies, or he abandons the struggle, or commits suicide. The history of the Russian revolutionary movement has as many suicides as martyrs."[19]

A powerful sense of helplessness runs through Weiss's play, helplessness which was similar to Weiss's own feelings as an *emigré* artist during World War II. And more than just helplessness, Weiss stresses the fact that his hero must certainly have questioned the value of his writing as a force for change, even when he was directly engaged in struggle. In one of the drama's most revealing passages Trotsky declares: "Sometimes I find myself thinking that the revolution is only hindering me from working systematically. As if the battle of ideas were more important to me than revolutionary activity. The writings, the printed impression of my thoughts more real than the action outside." Peter Weiss was, of course, asking the same question of his own work. Theory and praxis, detachment or engagement, the objectivity of analysis or the visceral response to needs, reason or absurdity—these paradoxes had been animators of Weiss's work since the time of *Marat/Sade*.

By using the expressionistic dream-vision as a production concept and by revealing the self-doubts of his hero Weiss succeeded in splitting his focus between a strong central character and the violent political arena in which that character moved. This approach to stagecraft, though, suggested important questions which the play didn't attempt to answer. For example, did the split in focus imply that mass movements were less influential than the efforts of one or two highly gifted intellectuals? Did the drama propose that a strong military planner (Trotsky) was the better leader for a revolutionary government than an intelligent Party theoretician (Lenin)? And was the failure of the Russian Revolution supposed to be indicative of the inabilities of leftist parties to overcome internal dissension and repressive totalitarian tendencies?

The most important of these questions was the failure of Trotsky as a revolutionary leader after Lenin's death, a question which causes a radical shift in the play's focus between the first and second acts. The first half of the drama is replete with documented statements, ideological arguments presented in detail, chronologically organized examples of the systematic growth of revolution. These nine scenes are eventful; the final six, however, are extremely spare in terms of external action. Each is simply another step in Trotsky's decline as he is chased across the globe by Stalin's agents.

Thus Trotsky's thoughts do not grow and develop as a result of this decline in the same way that we see his theories forged in the crucible of historical events during act 1; and this is a serious weakness in the script. Act 2 is mainly concerned with the hero's psychological condition as an exiled and, therefore, impotent radical and with laying out the applications of his theories to Third World students, visiting "fellow travelers" in Mexico, and others who follow his decline. This romantic, pathetic portraiture and sheer presentationalism of his beliefs sidetracked the movement of history in the second act, and it really did not yield a strong dramatic situation or climax where Trotsky could grow, change, or develop. Weiss realized this later and his comments in the *Notizbücher 1971–1980,* dating from March 1973, express his difficulty in figuring out a solution. In any case, the play's dramatic structure does demonstrate how strongly Weiss was concerned with the psychological problems of the revolutionary writer. In addition to being a political document dealing with the making of a revolution, the drama also became a tragic portrait of one heroic, misunderstood revolutionary.

Independence versus Political Parties

The conflicts raised in the Zurich coffeehouse scene in *Trotsky* between art and politics, between the apparently irrational zeal of the dadaists and the ruthless program of the Bolsheviks, sheds important light upon Weiss's feelings on politically committed art. In the scene Lenin argues for reason, objectivity, practical applications, and he rejects everything which is personal, everything which tries to remain independent of the great socialist upheaval. By contrast, the dadaists seek an even wider liberation which transcends political considerations entirely. In Weiss's portrayal, Trotsky straddles the fence, seeking a synthesis of the two positions.[20] Weiss speculated that Trotsky really had been willing to permit freedom of artistic expression within a new socialist society. This was a crucial point in defining the role of leftist intellectuals during the post–World War II period, and Weiss wanted to stress the issue:

> In a socialist country, especially one like East Germany where the society is still being built up, people seem to feel that only theatre directly involved in the political struggle should exist, that any other point of view distorts this struggle. . . . I've never understood why socialist countries fight against certain kinds of art—in a socialist society all forms of expression should be acceptable.[21]

The issue of surrealism and its corresponding implications of freedom for artistic expression are central to *Trotsky.*[22] In Weiss's mind, concern with the class struggle was not simply a political matter, at least not directly. Theater must and should be political, he believed. But within that definition there was still opportunity for a wide range of artistic responses to social problems. His own development as an artist was a case in point. He felt it had been necessary for him to explore nonpolitical subjective writing in order to understand himself and hammer out his artistic methods. Thus his abandonment of surrealist tendencies in his film work in favor of documentary feature films had "contained the seed of the work I am now doing in theatre."[23] Weiss knew that his freedom to experiment had produced positive results, and he tried to bring out this point too in the drama.

He attempted to connect this issue, the importance of artistic experiment, with the power struggles in which his hero had been caught. Lev Davidovitch Trotsky had tried to steer the great Russian socialist revolution on a progressive course during the 1920s, and he had been destroyed by a ruthlessly repressive man who was in every way his opposite. Where Trotsky was permissive, Stalin had been uncompromising; when Trotsky had urged spreading the Soviet Union's influence abroad, Stalin had branded him a tyrant bribed by Western powers who wished to lead the USSR down a disastrous road; and when Trotsky continued to write and publish, Stalin condemned and sentenced him as a deviationist. The artistic consequences of Stalinism for leftist writers at mid-century had been extremely unfortunate: artistic conservatism within already revolutionized states, repressive censorship in the satellite nations of eastern Europe, periodic purges of Russia's leading intellectuals, and the establishment of nineteenth-century bourgeois standards of pedestrian "realism."

A final point in Weiss's analysis of artistic freedom in this play is his emphasis upon the divisive effects of censorship. Weiss realized that when Trotsky abandoned the Party in 1928, he provoked a damaging split within the artistic ranks of the leftist European avant-garde, a split which was still apparent among postwar leftist intellectuals working in uncertain situations with regard to their political allegiances. Weiss traced the causes of this situation to their origin in the twenties, as a result of Trotsky's defection and Stalin's policies. At that time, Aragon and others separated themselves from the surrealist movement and joined the ranks of the French Communist Party. Of that large group of writers, however, it was André Breton and the other strict surrealists who had opted for Trotsky and Trotskyism. Thus in the play Weiss aligned himself with these counterrevolutionary followers of Trotsky and argued on behalf of individualistic art—even for the extreme subjectivity of the surrealists—within the socialist program for the sake of unity in the movement. He would return to this theme again in 1972 with the first part of his novel, *The Aesthetics of Resistance,* which would deal with the problem of the artist-intellectual's social commitment during pre-World War II Europe.

In conclusion, Weiss was hoping to demonstrate in the play that artistic independence and revolutionary activity could be brought into alignment. He realized this outlook ran counter to the political conditions in post-World War II Russia and China. He knew how individualistic tendencies are repressed in totalitarian societies (Czechoslovakia had been a recent example), and he stressed these points in his letter to Lew Ginsberg in defense of his play. But his own situation as a leftist writer was at stake here. Though he was living in the West and writing primarily for bourgeois audiences, he felt in solidarity with the socialist movement because he was trying to change the political assumptions of audiences. Indeed, it was only within the cultural context of political liberty found in the West that Weiss's own freedom of artistic expression could exist at all.

Like the earlier *Marat/Sade* which had revolved entirely around the issue of socialism versus individualism, *Trotsky in Exile* also concluded with an unsettling ending. Though Weiss's hero had displayed great foresight in his analysis of history and great courage in his beliefs, he had failed to bring about the needed sociopolitical changes. Weiss portrayed him as heroically optimistic—as he did Jean-Paul Marat—yet doomed to failure. The rebellious Trotsky—tolerant, critical, courageous—had been willing to leave the door open for two kinds of progressive social change: revolutionary art and revolutionary politics. Whether Trotsky's liberalism was truly viable in the postwar world, though, was something which Weiss was unable to answer. For Trotsky had died an unsuccessful martyr; his career had been as tragic as it was inspiring.

Hölderlin and the Writer's Independence

The drama on Trotsky had been problematical for Weiss. Of all his major plays between 1963 and 1971 *Trotsky* had the least success with audiences, critics, and the eastern European and Russian theaters. The play's commercial failure in the West reinforced Weiss's sense of political isolation and independence; he knew the play had failed to highlight such issues as revolutionary development in the Third World, or the political importance of artistic work. In a 1971 interview with Volker Canaris, just prior to *Hölderlin*'s premiere, Weiss referred to the Trotsky play as a piece which could never succeed, either with western or eastern European audiences: "Since the socialist countries are still under Stalinist taboos and cannot deal with the subject of Trotsky, the play must remain unperformed there." In fact the East German government refused Weiss an entry visa for two years because of *Trotsky*. On the other hand, the drama was much too long for Western audiences: "In its entirety it should be four or five hours long. In a shortened version the play fails. Can a bourgeois theatre risk doing that?"[24] Although the dream-vision concept of the staging supplied insight into Trotsky's personal tragedy, it did not function well in presenting historical material theatrically. The expressionist form proved to be dramatically flaccid in performance.

Although he was disappointed with this situation, Weiss had gained political insight from the play. He had clarified some political thoughts on the underdeveloped nations and he had also formed a clear picture of the impact of the Russian Revolution. But when all was said and done the most important question still remained: just what could be salvaged from the wreck of the Bolshevik Revolution which might be valuable for leftist intellectuals today? The play's subject had led Weiss into a blind alley as far as political activism was concerned. Trotskyism was a dead issue except for some loosely united, fiercely militant student groups. Only the idea of permanent revolution had connected the issue of Trotskyism with postwar concerns. But even this scant degree of social impact was limited. The developing countries were fashioning their own local variants of Marxist theory and many of these had little to do with Leon Trotsky.

The play was thus less important as a political document than as an examination of tactics which one socialist leader had pursued. Weiss was fascinated by the career of this man because of the ways in which Trotsky's struggles resembled his own. Trotsky had worked in isolation; he had used the pen as a weapon for socialist activism. When Weiss later turned to the subject of Hölderlin these concerns once again lay at the back of his mind:

> The impulse, the thoughts, and the ideas bound-up in the play stemmed from my earliest boyhood. As a twelve year-old I had lived for half a year in Tübingen, very near Hölderlin's tower—almost in the same Autenrieth family whose ancestors had operated the mental clinic in Hölderlin's time. The "disturbed" poet in his tower stuck in my memory long before I read his poems.[25]

Weiss believed that Hölderlin's madness and his retreat into isolation in order to work stemmed from the poet's political disillusionment. This connected Hölderlin the poet with the unsuccessful political theorists like Trotsky and Marat. "Hölderlin was concerned, like Trotsky and like Marat, with the movement of history, with discovering new insights into things. . . . We are all of us concerned with the struggle to change society and revolutionize art, we all find ourselves in this dilemma."[26]

Thus the value of Hölderlin's radical politics formed one of the play's central ideas. "Marat," Weiss explained, "is one of the end-figures of French Jacobinism. Hölderlin was the last German Jacobin. Marat was struck down before a new historical age emerged. Hölderlin too seemed to break down, to 'decay' into insanity" before the German social revolutions emerged in the latter part of the century. Weiss felt his new play would be "just as revolutionary as *Trotsky* or *Vietnam Discourse*," because the same political outlook conditioned all three dramas.

A final point of contact between Hölderlin's period and our own, Weiss felt, was the fact that his hero had been a historian who shared with modern historians the same perspective upon the past. Hölderlin's interest in the past, while typical of many nineteenth-century poets such as Novalis and Grabbe who cultivated a taste for classical antiquities, prefigured the work of twentieth-century historians. Hölderlin was not interested in ancient Greece "for its own sake." He wished to "contemporize" this past by applying nineteenth-century criteria to the study of ancient writers and political systems. His work on the Greek philosopher-poet Empedocles, Weiss felt, was one of the few nineteenth-century manifestations of German historicism which related to the twentieth century. As Weiss explained: "Hölderlin turned to antiquity in order to 'alienate' a contemporary problem by placing it into history . . . he meant that it held new meanings for the present, stemming from deep within his own personal experience." It was a strong challenge for Weiss to connect the ideas of a nineteenth-century poet to the concerns of the 1970s. Weiss sought this connection from the outset: "That Empedocles was involved with Hölderlin's world just as he [Hölderlin] is involved with the world of Che Guevara, is one of the play's key ideas."

Hölderlin: A Life of Frustration

To most English-speaking audiences the name of Hölderlin is unfamiliar, but to the Germans, acutely conscious of their classical heritage from the eighteenth and nineteenth centuries, he is one of that era's most famous writers. Contemporary and friend of Hegel, Goethe, Schiller, and many others who contributed to the flowering of German art and science, Hölderlin's life spanned both the classical and romantic periods; he was part of the most important social currents in Germany between 1788 and 1843. Though his work was unappreciated during his lifetime because of his radicalism and the ravages of madness in his later years, his importance—like that of Kleist and Büchner—has become widely recognized during our century. Certainly for Weiss, who was tracing the paths of socialist thought through the nineteenth century, Hölderlin seemed the most activist of the nineteenth-century German intellectuals. His poetry reflected many of the trends of the times, and thus Weiss saw him as a prototypical figure to whom the important sociohistorical developments of those years could be related.

Weiss relied heavily upon the large amount of data available on his hero and the times in which he lived. The drama is filled with historical incident and its central character is brought into contact with many important literary, philosophical, and political figures of the period. This gives the play a rich panoramic quality and strong historical texture. Weiss seems to have reached out successfully to the older German historical dramas of the nineteenth century for such inspiration. In these plays the movement of history tended to be embodied in a single heroic personality. Weiss's portrait of Hölderlin reminds one of Götz or Egmont, caught in their titanic struggles between personal disillusionment and the compelling force of the times, trapped between an outer world of necessity or moral duty and an inner world of self-conscious isolation, futility, and the sense of impending catastrophe. "I am trying here to silhouette one special person," Weiss remarked, "against the overwhelming necessity for social revolution."[27]

The drama highlights Hölderlin's importance as an individual typifying the cultural currents of his age. In the first scene Weiss shows his hero surrounded in his Tübingen school years by his classmates Hegel, Schelling, Neuffer, and Sinclair. They proclaim the ideals of the French Revolution by decorating the walls of their academy with graffiti and placards to greet the school's patron, Duke Karl Eugen. A riot breaks out when he arrives and the troublemakers are carried off under guard. The situation recalls the turbulent disturbances of young German radical intellectuals of that century who attempted to bring Jacobin ideals into near-feudal Germany. Weiss's opening scene establishes the historical context, stresses the political features of the situation, and introduces many of the major historical figures of the German nineteenth century.

From this scene we learn of the nihilistic tendencies of these young intellectuals. Their demands for terrorist acts are mixed with twentieth-century slogans: "The revolution marches on," "Down with the princes," "Power to the people," "Dispossess the landholders."[28] We also see how poets are inspired by political causes as Hölderlin proclaims the Jacobin ideals. He tells how he "saw the door thrown open wide / by the storm of the French Revolution / and soon rays of bright light / penetrated the swamp of German blindness." Weiss also sketches in the philosophical background by giving focus to Hegel who interprets the confusion of the scene in optimistic terms:

> On this earth
> God's kingdom democratically
> will emerge
> Thus try no longer to
> describe God
> rather
> describe man's existence
> and see how history
> by means of each reversal and every tragedy
> progresses step-by-step.

Weiss's second scene follows Hölderlin into the household of the von Kalb family where he served as a private tutor after his graduation from the theological seminary in 1793. Here Weiss shows the poet-radical attempting to tutor the scion of the Prussian Major von Kalb in the political realities of the nineteenth century. "It is not surprising," remarked one of Hölderlin's modern critics, "that he preferred the humble drudgery, but relative independence, of a private tutor to the clerical duties for which he was qualified, and which he would do almost anything to avoid in later life. This was due to Hölderlin's increasing Hellenism and political radicalism."[29]

Radicalism is indeed the issue in Weiss's scene. The major finds it impossible to talk with his son about his exploits in America because Hölderlin has taught his pupil how the Indian massacres and the slave trade made a mockery of the American Constitution. Weiss presents von Kalb's views as typical assumptions of European colonialism, as he shouts at Hölderlin: "Look my boy / we have decided / to conquer the world / You have had a better upbringing / than any savage / from the dark continent."

In the second part of the scene Weiss connects Hölderlin's political radicalism to his poetic alienation in order to stress the poet's personal tragedy. The hero reveals to Wilhemine Kirms, a family friend, his intention to leave the von Kalbs and enter the mainstream of political life. Wilhemine laughs and accuses him of taking himself too seriously. He should look around more closely, she argues; he should study everyday life instead of poetic ideals—the market, the milkmaid, the churches and farms: "Come and caress me now / Are you so surprised / when a woman / seeks a man / of her own choosing / out of a simple need / for contact?" Here Weiss adapted the historically documented romantic relationship between Hölderlin and Wilhemine in order to stress his hero's estrangement and his radical refusal to accept the world as he finds it.

In Weiss's third scene Hölderlin argues unsuccessfully with Goethe and Schiller on the subject of aesthetics. The scene is briefly and simply staged— "a rarified atmosphere" as Weiss described it. There is only a lectern upstage at which Goethe stands, leafing through manuscripts, as Schiller and Hölderlin argue. "But you must understand," Schiller pleads, "that your irregular meters / and tangled syntax / confuse us / Poetry should be / aesthetic / freedom arises from / the concept of the beautiful." "I cannot surpass your / classical notion / of beauty," Hölderlin replies. "I know it unsettles you / when I speak / about my world . . . how all the walls / must be torn down . . . all must be overthrown / torn down to the ground / before the new / can emerge." "That smells so much like a putsch," Goethe languidly interjects. "The truth is / that different classes / have different life styles / which cannot / be mixed together." A true patrician in Weiss's view, Goethe declares his preference for "the stillness / of my study" instead of Hölderlin's "great hammer" which will destroy society.

Weiss's fourth scene takes place in Jena, where Hölderlin, Schelling, Sinclair, and numerous students are attending a philosophical lecture by Fichte. The emotional climate intensifies when Fichte proclaims the historical necessity for revolution because "privileged classes / ride roughshod over the people." A riot breaks out between opposing student groups; Goethe and Schiller lead a police detachment onstage in order to supress the protests and thus restore academic tranquility. Weiss's fictitious scene scores a point against academic censorship and concludes with a satirical tableau of Schiller and Goethe smugly "standing downstage hand-in-hand, in the typical pose of famous individuals of the period," while the police brutalize the students.

Weiss's fifth scene concludes the first act and it occupies nearly 20 minutes of stage time. Hölderlin is once again a private tutor, this time in the employment of Gontard, a wealthy Frankfurt banker. This period of Hölderlin's life provided Weiss with excellent material for commenting upon the rise of European colonialism. The setting is a garden party attended by wealthy financiers and their families, as well as by cultural figures such as Hölderlin, Goethe, Hegel, and others. In small informal groups of two and three, the characters enter through the eighteenth-century formal garden. They move downstage as in a promenade where their conversations can be overheard by the audience.

Figure 18. *Hölderlin*
The von Kalb family house. Matthias Meyer as Hölderlin
and Christine van Santen as Wilhemine Kirms. Volkstheater
Rostock, 1973, directed by Hans Perten.
(*Photo by Hildegard Levermann-Westerholz*)

The scene is carefully choreographed in the stage directions and "should resemble a dance of death," as Weiss notes. Hölderlin is caught in this scene between the affections of Gontard's wife (with whom he had an intimate relationship) and the political-economic factions which were shaping Germany's future. Hegel, for example, chats amiably with Gontard and reminds the banker that it would be unrealistic "to ignore / the imperialistic trend of the times." The French Revolution is treated simply as an economic phenomenon: Napoleon's Egyptian campaign has weakened the stability of the franc, workers produce more when they are granted token rights and minor privileges, bloody revolts have been forgotten because of the growth of industry and the rising middle class.

The conclusion of the scene stresses the isolation and helplessness of the writer-hero who struggles to change the course of his times. Hölderlin confesses to the unsympathetic Goethe and Hegel: "so long as / I can do / nothing better than to write / I shall continue my work . . . This country / is a dungheap." The writer with true sensitivity, he declares, is shut out from the secret meetings of financiers who plan the future. "And nothing remains for us / other than like Ulysses / to wander the earth / and seek out wider worlds." The scene concludes with all the characters arranging themselves into semichoruses. Accompanied by court musicians they sing of "business, trade, and busy factories," of "our cannon / and caissons rolling" across Europe, "thundering" over the globe, in fact. "O God and business," they conclude, "We expand, produce / and accumulate."

In the second act Hölderlin and the Jacobin cause are shown in historical defeat. The final three scenes retreat from the arena of external political affairs as Weiss focuses upon Hölderlin's internal development as a poetic visionary between 1799 and 1843. Scene 6 represents a literary club meeting in which Hölderlin explains his interest in the exiled Greek philosopher Empedocles. Hölderlin admired Empedocles because he could have brought political reforms to ancient Greece had it not been for the machinations of the Athenian government. Empedocles had argued for freedom and human rights in a period when tyranny was the order of the day, and Hermokrates banished him to a life of wandering about Attica. Empedocles lived alone in the mountains for many years, hoping for the dawn of a new age, but growing increasingly cynical and withdrawn. He committed suicide by hurling himself into the volcano of Mount Etna.

Scene 7 develops this theme of the disillusioned revolutionary by showing Hölderlin confined in a madhouse, raving prophetically and philosophically. Straitjacketed in the asylum, his face behind a leather mask, abused by psychiatrists and warders in a situation reminiscent of Ibsen's *Peer Gynt,* Hölderlin's hallucinations emerge surrealistically from the rear of the darkened stage as living characters. First Buonarotti, the Italian freedom-fighter, greets Hölderlin in a dream of revolutionary France. "Comrade," says Buonarotti, "you came to

Paris in the final hour / when theft and slavery were the laws / and the great period of the Republic was over." Hölderlin screams at the mention of the Terror but the Herald/Warder beats him into silence. Next appears Susette Gontard who dies before the madman's tortured eyes, calling for him; Sinclair is with her and tells Hölderlin: "You are true to the last / You are true to the last." Finally there appears Hölderlin's old friend Schmid, killed while fighting for "freedom" in the Napoleonic wars.

The play's final scene is set in Hölderlin's tower on the Neckar, where he lived until his death in 1843. Several old friends come for brief, unsatisfying visits; but the most unusual is the final visit of Karl Marx. It is obviously an unhistorical encounter but the theatricality of the situation allows Weiss to resolve the question of the writer's revolutionary influence in the only way possible—from the standpoint of future history. The two "radicals" sit peacefully together in the garden smoking their pipes and speaking of historical developments. Marx translates the half-mad poet's visions into socioeconomic terms, and Hölderlin hangs on Marx's every word. At the end of the scene Marx delivers what are plainly Weiss's own reflections upon the role of leftist intellectuals in the socialist movement: "Two roads lie open / for the development of / fundamental changes," he declares.

> The first road is
> the analysis of concrete
> historical situations
> the other road is
> through visionary ideals
> of the deepest personal experience . . .
> Before you
> I set both roads
> as equally important.

In the brief epilogue which follows, the actor playing Hölderlin moves downstage while Hegel, Neuffer, Schmid, and Sinclair group themselves around him. They remind the audience that

> We have given you a portrait of Hölderlin
> in which you can see him
> not as a reflection of past history
> but as though he had before him the same
> problems we have today.

Sociotypical Handling of Characters

Unlike Peter Weiss's *Mockinpott* and his *Trotsky in Exile, Hölderlin* was greeted by a storm of controversy following its Berlin premiere. The drama was judged "Play of the Year" by West German theater critics, and the following year Weiss was awarded the Schiller Prize for Literature from the German

Academy of Arts for the drama. Weiss's hope, however, that the play would have a strong impact on Western audiences has not been borne out. Although 16 other productions were mounted in German-speaking nations within a few months of its premiere, and an experimental English translation was performed at the Edinburgh Festival in 1973, the drama has remained largely unproduced and no English translation is currently planned.

Undoubtedly the strong German flavor of the play is mainly responsible for this situation. Despite Weiss's innovative methods of combining political, economic, and cultural trends in unhistorical situations in order to yield surprising perspectives, and despite his deft manner of reducing issues and characters' viewpoints to clear political terms, the historical events and the characters remain firmly locked within German cultural history. Unlike the episodes in *Marat/Sade,* the scenes in *Hölderlin* are not presented within a metaphysical context such as the madhouse. They are enacted in definite locales and in specific historical situations which make it difficult for audiences to connect the action to non-German, twentieth-century conditions.

Two productions of the play in Frankfurt and Hamburg tried to modernize the play's political pertinence even more—with some public success but also with the author's disdain—by heightening its presentational features: "alienating" certain historical roles by reversing the sexes of the performers in the Goethe-Schiller scene, by surrounding the stage with projected materials, and by introducing twentieth-century radical jargon with political placards, graffiti, and the like.

Much of the hostile criticism was predictable and the negative press which the play received did not dampen the enthusiasm of many Germans for the drama.[30] From the historical purists, however, came the charge that Weiss had misrepresented the role of Hölderlin as an early Marxist—a view propounded in one of Weiss's major sources for the play, Lawrence Ryan's 1968 tract *Hölderlin and the French Revolution.* German classicists were outraged because Weiss had pilloried their sacred cows (Schiller, Goethe, Hegel) on account of their supposed "indifference" to the political uprising in France in 1789. Ulrich Schreiber complained of Weiss's retreat into "idealistic mythologizing" by his argument that the insane poet had actually been a political visionary.[31] Siegfried Melchinger, on the other hand, noted a few structural weaknesses in the script but heaped praise on Weiss for what he regarded as "a wonderful scenic imagination" which "surpassed even that of *Marat/Sade.*"[32]

Perhaps the most telling comment, which explains much of the critical furor as well as the drama's lack of international attention, was made by Henning Rischbieter (who admired the play a great deal): "Peter Weiss's *Hölderlin* has fallen a victim to our national theatres . . . as a rich man is thrown to the dogs. . . . It was the directing which was at fault. . . . Our national theatres and our State Theatre are totally incapable of producing this play."[33]

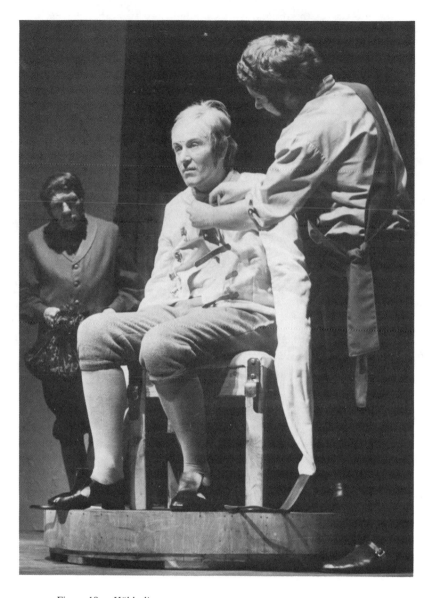

Figure 19. *Hölderlin*
The Warder removes the hero's leather mask in the
Tübingen madhouse. Gerd Michael as the older Hölderlin,
Hermann Wagemann as the Warder, and Egon Bremmecke
as the Singer/Herald. Volkstheater Rostock, 1973, directed
by Hans Perten.
(*Photo by Hildegard Levermann-Westerholz*)

By and large, most of the critics had trouble accepting the way in which Weiss constructed his characters—particularly the central character—according to their political outlooks. Friedrich Hölderlin emerged as a focal point of many cross-currents in nineteenth-century Germany. Weiss presented historical situations through Hölderlin's eyes; he used the political outlook of his hero as a yardstick for measuring the activities of Hölderlin's contemporaries, and as a point of contact with modern concerns. Weiss described his approach to the character of Hölderlin thus: "I am trying here to silhouette one special person against the overwhelming necessity for social revolution. The entire conflict will be summed up in his personality."[34] The important issue for Weiss was revolution; his poet-hero typified that concern for social reform during the times; and the historical period was discussed in relation to that concern.

In order to achieve this split in focus between the central character and the historical developments of which he was a part, Weiss used three dramaturgical strategies. The first of these was to create a clear form for the action by sharpening the play's presentational features. Weiss wanted to avoid problems with ambiguity which the surrealistic features of *Marat/Sade* and *Trotsky* had produced. He began *Hölderlin* and concluded it with ceremonial scenes set up as dramatic tableaux (an idea he had discarded when he had written the Charenton drama). The prologue introduced all the radicals who delivered directly to the audience key statements encapsulating each one's personal standpoint towards historical change. As they spoke they decorated the stage for the play's first scene, literally "setting the stage" for the action. In the epilogue, the characters were arranged presentationally in choral groups in order to sum up in narrative fashion the play's major ideas. In addition to using emblematic scenes, Weiss made the herald figure more prominent in performance. This character provided a formal narrative introduction and assigned an historical date to every scene; he also filled in as an extra on several occasions in order to provide commentary during a scene with a minimum of interruption to the flow of the action.

Weiss's second strategy for developing the play's historical context was to present each character first as an individual, and then to show him as a member of a choral group which expressed a particular socioeconomic outlook. This approach to characterization worked extremely well with only a minimum of artificiality in setting up the choral groupings and it was consistent throughout the play. The garden scene which concluded the first act was an excellent example of this skillful character portrayal. All the characters were first seen in groups of two or three engaged in conversation as they moved in and out of the scene. Then at the scene's conclusion and within the festive atmosphere, the semi-choruses formed for a chorale activity. Using such techniques in numerous scenes, Weiss's characters were able to move freely between their individual stage identities and their emblematic, typical identities as proponents of socioeconomic attitudes. Character traits were sharpened in good detail, while political perspective was sustained.

The third way in which Weiss strengthened the historical context was by inventing dramatic situations within which his central character could engage other historical figures in discussions of a political nature. Goethe and Schiller, for example, were allowed to express their ideas on the nature of art, but only in relation to Hölderlin who stood before them insisting that they reduce their terms to practical, political realities. Hegel, too, came in for his share of criticism in the garden scene when his theory on the German *Zeitgeist* was directly connected to the rapacious colonial policies of the industrialists who accompanied him throughout the scene. The most striking example of such fictitious confrontations came in the play's final scene when Weiss brought Karl Marx into conversation with the exiled Hölderlin. Marx's speech on the "two roads" of socialist progress neatly summarized the course of events during the nineteenth century, celebrated the long struggle of the disillusioned central character, and propelled the drama into the modern period.

In these three ways Weiss encouraged the audience to regard history from a contemporary, politically based standpoint. The crisis in Hölderlin's life thus became the result of "future shock," of political shock, because Hölderlin was shown in possession of a modern historical consciousness which his contemporaries did not share. In the dramaturgical balance of focus between the central hero and his historical circumstances, we can see reflected the playwright's own position as a postwar writer caught in the contemporary situation of uncertainty between artistic self-expression and political commitment.

Hölderlin and the Twentieth Century

Weiss's assessment of Hölderlin's importance for the twentieth century accords with recent critical opinion on the development of German Romanticism. Several contemporary scholars have observed that the modern artist's revolt against social values and the political concerns voiced in so many avant-garde works can be traced to the rise of Romanticism in European literature—of which Hölderlin is Germany's best example. The "romantic rebellion" of these writers signalled the beginning of the artist's alienation from society which has carried down to modern times. Renato Poggioli, for example, has described this critical observation as "a new historical fact of incalculable importance and profound meaning" for the modern period.[35] It helps explain to a certain extent the rebellious antisocial and independent attitudes of modern artists towards contemporary society. In terms of the stage, the critic Tom Driver has described the modern situation as one in which "the stage has become a mirror of human consciousness imprisoned within itself . . . an extraordinary representation of the alienated psyche of modern man."[36]

The note of alienation is especially keen in this play, as it was in the drama on Leon Trotsky; and it reveals much about Peter Weiss's own sense of dislocation as a postwar writer. Weiss described Hölderlin's *personal* estrangement from the life of his society in terms of the betrayal of Hölderlin's friends, most of whom rejected him because of his radical views. "All of his friends," Weiss commented, "Hegel, Schelling, and the great historical personalities Goethe, Schiller, and Fichte mention nothing about him, separated themselves from him and adopted conservative stances." Weiss also illustrated Hölderlin's *economic* estrangement from society by portraying his hero's awkward attempts to secure for himself a place as a teacher or poet within respectable society— overtures which failed miserably and only alienated him still further. Finally Weiss stressed Hölderlin's *artistic* alienation through his hero's frustrating encounters with writers like Goethe and Schiller who dominated the German literary scene during Hölderlin's early life.

Weiss thus created a sad portrait of the lonely artist, a pariah within society because of a continual concern for social reform which his contemporaries did not share. The misunderstood poet was forced to retire to his tower on the Neckar and write visionary verses. Weiss understood him as a martyred intellectual: "He stood alone with his revolutionary consciousness, awaiting a kind of restorative period. . . . After running the gauntlet, only imprisonment seemed real to Hölderlin."[37]

Despite this tragic treatment of Hölderlin's career, Weiss did approach his hero's situation in a positive frame of mind. He refused to end the play on a tragic note; he did not leave the conflict between activism and noninvolvement unresolved. He wanted to affirm value for the solitary writer who pursues his own beliefs despite society's hostility, and to demonstrate how many artists are vindicated by later historical developments. Weiss's hero expressed confidence that a "restorative period" would eventually emerge to justify his efforts; Weiss, too, felt the same with respect to the situation of twentieth-century writers. Karl Marx's presence in the drama makes this point unmistakable because of his observation about the coming social revolutions during the latter part of the century. As one reviewer, Georg Hensel, pointed out: "Marx is enthroned by Weiss as the analytical and prophetic embodiment of Hölderlin's mythological fascination."[38] Despite the personal tragedy which governs the outward circumstances of Hölderlin's career, the play does affirm a confident, uplifting outlook in its conclusion. Unlike *Marat/Sade* where absurd faith and historical skepticism co-existed in unresolvable tension, *Hölderlin* fuses hope and despair into long-range optimism.

This represents an important development in Weiss's thought after the unsuccessful years of propagandistic writing, and his ambiguous assessment in *Marat/Sade* and *Trotsky* of the writer's importance. "In my personal life," Weiss remarked, "I know I'm not working in the arena of politics. I haven't the time or energy. I realize just how little I can accomplish with my plays and books. But writing is my occupation . . . we must continue nevertheless."[39]

On another level we should realize that Weiss was able to speak very precisely in the play about where the writer's contribution to society rests: in his visionary perception of social conditions and society's needs. This was a point which Weiss had introduced in *Trotsky* with the scene in the Zurich coffeehouse. Like the totally rational creation of a revolution by Lenin and the Bolsheviks, the intuitive or irrational contributions of the dadaists were equally important for advancing socialism. Artistic independence within revolutionary societies was therefore necessary, and the dadaists—like Hölderlin—had major insights to offer. Thus it was personally important and historically appropriate for Weiss to conclude his drama on the nineteenth-century poet by coupling his hero's mystical understanding of social change with Marx's rational interpretation of historical development.[40]

There are numerous points in the play at which Hölderlin's visionary understanding of history is underscored. The most important is the play's penultimate scene, which explains the hero's experience in the asylum. Weiss uses madness as a device for compressing several years of historical development and for commenting upon that development from a radical standpoint. In the scene, the Herald-Warder beats the straitjacketed poet to induce hallucinations, and Hölderlin raves at his memories of revolutionary Paris. He recalls the initial ideals of the Jacobins with admiration, but then suddenly recoils from a glimpse of the terror which followed. He despairs when seeing Napoleon at the head of the Republic, and Buonarotti appears in order to reassure him that the cause is being carried forward. Hölderlin's old acquaintances (Susette Gontard, Sinclair, Schmid) and his mother also appear to his disturbed mind and remind him of all he has personally suffered because of his commitment to Jacobinism. The history of the revolutionary movement which began in 1789 is therefore recounted through a poet's eyes. It is criticized nearly 30 years after it began by a visionary living in Germany who is trying to reform his own society.

It is noteworthy that Weiss concluded this scene with the words of Hölderlin's lifelong friend, Sinclair: "You are true to the end." Weiss leaves the audience in no doubt about how to assess Hölderlin's achievements. Despite the likelihood of failure, the heroic individual is shown pursuing his own course: independent of political parties, unconcerned with his economic situation, abandoned by his acquaintances but not entirely friendless, and striving to relate his work to the political trends developing in the nineteenth century.

This final point, the way in which the visionary writer maintains contact with important historical developments, is extremely important. For Weiss it represented the solidarity which all committed writers share because of their concern for social progress. This solidarity is directly mentioned in the words of Marx, and it is also a note sounded in the dramaturgical handling of many of the play's situations. In the very first scene, for example, Weiss portrays his hero at the hub of cultural developments not only in Germany but in Europe, not only in a Tübingen classroom in 1792 but also in the context of history between 1789 and 1801. In this scene, historically set in 1792, Hegel has already developed his theory of the *Zeitgeist*. "The world as such is idea," he expounds to his classmates, "in our minds / it manifests itself / as eternal process." Sinclair too is part of this student group though historically he did not meet Hölderlin until 1798. Marat's death is announced (1795) and the French armies are on the march in the campaigns of 1801 and 1802.

Such compression of historical time within a single scene permits the spectator to form a clear idea of the *context* rather than the *sequence* of historical events. It opens up the scene to more than just the narrow concerns of German students in 1792, and stresses the ability of the artist and intellectual to sense the pulse of the times in order to write and to act effectively. This solidarity which Hölderlin feels with the Jacobins in 1792, and which he will feel in 1843 through prophetic visions of the coming revolutions at the end of the century, is a solidarity which exists only in the mind of the writer. Hölderlin—like Peter Weiss—could not build a political base from which to influence practical reforms in his society. He was politically impotent, and he could make a contribution to social progress only through poetic visions of the future. He pointed the way, therefore, for those coming after him. The modern writer *engagé*, Weiss suggests, the independent leftist artist who is working to improve society, must work in isolation and must await a "restorative period" which will emerge eventually through combined effort.

Brecht's Influence upon Weiss

In reviewing Weiss's career over these busy and productive years between 1964 and 1971, the similarities between the thrust of his plays and those of Brecht are very apparent. Indeed few postwar playwrights have remained untouched by Brecht's influence, and Peter Weiss is certainly no exception. Numerous techniques which recur in Weiss's plays bear an unmistakable Brechtian stamp: the use of ironic narrative commentary between and within scenes, the dialectical development of the dramatic action, the conscious theatricality in the handling of technical elements, the frequent use of direct political statement to the audience are only a few such devices. Weiss borrowed freely from Brecht in his dramaturgy and staging, just as he adapted post-World War I avant-garde concepts for his prose and film work early in his career.

In order to appreciate Brecht's influence upon Weiss, especially as it concerns the theme of the writer and society in Weiss's plays, we should not emphasize their dramatic methods because technique alone is no sure indicator of a playwright's importance. For purposes of this study we need to understand the similarity of these playwrights' approaches to the theatre. As Ronald Gray pointed out about Brecht:

> The truly valuable thing about Brecht's dramatic work, I submit, is not his extraordinarily wide range of theatrical invention and innovation, nor the cogency of his political message— though both of these may yet be more effective outside Europe and North America than we

are inclined to suppose—but in . . . looking for a more than personal solution to the problems of the society in which Brecht had to live.[41]

The plays of Brecht and Peter Weiss were strongly conditioned by the need these writers felt to respond politically to their world, by their decision to examine their societies through literature and to portray effective and ineffective political choices onstage. Thus I would like to conclude this chapter with a brief discussion of their political orientation towards playwriting, and particularly towards their use of historical material as a major method of social criticism.

One of Peter Weiss's earliest public references to Brecht occurred in 1965 when he described literature as a force for social change, as a practical method of producing reform: "I don't think it's enough just to write," he remarked to an interviewer, "and it's not enough to write my individual stuff. I think it's absolutely necessary to write with the point of trying to influence or to change society."[42] It is plain that all his dramas between 1964 and 1971 reflected this attitude in some way. Occasionally he explored the possibility of direct social influence by writing plays on current events in Angola and Vietnam, and by prescribing rules for a documentary theater which would highlight the need and the strategies for taking political action. As I have tried to show, however, his most important and successful works were those which examined the careers of writers—both poets and political theorists—who had sensed the development of historical change during their lifetimes and had tried, unsuccessfully, to assist with that process.

The general thrust of all Weiss's plays during this period can be described as an attempt to uncover what Brecht defined as the political-economic causal structure of modern society, and closely related to this point is the correlative need to encourage in his audiences the attitude that social systems—no matter how familiar or strongly entrenched—can be modified. Even in *Marat/Sade,* where Weiss's political sympathies were undecided and where he was able to hold both sides of the argument between individualism and socialism in an unresolved tension, he demonstrated quite clearly the transitory nature of beliefs, institutions, political causes, and social systems. Despite the range of controversial interpretations which the play received, Weiss was able to express the notion that history is a developing—though not necessarily progressive—process and that, as Brecht believed, a human being is not "a temporarily fixed point in Newtonian space, but a future-oriented vector in Einsteinian time-space. . . . The world as process and man as emergent."[43] This stress upon future possibility propels the drama forward because it compels Marat to keep searching for answers despite setbacks and despite Sade's skepticism. We find this emphasis, of course, not only in Marat but also in Weiss's later portrait of Hölderlin and most especially in Trotsky who declares that he cannot "surrender his faith in reason and in human solidarity," that "the failures and disappointments can't stop" him from seeing the socialist future.[44]

Another major point of contact between these two writers is the fact that both Brecht's and Weiss's attitudes towards social change developed as a result of their contact with global war. Brecht's experience as a German medical orderly in World War I produced a bitter reaction against the callousness and waste of the German war managers. And as a boy of 14 in Germany, Weiss had already come into contact with Brecht's early poems, and was personally inspired by them. He was also exposed to recordings of Brecht's *Mahagonny* and *Threepenny Opera* as a young man, and they influenced him very much. Weiss's own responses to a wartime situation were similar to those of Brecht. In 1966 he described to Americans his strong reactions to "the dead lying in the streets," "wagons laden with bodies," "bombed homes," "whole countries reduced to ashes."[45]

Both men, too, were driven into exile by the Fascists and this experience had profound effects upon their writing. Brecht emigrated to America in 1935—by way of Stockholm where Weiss would later reside—and was able to collaborate with other artists in New York and southern California until his return to Europe in 1948. Some of his finest plays—*Galileo* and *Good Woman of Setzuan*—were written in exile. Peter Weiss, though, went to Sweden where he worked in exile until well after the war. He developed his art as a method of self-analysis, expressing his visions in painting and intermittent writing. "What mattered to this man was self-realization and nothing else," he remarked about himself in 1965, "to battle against outside resistances, to do only that which he felt corresponded to his inner self."[46]

The difference between their experiences as exiles lay in the type of work they produced during this time. Brecht remained a man of the theater while living in the United States, and he eventually realized that his freedom as a political writer was severely curtailed by the necessity of having work produced by unsympathetic individuals and technically limited production organizations.[47] Hence after the war's conclusion in 1949 he accepted—albeit reluctantly—the offer of the East German government to supervise the Berliner Ensemble. He realized that he would have to work under difficult conditions of political censorship but he also knew that he would be able to exert total *artistic* control over the production of his plays.

Weiss, on the other hand, always wanted to remain politically and artistically independent, and he always regarded his *political* exile as a reflection of his *existential* "exile" as a human being. In a speech in 1983 accepting the Büchner Prize for Literature on behalf of her deceased husband, Gunilla Palmstierna stressed this dilemma in Weiss's career. She pointed to Weiss's difficulties with the German and Swedish languages after his exile: he was able to write in literary German but did not know conversational German, "street language." Conversely, his daily "street language" was Swedish. She said that throughout Weiss's career he was continually troubled by this "double perspective," the Swedish and German ways of regarding history and human experience, and that it formed the subject of many of their conversations. She concluded: "In my opinion this dilemma of his emigration had begun much earlier in his life, namely as an artistic emigration—not as an escape but instead as an inner compulsion. The external emigration was a reflection of his inner one, which had arisen long before."[48]

The impact of exile upon Weiss's writings was more than just this personal, philosophical dislocation. More than Brecht, Weiss seems to have fretted throughout his career over the difficulty of producing his plays for Western audiences. Unlike Brecht who eventually returned to Berlin, Weiss remained in Stockholm and was forced (until 1982 with *Der Prozess*) to submit all of his plays to the interpretation of Western directors—many of them gifted—but he often disagreed with them. Additionally, for eight years after *Night with Guests* he was compelled to rely upon commercial theaters in the West for the technical and financial support his plays required, and these theaters did not serve audiences who were sympathetic to radical political plays.

Thus both writers' artistic situations became difficult for them, Brecht's for political reasons and Weiss's for personal and artistic reasons. Weiss remarked upon this point in 1965 when he complained that his "artistic work in the West is very marketable if it provides consumers with aesthetic and spirtual rewards, or with emotional stimulation" and when it does not carry any practical weight towards social reform.[49] But he grew tired of writing for political sympathizers in certain agit-prop plays, and impatient when seeing his dramas produced mainly for bourgeois audiences who could afford the high admission prices to expensive theaters. Although productions of his plays attracted the talents of some of the finest contemporary artists—Peter Brook, Paul Dessau, Glenda Jackson, Erwin Piscator and others—there was no question in his own mind that his political impact was limited because of his audiences. What is remarkable for our study, though, is the way in which he turned this situation to his advantage by writing plays about poets and revolutionary theorists whose ideas had also been abused, misunderstood, or ignored during their lifetimes.

Brecht did not—often could not—express his political and personal thoughts in this way, and this reveals a major distinction between the types of dramas these two playwrights produced. It was only in Brecht's short stories, in his private correspondence, and especially in his later poems written from East Berlin that we find "a kind of spiritual autobiography and a record of his political attitudes and views on a number of subjects" which reveal him as a political writer "of deep melancholy."[50] He was profoundly shaken by events in the socialist nations—events which he could not openly discuss because of the political controls under which he was forced to work. The East Berlin workers' uprising of 1953 was the most obvious example of this, and Günter Grass severely criticized Brecht's silence over the uprising in his 1966 drama, *The Plebians Rehearse the Uprising*.

Despite Peter Weiss's difficulties in writing political plays for Western audiences, it is clear that he never felt it necessary to suppress his political views, nor to couch them in the indirect form of parables which "lifted Communism from reality to a Utopian plane, an idyllic realm in which a rosy glow of human wisdom and kindness dissolves all contradictions."[51] His plays and especially his prose novel, *Ästhetik des Widerstands,* all display a clear pattern of self-analysis through self-identification with the central characters.

More important than the different kinds of plays which these writers produced is the question of the pertinency of their literary views the world situation during the last quarter of this century. As Weiss always maintained, his dramas on great historical individuals were not simply exercises in personal self-expression, but attempts to clarify the situations in which leftist intellectuals were trapped and compelled to remain for some years. In this respect it is crucial to recognize that Weiss borrowed little or nothing of Brecht's personal policy of enlightened self-interest, what Martin Esslin and others have called his "Schweykean ethics,"[52] vis-à-vis the societies in which he had to work. Weiss always spoke boldly and often critically of Western capitalism and he never felt it necessary to hide behind an ironic mask as Brecht did, writing in the German Democratic Republic.

Brecht's policy was most succinctly stated in the famous passage written in 1935, "Five Difficulties in Writing the Truth," in which he spoke of "the courage to write the truth although it is everywhere suppressed; the shrewdness to recognize it, although it is concealed; the art of making it available as a weapon; the cunning to disseminate it; and the judgment to choose those in whose hands it will be most effective."[53] In light of contemporary needs, it is plain that such directives hold little value for modern authors. Our problems with writing the truth do not arise from the suppression of facts but from the bombardment with facts and the debasing of "truths" on the part of what Hans Magnus Enzensberger has dubbed the "mind-making industry."[54]

It is in Weiss's documentary dramas that we find his rejection of Brecht's "Five Points" most clearly reflected. Although they may appear to be plays which reveal the "true facts" about Angola and Vietnam—and the distortion of supposedly "true" facts was an accusation which many critics levelled at Weiss from the time of *The Investigation* through *Hölderlin*—a closer examination reveals them to be attempts at providing a meaningful interpretation of historical fact, at supplying what Weiss believed to be a valid (socialist) perspective upon the facts.

Few critics have noted this in their haste to condemn Weiss's documentary plays as biased propaganda or dull agit-prop moralizing. Otto Best, however, has explained this problem with respect to Weiss's plays in very precise terms. In referring to Weiss's rejection of Brecht's "Five Difficulties," he remarked:

> It is obvious that these postulates have become meaningless . . . because our truth is not foundering nor is it suppressed, but rather any 'truth' can be bought in today's marketplace

and its customer can be found. Our dilemma is pluralism, as well as the unmistakable assumption of our freedom. The weapon of art, if one wishes to speak of weapons, is a dead issue because a consumer society has no need of courage or cunning. Furthermore, art is now more than ever a consumer item; the need for culture can be met and enlightenment can come about only insofar as these goals may agree with consumerism.[55]

Any comparison of Brecht's and Weiss's stagecraft must begin with this point in mind. It is not a question of whether Brecht's methods are dated and therefore inapplicable to contemporary conditions. On the contrary, there is a great deal in Brecht's later work which is enormously provocative and which still remains unexplored. Instead it is a question of Peter Weiss's attitude towards Brecht's methods, that they could not generate the kind of direct statement upon the late twentieth-century political situation which he felt was more important. He referred to this point in an interview following the premiere of *Marat/Sade* when he remarked that he would not have been able to "get the strong emotional effects" he wanted had he used Brecht's "pedagogic way" of writing plays.[56] Brecht's technique of *Historisierung,* Weiss realized, portrayed social events by showing them as unique, transitory, and tied to certain eras, and thus pointed out the particular past nature of those events. Such an approach, though, tends to "lock" the issues within history and thus to weaken their applicability to present-day problems.

If there is one feature of Weiss's playwriting which radically departs from that of Brecht it is the way in which Weiss at all times "modernized" and "relativized" history by directly pointing to its contemporary features. The Marquis de Sade is not the familiar sexual libertine of literary history but a dynamic embodiment of contemporary existentialism and modern historical skepticism. Jean-Paul Marat is not the French national hero of historical record, but the modern leftist intellectual trapped within the "madhouse" of political argument and counterargument. Weiss's portraits of Trotsky and Hölderlin are modified in similar ways in order to create what Weiss's Hölderlin states directly to the audience in the play's epilogue: "a reflection not of past history / but as though he had before him the same / problems that we have today."

Although Weiss's approach to history laid his plays open to accusations of distortion and falsification from many quarters, he was also supported by certain critics who realized just what he was trying to do by updating Brecht. Ernst Schumacher is one such critic and it is helpful to recall his remarks about *Galileo* in order to stress the significance of Weiss's innovations:

> *Galileo* could clarify historical types . . . but it could not make the contemporary point of reference of this typical failure understandable, which was the issue from which Brecht was operating and about which he wanted to write. . . . An historical analogy cannot be substituted for an analysis of the actual historical problem. . . . In order to make modern history transparent by a selected historical "medium," that medium must be greatly enriched with techniques which strive for a direct practical effect on socio-historical reality.[57]

To free his dramatic issues from history and connect them to modern problems, Weiss devised a number of innovations, many of which Brecht did not or could not use to any extent. The dream-vision concept for *Trotsky,* which Weiss borrowed from the expressionists, enabled him to portray the effects of the fast-changing nature of modern history on the leftist intellectual intent on influencing historical processes. The blatantly unhistorical presentation of historical characters was another method which permitted Weiss to point out the contemporary focus of his arguments. In his documentary plays he used many emotionally charged methods which greatly intensified the plays' impact on current topics: the grotesque figure of the Lusitanian Bogey which tumbled in pieces to the stage, or the gigantic photos of combat scenes during the Vietnam war. Certainly Brecht developed many methods that Weiss could not employ: acting training methods, or the extraordinarily wide range of dramatic forms which Brecht explored over his long career including parable, epics, learning-plays, operas, and others.

The full extent of Brecht's impact upon the modern theater is still not completely understood; like Stanislavsky, Brecht contributed not only a rich repository of practical methods but he also left a significant body of theoretical work and created a dynamic theater ensemble which is still alive and operative today. During his comparatively brief period as a major playwright, Peter Weiss limited his focus to the concerns of writers and their relationship to society, and in so doing he has perhaps contributed more than any other modern playwright to our understanding of the complexity of the problem of social reform in our pluralistic age. He produced plays as well as significant pieces of criticism which bear upon the problems faced by leftist writers, and which also throw important light upon the political-industrial makeup of our contemporary world. Brecht's dictum that "the world must be changed" is surely a directive which has been adopted by a number of playwrights; but few have pursued it so consistently and productively throughout their careers as Peter Weiss.

Figure 20.   Peter Weiss, 1980
(*Photo by Isolde Ohlbaum*)

5

Dramatic Themes and Ideas

The Issues and the Plays

In looking back over Peter Weiss's career as a painter, filmmaker, novelist, essayist, and playwright, it is fascinating to note how consistently certain themes have been taken up and worked over again and again in his writings. I would like to conclude my study by focusing upon a few such themes which I have traced in this book.

Weiss's examination of the relationship between writers and society in his work led him into three major avenues of thought: an exploration of the problem of absurdity, particularly in regard to the limitations experienced by ordinary individuals and by political writers and activists; a consideration of writers and of radical literature as a force for social change; and an assessment of the relationship between artistic independence and the political choices afforded writers in the modern world.

The most important of these themes derives from Weiss's firm belief in the writer as a sort of political prophet, as an artist who often perceives the proper direction for historical development but whose influence upon change is only indirect. Weiss stresses the importance of understanding the restrictive conditions under which politically inspired writers must function, and he dwells on the impact of leftist thought in understanding the present and in planning for the future. We find such themes not only in dramas like *Trotsky* and *Hölderlin* which investigate the problems and solutions which leftist intellectuals have chosen in different historical periods; but also in Weiss's documentary plays and in his own stated objectives as a writer seeking to influence changes in his own society.

These three themes troubled Weiss from his earliest years as an artist; he continually explored new terminologies, new opportunities, and new challenges for testing himself and for refreshing his thoughts upon these issues. Late in 1971, in fact, he himself stressed the importance of this "evolutionary" quality to his total work. Shortly following the premiere of *Hölderlin* he wrote, "Just as history is a continuum, so too are all these plays part of an evolutionary process. Motives are taken up, then worked over and changed."[1]

A study of his writings over the years reveals clear patterns of self-evaluation. For example, Weiss's political difficulties as an artist "caught between the two stools" of East and West was the question which inspired his first major play in 1963, *Marat/Sade,* and which underlay his political work in the decade which followed. At the end of his career we also find this same note of self-examination occupying his thoughts as he describes the role of the first-person narrator in his novel *Äesthetik des Widerstands:* "The central figure of this novel, the narrator, is perhaps an abstraction for many readers, but not for me, the author. For the author it is self-discipline. I narrate the story as myself in order to pose these problems as clearly as possible to myself by identifying with this narrator."[2]

Weiss's trilogy of plays on the careers of revolutionary intellectuals— *Marat/Sade, Trotsky in Exile, Hölderlin* —are especially important because they are the most obvious reflection of his lifelong concern for politically inspired writing. In these dramas Weiss focused attention upon historical figures who struggled to bring about the same kinds of progressive social change that Weiss did. Thus in his plays he not only analyzed historical conditions which paralleled post-World War II political situations, but he also stressed the importance of literature in relation to social activism. Weiss always made it clear that he regarded his profession as an activity directed towards understanding himself and influencing society. His choice and his manner of presenting the dramatic heroes of his plays, therefore, reveals much about his feelings towards the value and the potential of politically inspired writing.

The attention Weiss devoted in these three plays to the literary work of important revolutionary figures is counterbalanced by his concern for the issue of political oppression and resistance in his other four plays, *The Investigation, Song of the Lusitanian Bogeyman, Vietnam Discourse,* and *Mockinpott.* The figure of Weiss's writer–hero has an opposite in the figure of the little man— the Angolan native without travel papers trying to visit his family, the credulous German Jew bewildered by the callous treatment he receives at the train depot, Mockinpott puzzled by his employer's indifference to his plight—although such portraits are never drawn as convincingly as are the heroes of his major plays. In all his documentary dramas, with the exception of *The Investigation,* Weiss optimistically celebrated the struggle for political freedom and the achievement of political consciousness through movements of the masses. Thus, while his search for identity as a leftist author is reflected in *Marat/Sade, Trotsky,* and *Hölderlin,* his search for direct political influence through his art is mainly reflected in his documentary plays on current events.

In creating the characters of the documentary plays, Weiss did not concern himself with the dividedness of human nature as he did in his dramas on leftist intellectuals. This is an important point of distinction between the mass heroes of the minor dramas and the writer–heroes in the other plays. The natives and peasants in *Bogeyman* and *Vietnam Discourse,* for example, must concern themselves with problems of an immediate, practical nature. They must form a rudimentary political consciousness in order to become aware of their oppressed condition and take action to improve it. Unlike the great historical personalities of Marat, Sade, and Trotsky, who must combat restrictive forces both outside of and within themselves, the mass heroes must single out and combat only the external forms of their oppression: colonial domination, exploitative economic relationships, military invasions, and foreign influence. They are not concerned with analyzing mistakes made in the past nor with the future development of socialist thought; they are forging new socialist programs in the immediate present. Although it must stand to Weiss's credit that he was astute enough to recognize and celebrate this quality of "history in the making" which he perceived in the underdeveloped nations, nonetheless the absence of critical analysis in the documentary plays helps to explain their commercial failure. Additionally, these dramas lack depth of characterization, a clear theoretical understanding of the issues, and a broad perspective on problems which are both geographically and culturally remote from Western spectators.

Weiss's major dramas, on the other hand, link more overtly with his understanding of himself. Not only do they celebrate historical figures who became socially committed in their literary work, they also helped Weiss to define a proper social role for himself. Each of the writer–heroes was a model for Peter Weiss's own situation, even though only Hölderlin and Sade were historically prominent as artists. Of course Weiss modified the ideas of these men and delimited their careers by stressing this literary aspect of their work in order to express his own beliefs on the subject of the writer *engagé*. But this is only to be expected and is part of what we customarily understand as poetic license. Weiss always sought something contemporary in his studies of the past: an understanding of the roots of social violence, of the extent of human influence upon historical development, of the restrictive conditions which bear upon modern artists and how to overcome them, and, most especially, an understanding of the roots of the seemingly paradoxical faith of certain individuals who struggle unsuccessfully to improve apparently hopeless situations. Let us now examine more closely the personalities of the dramatic heroes Weiss created over the years.

The Writer's Independence

Peter Weiss's dramatic heroes are rebellious intellectuals committed to the struggles of their times. They are men of action and extreme if not ruthless in their political choices. Weiss presents them dynamically and rarely allows them moments of quiet reflection during which they can share their less urgent feelings with audiences. As Sade pointed out to Marat early in their argument: "No small emotions please. . . . For you just as for me / only the most extreme actions matter." The arguments in which Weiss's heroes are engaged are brutal and relentless. When they analyze their own motives one rarely hears from them overt sentimentality. They struggle against self-deception and despise those who are motivated by self-interest: the Parisian *sans-culottes,* the political powerseekers such as Hegel who place themselves at the service of financiers and politicians. Marat and Sade are vivid examples of such dynamic, rebellious heroes locked in a struggle for ultimate goals. They grapple with discovering the layers of implications in all their decisions.

The "most extreme actions" of which Sade speaks, though, are not limited to strictly political activities. All Weiss's heroes are political extremists, but they are more concerned with the worth of their ideas than they are with the efficacy of their acts. These men are rational political leaders even in periods of crisis and tragic defeat. They crave upheavals and insurgent causes in order to test their theories. Hölderlin is consumed by the fervid goals of the French Jacobins, but in the absence of any clearly defined German revolutionary movement at the time, he must therefore work out his own theories by urging civil protests wherever and whenever he can. His struggle resembles Marat's in this regard because both men must hammer out theory in light of the political struggles in which they are engaged, and which they have largely provoked. At times, such as in Trotsky's case, Weiss shows the writer in a state of indecision over which of the two modes of action—theory or practice—is more appropriate. But the complementary nature of these two forms of activity is always stressed. As Marat indicates in scene 28:

> When I investigated a wrong it grew branches
> and every branch grew twigs
> Wherever I turned
> I found corruption
> When I wrote
> I always wrote with action in mind . . .
> I always wrote in a fever
> hearing the roar of action.

Despite their involvement in political movements, however, these are all men who work alone, often by choice. Trotsky distances himself from contact with the proletariat and refuses to participate in Party struggles. During his later years, even though Weiss shows him in a close relationship with his wife and a few friends, he is forced to flee from one temporary asylum to another, rootless and constantly watchful. Sade is alone, surrounded by madmen. Marat is alone in his bath forming his "ideas about the world / which no longer fit the world outside." And Hölderlin's pathetic sexual encounters and the falling away of his friends leave him with a profound sense of alienation in a world which refuses to understand or accept him. This solitary condition of the writer is reflected in his political status as an exile, pursued by enemies and forced to work conspiratorially. Even Marat "at the head of the movement" is psychologically exiled and paranoid.

Isolation and solitude do have worth. All of Weiss's heroes are men of international outlook precisely because of their experiences of life as exiles. The conditions of exile account for their independence and their courage. Bound to no country, they are permitted to observe events from an intellectual distance. Even Marat, the most "patriotic" and politically powerful of Weiss's heroes, finally defines the revolution's ultimate goal in existential rather than in ideological or nationalistic terms: "The important thing / is to pull yourself up by your own hair / to turn yourself inside out / And see the whole world with fresh eyes." Their international and humanistic outlook allows Weiss's heroes to rise above regional objectives in order to promote universal goals, and this is a strong point of appeal for audiences. Because of this they become men whose concerns are shared by many writers, whatever their political persuasion, who attempt to influence historical change.

The artistic and political independence of Weiss's dramatic heroes is important because it allowed Weiss to analyze their struggles and to understand the context of their achievements and failures in more than just political terms. Specific political programs were less important to Weiss than the impact of his heroes' actions on the development of humanitarian principles of government. For example, some of the obstacles which obstruct his heroes' efforts—the French clergy, Coulmier's censorship, Tsarist nobles, literary conservatives such as Goethe—are the product of socioeconomic class determinations. Other forces, though, which contribute to the writer's oppressed condition, stem from causes which are only partly political in nature: parental upbringing, personal biases, or intellectual limitations. Weiss always portrayed the common people as limited by narrow concerns, by violent and often self-destructive tendencies, and by ignorance. Such influences, which are not dealt with in the documentary plays on Angola and Vietnam, arose from Weiss's concern for humanity's existential dilemma and in many cases they posed more formidable obstacles to the hero's self-development and the realization of his goals than his political circumstances.

It is difficult to connect the rebellious and independent outlooks of Weiss's heroes to any specific political movement in the modern world. These men seem to be generally inspired by socialist principles; certainly they laid the groundwork for ideas which Weiss regarded as central to modern socialist thought: fair distribution of wealth and resources among all social classes, national self-determination without pressure from foreign entanglements, democratic broadening of the political base which would prevent special interest groups from exercising control. Thus Weiss seemed to identify them as socialist planners, but the term "radical intellectuals" is more appropriate for describing their political acumen. His heroes are supranational in their outlook as well as in their struggles against forms of socioeconomic oppression, particularly capitalist systems of government. Jacques Roux praises Marat for destroying the blindness of class outlooks; Trotsky assails the ruthlessness of strongmen like Stalin who manipulate political parties and control world super-powers; and Hölderlin disapproves of the industrial-political system of mutually supportive alliances which defies his attempts at social reform.

One must conclude that the greatest strength of Weiss's writer–heroes lies in their independence, artistic and political. Independence—in the stance of a concerned leftist author—was also Weiss's greatest asset. His heroes strive desperately to free themselves from national ties. Their success is not measured in political terms in the plays, but rather in the soundness of their views. They are dynamic, highly rational men, meant for action even though Weiss often showed them as incapable of taking action. The universal nature of their goals—freedom from exploitation, vigorous pursuit of theoretical understanding, self-knowledge, political engagement—are features which recommend them to audiences on a prototypical basis. While presenting them within the context of their times, Weiss also sketched them with an eye to modern concerns, and he stressed the similarities between their political activities and the socialism of the present.

The Writer's Self-Doubt

The intellectual independence of these heroes stems from their solitary condition as rebellious exiles, and their common weakness of self-doubt also arises from the same source. These writers and intellectuals are continually threatened by the knowledge of their partial successes, their political failures, their ultimate inability to influence history in a controlled, predictable fashion. Marat is forced by Sade to witness the betrayal of his cause by Napoleon's dictatorship; Trotsky must watch helplessly as Stalin ruthlessly eliminates political opponents and bends the course of Marxism to his own will. The control of history is something which continually troubles and eludes the hero in Weiss's plays, just as it eludes leftist writers in today's world. Sometimes, as with Marat and Trotsky, a visionary leader may initiate action and temporarily direct events. At other times, as with Hölderlin, political power remains out of the hero's reach precisely because he criticizes society. In every case, though, these men are brought to a recognition of their failure, and they continue to work with that realization in mind.

This lack of political success is a curse upon all Weiss's heroes. It forms a strong bond between their historical situations and Weiss's personal objectives as a leftist writer. Peter Weiss, like his heroes, could not debase his political ideals by placing them at the service of any particular party or national program. It is noteworthy that Weiss never chose to celebrate the achievements of revolutionary leaders like Castro or Mao Tse Tung. For Mao or for Castro, the goal of their initial efforts was the consolidation of a particular nation–state. In Weiss's analysis, though, what made Trotsky greater and more appealing than such men is the fact that his concerns were more than patriotic; he sought universal permanent revolution through a combination of theory and practice.

Weiss found that there were two advantages to be gained from this supranational, independent approach to revolution: the avoidance of a reliance upon dictatorship and the escape from destructive internal power struggles. Weiss was not, as Enzensberger and other critics charged, an ideological dilettante who avoided political commitment to a Communist cause or party. He witnessed at first hand the repressive conditions in eastern Europe, and he had barely escaped with his life from conditions of Fascist dictatorship which nearly engulfed his entire family in Czechoslovakia in 1938. Weiss first raised the question of dictatorship in *Marat/Sade* and explored it even more fully in *Trotsky*. There Trotsky explained to Lenin's ghost the reasons behind Stalin's unchallenged rise to power. The power struggle after Lenin's death disgusted Trotsky because he regarded internal bickering as counterproductive in achieving permanent revolution. Judging from Peter Weiss's own indifference to ideological disputes among socialist parties, it is clear that he shared Trotsky's international concerns.

Weiss also emphasized that despite political failures, his heroes' radical outlooks on social change deserve serious consideration today. Weiss presented all these men as individuals who relied on their imaginative grasp of universal socialist principles to guide them in their progressive approaches to historical change. And Weiss assigned his heroes a prophetic understanding of historical trends. Trotsky's inner certainty about the important role which the underdeveloped nations would play in the emergence of socialism, and Hölderlin's recognition of the disastrous implications of a militaristic, industrialized Germany—these were ideas much too radical to be accepted by their societies. Such concepts reflected an historical understanding out of step with their times or far in advance of them. Weiss shows, however, that his heroes' views would have been more valuable for achieving socialist progress than pragmatic social or political planning. Had Trotsky's ideas been adopted by the Bolsheviks, the face of the contemporary Soviet Union would have been profoundly altered. One of the most important conclusions Weiss drew from this point is that avant-garde ideas on culture and politics must find free expression in any society which regards itself as progressive and revolutionary.

Despite their failures, all Weiss's heroes act within the political arena as though success were attainable. His plays celebrate heroes caught in the paradoxical situation of acting politically in order to dispel the fear of meaninglessness. The conclusion to the first act of *Marat/Sade* shows Marat struggling to continue his revolutionary work while trapped in a nightmare. He desperately calls for Simonne to bring his manuscripts, and it is only the need to write a patriotic speech for the fourteenth of July which breaks the spell that holds him trapped in dreams, fears, and hallucinations. The madmen mock his desire to write by plunging him into human feces, but Marat screams for his secretary and emerges from the nightmare to take up the pen again. This moment in performance is particularly dramatic. We see Weiss's Marat driven by an inner compulsion which he cannot deny, and which stems from his deepest fears of failure and pointlessness. Provoked by the vast indifference and confusion of experience surrounding him, Marat struggles angrily and heroically to "invent a meaning." Roux, in fact, points this out in the final speech of that scene.

In *Trotsky* Weiss restated this need for prophets—political or cultural—to invent meaning by introducing the scene between the dadaists and the Bolshevik leaders. Unlike *Marat/Sade*, however, the issue was not stated in terms of radicalism versus skepticism, but instead between political versus aesthetic contributions to revolutionary work. In *Trotsky* the avant-garde artists directly opposed the pragmatic and culturally repressive programs of Lenin and Trotsky. Both groups were inventing meaning for the twentieth century, one of them artistically and the other politically. In this scene Weiss voiced the necessity for an alliance between visionary understanding and reason, between the artist and the revolutionary, in remaking the world. A synthesis of the two approaches to revolutionary reform (which Weiss believed Trotsky dimly perceived) was finally set forth in *Hölderlin*. Karl Marx, Weiss maintained, *did* conceive of the possibility of two approaches towards historical change: "the analysis of concrete / historical situations" as well as "a visionary conception / of the deepest personal significance." The artist's concern for social reform is thus critical, both for his own development as well as for that of society.

Skepticism towards the efficacy of political action can either force the writer into a withdrawal from political affairs (as Sade retreated into an aesthetic experience of life), or else skepticism can spur the writer to develop a sound theoretical understanding of his social purpose and of the laws of historical change. In both cases the writer must work in isolation, exposed to the dangers of madness, paranoia, and despair. His solitary condition, however, places him in familiar contact with the irrational side of his nature, a fact which can produce valuable visionary insights into experience. All of Weiss's heroes struggle against self-doubt and political skepticism by hammering out their ideas through writing and by testing their theories in action of some kind: Sade argues his viewpoint in the confusion of the madhouse and shows Marat continually preparing his "calls" to the French people, Trotsky is portrayed with his books and papers wherever exile leads him, and Hölderlin continues to write visionary poetry despite his ruined career and frustrating life.

Peter Weiss, like his Hölderlin, wrote "visionary" dramas; he refused to celebrate any particular political system in his plays. Instead he recommended ideal possibilities, ideal choices for socially concerned artists. Weiss could neither accept the world as he found it nor could he identify himself with nationalistic or ideological causes. He created through his plays a complex of ideas which reassured him in his role as an independent writer hoping to guide others. This, then, was the major function of Weiss's dramatic heroes: to provide socialist models whose values could stand in sharp contrast to the destructive political tendencies of our time, both East and West, and whose choices can contribute insight to problems shared by countless other artists and intellectuals.

The Need for Self-Liberation

The first aspects of the writer's condition we must consider are the parental and class limitations which stem from familial circumstances. These are obviously the first and most crucial determinants of the writer's condition. Weiss's early work was heavily influenced by his authoritarian upbringing. His bourgeois environment confined him to a domestic situation in which parental expectancies suffocated creative ability. Weiss felt that his family did nothing to encourage his artistic inclinations, and the lack of communication between the family members was a continual source of pain and frustration for him.

Two effects of Peter Weiss's familial background reflected in his plays were the intimidation he experienced at the hands of his parents, and the withdrawal into a fantasy life which he pursued as an escape from parental domination: solitary activities which separated him from social experience and bred in him a lasting distaste for authority figures. Weiss dealt directly with the problem of parental authority in his first play, *The Tower*. Here the split between the child's psychic life and the world of parental demands assumed tragic form, and the strongest feature of the drama was its expression of the hero's situation of an entrapment from which he tried unsuccessfully to liberate himself. Pablo's bondage consisted in having to remain in the tower cut off from the outside world, just as Weiss had felt condemned to a solitary existence as a child. Within Pablo's tower the inhabitants were confined to a never-ending routine of self-abasing activities, imprisoned in a world lacking all hope of improvement. Escape was impossible; there could be no contact with normal society, contact with new ideas, and different ways of living.

Weiss's need to find relief from his painful situation in the fantasy world of his imagination was first reflected in *Marat/Sade*. The Marquis de Sade boldly affirmed a preference for the world of the mind in opposition to outer reality. "The revolution no longer interests me," he defiantly tells Marat. "For me the only reality is imagination / the world inside myself." Weiss's Trotsky echoed this same concern five years later. According to Weiss, he was a man trapped in his solitude because he was exiled and cut off from all avenues of political action. "Sometimes I find myself thinking . . . as if the battle of ideas were more important to me than revolutionary activity. The writing, the printed impression of my thoughts more real than the actions outside." In presenting Hölderlin's career, Weiss laid great stress upon the hero's withdrawal from social intercourse during the later period of his life. He demonstrated how Hölderlin's retreat into the tower led to inspired poetry which enabled him to foresee historical developments many years ahead of his time. In each of these examples it was the strength of the hero's inner convictions, the determination to pursue one's private beliefs despite social rejection which Weiss recommended to writers of the post-World War II period.

In addition to these effects of a repressive parental upbringing upon Weiss's writing, his plays also reflect his class influences. It took Weiss many years, for instance, to rid himself of a painful sense of uselessness as an artist. In the Jewish bourgeois environment of his home, he claimed that his interest in painting was treated with condescension; his family rebuked him because such activities were totally unproductive. All of Weiss's heroes suffer from similar feelings of doubt about the value of their work. They respond to their situations as Weiss responded to his, by inventing meaning through intellectual pursuits. The failure of their efforts in the political arena underscores what Weiss regarded as the most valuable aspect of their work: self-understanding through socially concerned writing, and a perception of the future possibilities of socialism. Thus Weiss's rejection of bourgeois attitudes towards the social importance of art contributed to his need to fashion hero-models whose careers demonstrated that art can and does influence social change.

A second reflection in Weiss's plays of his youthful antibourgeois feelings can be found in his hatred of class institutions which impede social progress by serving those in power as instruments of oppression. The asylum of Charenton is a place of entrapment similar to the prison of Pablo's tower and comparable to Weiss's appraisal of his own familial incarceration. Weiss suggests that the socially concerned writer act pitilessly to tear down existing social forms and appraise those set up to replace them. He suggests that churches, schools, and scientific academies have vested interests in maintaining the status quo and in suppressing social reform. In *Marat/Sade*'s bitterly ironic scene entitled "Marat's Liturgy," the chorus of patients repeats the refrain, "The kings are our dear fathers / under whose care we live in peace"—while Marat undercuts this with rebukes of the church's hypocrisy in maintaining the status quo. In the scene entitled "Marat's Nightmare," the writer–hero is tormented by the authority figures of his petit-bourgeois schoolmaster, by literary pundits like Voltaire, and by members of the French Academy who ridicule his early work and fail to appreciate his unconventional criticism. Marat cries out that such people "laugh like executioners," and he responds by hurling abuse into the "puffy bourgeois faces / which are now all twisted up with anger and disgust."

Weiss also criticized class restrictions upon the writer's creative work in *Hölderlin*. Unlike Weiss's other heroes, Hölderlin is portrayed as a product of a definite social class; and in the first half of the play he must struggle to free himself from this influence. He is a clerical functionary in nineteenth-century German society, and he tries to improve his wretched condition by rebelling against the social restraints imposed by his occupation as a tutor and lecturer. He is dismissed from the von Kalb household because of his criticism of the major's military activities against the American Indians. Goethe and Schiller, apologists for the ruling class, treat the hero with scorn because his radical ideas and impassioned literary style are out of step with Weimar classicism. In the garden scene Weiss shows how such intellectuals as Goethe and Hegel who place themselves in the service of the establishment receive power, honor, and social rewards, while others who criticize the class system are driven into minor posts outside of respectable society. Hölderlin's attempts to find work, to obtain sponsorship for his literary efforts, and to plan a useful career are frustrated and jeopardized by his rebellion against the influence of the economic ruling classes in nineteenth-century Germany.

Sociopolitical Pressures and the Writer

The sociopolitical restraints against which Weiss's heroes must struggle are far more formidable than the repressions that issue from parents and class upbringing—although they are often interrelated. Weiss usually defined the writer's sociopolitical environment in terms of particular institutions such as law, medicine, religion, and, of course, government and business which are commonly presented as riddled with political bias and in desperate need of reform. In his criticism of social institutions Weiss often tried to explain the reasons why institutional reform is dependent upon changes in man's psychological and philosophical outlook. As Jacques Roux points out in the conclusion to the first act of *Marat/Sade,* revolutionary planners must seek to change fundamental outlooks in human experience if social reforms are to succeed:

> You wanted enlightenment and warmth
> and so you studied light and heat
> You wondered how forces could be controlled
> so you studied electricity . . .
> And you came one day to the Revolution
> because you saw the most important vision
> That our circumstances must be changed fundamentally
> and without these changes
> everything we try to do must fail.

Weiss's optimistic attitude towards the possibility of reforming social institutions was tempered by his awareness of the likelihood of failure, and especially by his conviction that only partial successes were immediately attainable. At times he attacked a political target in his plays directly, such as the Fascist mentality and the nationalistic fervor which inspired the death camps of Nazi Germany. At the same time, though, Weiss recognized that those targets were only a reflection in miniature of more complex problems. In *The Investigation* Weiss presented Fascism as only one manifestation of harmful nationalistic trends which were very much alive in the post-World War II period. This, of course, led to difficulties with his audiences. Though the villains seemed to be on trial, Weiss argued that their guilt was also to be shared by the judges, the victims, and ultimately by the audience. Considered in these terms, the war crimes trials could produce only superficial results, which almost amounted to a political coverup. Weiss implied that the judicial process might deal effectively with a few notorious criminals, but it was powerless to address itself to correcting the underlying frame of mind and the xenophobia which always produces totalitarianism.

Other plays also express doubts about the possibility of reforming social institutions. In extolling Marat as the precursor of modern socialist revolutionaries, Weiss also pointed out that the order which Marat created led directly to the disastrous emergence of Napoleon. In *Trotsky* we find the interesting suggestion of Weiss's own self-doubt as to the efficacy of literary work. Weiss may have called the play an attempt to celebrate the creation of the greatest social revolution of our century, but his choice of hero sharply contradicted this professed intention. Trotsky was the one man who had let the movement slip through his fingers when he could have led it. Instead of tracing the fulfillment of revolutionary principles in the play, Weiss demonstrated the betrayal of these same principles and the emergence of dictatorship.

Despite the fact, then, that these plays reveal the difficulty of constructing viable social institutions, Weiss did affirm the value of the writer who works to improve the social circumstances of his time. The writer's compulsion to work for progressive social change is an important—if tragic—feature in all his major dramas. Here we encounter Weiss's admiration for the heroic rebellion of certain men who refused to give in to nihilism, who continued to work and to create despite the all too obvious sense of absurdity which crowded their efforts. The intricate and imbecilic web of sociopolitical interrelationships of which Hölderlin gradually becomes aware stimulates the hero to create meaning through his literary work. In the garden scene the hero watches the alliances being formed between Hegelian philosophy, laissez-faire capitalism, and scientific experimentation. He realizes that his political position is untenable; but he continues to work in isolation in the second act, remaining "true to the end" in voicing socialist ideals through his visionary poetry.

It is noteworthy that despite Weiss's socialist outlook on contemporary political affairs, he cautioned writers against the dangers of committing themselves to any particular cause. In his plays he revealed how philosophical goals and ideals are invariably compromised by the writer's abandonment of his independent stance, by his identification with political parties. The betrayal of justice, of progressive educational systems, of a fair distribution of wealth, of free speech and a sharing of political power is certainly common to both capitalist and socialist societies. Despite the immediate vigor and challenge which political activism affords, there is no advantage to be gained from identifying oneself with a system. Weiss himself chose to live in Sweden, thus remaining neutral in his political allegiance. His heroes also avoid identification with political systems and parties, and even with political action in the form of "praxis." Sade confines himself in the asylum, Marat continually finds new factions to be attacked, Trotsky flees and works in isolation, and Hölderlin retires into social obscurity. Society in all Peter Weiss's plays seems eternally corrupt and in need, therefore, of constant reform.

The Unpredictability of Human Nature

The strong feeling of being trapped which the heroes and many other figures in Weiss's plays experience is not only the result of parental-familial oppression or of sociopolitical oppression, but also of the writer's own human limitations. Weiss's attitude towards human nature is overwhelmingly negative, whether he expresses it in terms of the individual or especially in terms of national groups or "the masses." While his heroes might succeed to some extent in bearing with parental and familial oppression, or while they might achieve partial victories in overthrowing the tyranny caused by social institutions, these men never escape their feelings of failure, guilt, selfishness, or ignorance. Nor can they ever optimistically regard their fellow man as capable of shedding destructive psychological tendencies which betray social progress.

This grim view of human potential receives its tersest expression at the conclusion of *Marat/Sade*. Immediately before the murder is committed, Sade insists to Marat that political reforms can only follow upon the reformation of each individual within society (a point reaffirmed by Roux when the berserk patients trample him):

> these cells of the inner self
> are worse than the deepest stone dungeon
> and as long as they are locked
> all your revolution remains
> only a prison mutiny
> to be put down
> by corrupted fellow-prisoners.

Sade's prison of human nature recurs in all Weiss's writings: in the confinement of Pablo's tower, in the tunnel vision literary perspectives of the early novels, or in the universal guilt implied in *The Investigation*. Social change is always hampered by the unpredictability and inherent destructiveness of human nature, and all Weiss's heroes feel the need to shun society at some point in their careers in order to work in freedom. Let us approach this theme of the writer's human limitations in two ways: Weiss's appraisal of the violent tendencies of human society, and his stress on the irrational aspects of the writer's creative work.

The imperfectibility of man's social relationships is almost always demonstrated in grotesque terms. Weiss's plays are replete with descriptions or enactments of brutal violence. Sade's catalogue of the excesses provoked by the revolution overwhelms the arguments of Marat, and it is reinforced by the dismal existence in the asylum of Charenton. The kicking and beating of pregnant women in scenes from *Bogeyman,* and the interminable and gruesome descriptions in *The Investigation* indicate how frequently Weiss returned to dwell upon the theme of imperfectibility in all his plays.

The unpredictable behavior and inconsistent ideals of Weiss's characters are a strong indication of the violent tendencies which influence social reformers who lead them. Weiss's characters often vacillate between cruelty and kindness, loyalty and betrayal, and thus suggest that self-contradiction and ethical ambivalence are staples of human relationships. In *Hölderlin* Weiss established a strong contrast between the behavior of certain characters as idealistic young men and their actions as older, established public figures. Hölderlin's fellow student, Schmid, is a pacifist at the university, but years later he is killed while fighting patriotically in the Napoleonic campaign. Hegel is portrayed exchanging his youthful egalitarian principles for financial rewards later in life: German industrialists of the nineteenth century enjoyed his theory of the *Zeitgeist* as a justification for their rapacious colonial practices. In *Marat/Sade* the four singers vacillate between the expression of humanitarian sentiments and the encouragement of bloodthirsty acts. Violent tendencies can unpredictably burst forth from ordinary German citizens assigned to guard duty at Auschwitz, or from Sade's mild-mannered tailor. The humanitarian tendencies in individuals, no matter what their station in life, are shown to be just as unpredictable as their violent cravings.

Weiss also stressed the significance of violence by presenting atrocities and crimes in the form of rituals. This method scores a powerful impact on spectators and permits the theme of brutality to function as a *Leitmotif* to the dramatic action. Corday's three visits to Marat are represented with formalized, ritualized movements and patterns of dialogue. When Corday finally approaches Marat in the third visit, the sexual-religious imagery of Sade's language stresses the archetypal features of political terrorism:

> Marat
> an untouched virgin stands before you and offers herself to you
> See how she smiles
> how her teeth shine
> how she shakes her auburn hair aside . . .
> a maiden
> from the rural desert of a convent
> Imagine
> those pure girls lying on hard floors
> in rough shifts
> and the heated air from the fields
> forcing its way to them through the barred windows . . .
> And then she was tired of her isolation
> and stirred up by the new age
> and gathered up in the great tide
> and wanted to be part of the Revolution.

Inasmuch as ritual implies a repetition or reenactment of events holding special significance, Weiss's use of ritual, here and elsewhere, suggests a cyclical recurrence of violence and brutality which strongly conditions our historical experience. It also provides a countermelody to the threnodies of idealism and optimism voiced by many of Weiss's principal characters.

It may seem inappropriate for a dark view of human nature to run through the work of a "socialist" writer, but Weiss's use of dramatic tableaux, just as his use of ritual, also asserts the presence of violence and cruelty in the writer's milieu—as a condition against which the hero must always be watchful. This is a point often overlooked by critics who regard Weiss's plays as optimistic statements of socialist doctrine. On the contrary, his dramas often suggest that injustice and cruelty are the staples of life. He shows Marat stabbed while writing manifestoes, and Trotsky is revising manuscripts while the assassin's hatchet is poised. Weiss includes huge, often grisly documentary photographs for the background behind the *Discourse on Vietnam;* and he depicts Hölderlin trussed up in a crucifixion pose raving behind his leather mask. These are powerful statements which undercut any optimistic expectation of the writer's ability to prevail for very long over the destructive tendencies in his society.

Weiss is only slightly less pessimistic in his attitude towards the writer's own self-limitations. The most notable image of entrapment which Weiss employs in this regard is that of madness: the inner world of confused subjectivity and individual pathology encased by a sociopolitical madness. Weiss presents two of his heroes actually living in a madhouse, Sade and Hölderlin, and the ideas of Marat are sharply criticized by the fact that a lunatic plays the role. Though lunacy is not a key feature of Trotsky's situation, Weiss's dream vision production concept suggested that the hero was trapped within the prison of his own mind. In *Marat/Sade* madness is the means whereby Sade can illustrate the senselessness according to which historical events take place, while in *Hölderlin* the hero's insanity is not only historically based, but also stresses his condition as an exile. Weiss uses it in his play to demonstrate the rootlessness of the thoughts of the writer who is detached from social efficacy.

In Weiss's plays the condition of madness is always analogous to sociopolitical conditions. Sade, for example, enjoys having madmen enact revolutionary events because that situation accurately reflects his view of historical experience. Hölderlin seems more inspired than insane in his confinement because lunacy provides insight into the French betrayal of Jacobin ideals or the role of Buonarotti in the history of the socialist movement. Trotsky's prison of the imagination also becomes a positive feature of his condition because it continually provides him with hallucinatory visions and radical perspectives upon past events.

Through the image of madness in his plays Weiss often directs his discussion at subjects which lie beneath the surface of sociopolitical events. Though his heroes are invariably bound up with political causes, Weiss does not attempt to explain the worth of these men solely in terms of their political choices. With the possible exception of the lunatic playing Marat, Weiss's heroes are everywhere conscious that historical reality is a phenomenon quite different from the world of their imagination. In Weiss's prose novels he dwells upon the limitations of human consciousness in grasping phenomena in the outside world. In *Shadow of the Coachman's Body* the image of the flickering shadows thrown by the bodies of the cook and the coachman in violent copulation presage Weiss's view of human consciousness in all its confusing limitations. And as late as 1975 in the first volume of *Ästhetik des Widerstands,* Weiss is still preoccupied with the problem that one critic described as "the continuities and discontinuities of his experience of himself and the world about him."[3]

This confusing inner world of the mind is a powerful force against which Weiss's heroes must struggle; the effectiveness of their political activities is often directly measured against their sense of doubt, failure, and partial knowledge. Thus at the conclusion of *Marat/Sade,* Weiss gives his martyr–hero revealing statements about the nature of political activism:

> Why is everything so confused now
> Everything I wrote or spoke
> was considered and true
> each argument was sound
> And now
> doubt.

Self-doubt is not the only limitation which Weiss's heroes suffer, although it is certainly the most unsettling. There are other weaknesses such as Marat's paranoid hatred of all who oppose his viewpoint, or the criminal tendencies in Sade's own personality which disgust Sade, or the self-degradation of the Jewish prisoners who unprotestingly accept their fate. Only in the Angolan and Vietnamese dramas (and in *Mockinpott*) where Weiss focused upon heroic popular struggles did he ignore the equation between private pathology and political freedom-fighting.

This situation of entrapment within parental, familial, societal, political, and psychological restrictions confirms the heroic stature of the writer because Weiss's dramas make clear how difficult it is to remain true to one's inner convictions within an oppressive society. The violent death of the hero and the betrayal of his goals are crucial features of Weiss's view of history, and this agonistic aspect of heroism is a recurring feature in the major plays. In the minor dramas, Weiss does not deal with entrapment in a personal sense; he is solely concerned with the external, political forms of oppression. In his trilogy of major plays, though, Weiss demonstrates that political activism is necessary and valuable for the writer's self-fulfillment, and therefore his heroes' values cannot be measured simply on the basis of their political successes or failures.

Socialism and the Writer's Political Choices

If, then, Weiss's dramatic heroes reflect his own search for meaning as a writer *engagé,* we need also to ask what answers Weiss was able to uncover for himself and for others. Just what was the relationship Weiss was able to recommend between the writer's aesthetic and political choices?

In the documentary plays, and in *Mockinpott,* Weiss adopted a socialist stance in order to criticize the policies of Western nations and to sharpen his own leftist sympathies. In his major historical dramas Weiss dealt with the influence of socialist ideas upon three different political systems in the Western world. To describe Weiss as a socialist, though, is somewhat misleading because one cannot identify him with any specific party. As one interviewer observed in 1966, Weiss continually used the terms "socialism" and "communism" interchangeably. He insisted that his literary work "is for the salvation of all humankind, and indeed he termed the key to it 'Socialist humanism' or 'humanistic Socialism.'"[4] It is probably most accurate to regard Weiss as a member of what Sartre calls "the Left in Western Europe," whose general task is "to answer the fundamental question of our time: how to unite all the exploited to overthrow the old ossified structures of our own society, how to produce new structures which will ensure that the next revolution does not give birth to *that sort of socialism.*"[5]

Sartre's broad definition of the mission of the leftist intellectual offers helpful insight into Weiss's work. Sartre suggests two courses of action for the modern writer: criticism of the political status quo, and theoretical planning for the future. Weiss's analysis of the writer's existential condition is a reflection of Sartre's call for critical understanding; and all Weiss's portraits of writer—heroes stress the importance of Sartre's second demand for a sound understanding of Marxist thought in influencing social change.

Sartre's comment also suggests that the writer must exert influence on society in an indirect manner, primarily planning rather than directly molding political struggles. Weiss echoed this suggestion in his plays because political possibilities for effecting social change are not always available to his heroes. The political failure of these men, the universal guilt implied by *The Investigation,* the betrayal of revolutionary causes which forms the background of his trilogy—such things demonstrate the limitations of political freedom-fighting and stress the importance of the writer's own self-integrity and his indirect contribution to social reform. Because Weiss's heroes evaluate their programs in light of the *horizons* of socialist development, and because they speak for universal, broadly humanitarian goals, they provide what Sartre calls "the experience of being in a world which crushes us . . . and an appeal for freedom addressed to all other men."[6]

The writer who is seriously concerned with the social impact of his work must first of all accept and learn to live with the paradoxical nature of his activity. According to Weiss, he occupies an uncomfortable position in the modern world. He exists as an island in an uncertain sea of political crosscurrents and historical backwaters, struggling to sustain his artistic integrity while responding to the need for assisting progressive social change. All of Weiss's heroes are men compelled to work under lonely, chaotic, and dangerous conditions while maintaining their faith in the importance of their work.

This paradoxical combination of skepticism and historical optimism which inspires the writer's work must be affirmed simply because it is suicidal to deny either side of the paradox. Although his attempts to improve life may fail, the writer nevertheless must pursue his work not despite but because of his consciousness of human limitations. As one critic has remarked concerning this feature of the writer's situation as expressed in *Marat/Sade:* "No one wins! The aristocrat, the bourgeoisie, the proletariat, the romantic idealist, the social worker, the hedonist, or the socialist theoretician, the existential theoretician, or the anarchist . . . *all of them* live out the failure that is the human condition. Their ideas perish as certainly as they themselves."[7] Such never-ending fratricidal combat between social reformers and political skeptics will be repeated in all historical periods and with many different protagonists. Weiss himself points this out: "It's usually the same conflict—the dualism of Utopia, wishes, dreams, poetry, humanism against outer reality, dogma, the status quo, power, compromise, repression."[8]

In this situation the writer's primary task is to refine revolutionary theory in light of past examples, present problems, and future possibilities. Weiss's documentary plays suggest that the modern writer may occasionally adopt a journalistic stance by commenting upon or by celebrating freedom struggles. In this case, though, Weiss recommended that the writer be cautious about aligning himself with a political party since the results of such upheavals are not likely to duplicate the goals of the initial struggle. The modern writer, he suggested, must function as a focal point of information—historical and contemporary—and must synthesize that information in order to extrapolate the important issues for his public.

Weiss also suggested that the committed writer must learn to accept the fact that he stands in solidarity with many others, despite the remote or indirect influence he is exerting. Trotsky has no real hope of reversing the course of Stalinism, nor have Marat, Sade, or Hölderlin any expectations of immediately or profoundly influencing the course of history by their literary work. Each discovers that writing is only a partial substitute for political action and they all find this knowledge painful. But Weiss recommended that the writer take pleasure in celebrating others' achievements and in speaking on behalf of long-range goals. Trotsky, for example, writes of the future of the underdeveloped nations; Hölderlin expresses his faith in poetry as a vision of future possibilities, and he celebrates the work of early pioneers like Empedocles.

The writer–hero in Weiss's plays thus performs an ancillary function with regard to his society. He may inspire or criticize popular movements, he may add some leverage to them by publicizing their importance, or he may point up their implications for the benefit of other leftist freedom-fighters. Through all such activity the writer increases his self-understanding and reaches an awareness of his social role. Though he cannot directly influence change, he can discover how change must eventually come about, and often with the help of his efforts. This long-range focus to his work helps him distance himself from the dangers of political involvement. As Weiss observed in 1971: "I know that I'm not working in the arena of practical politics. I haven't the time or the energy. Certainly I realize just how little I can accomplish with my plays and books. But writing is my occupation. . . . Besides, in the political arena we always take the risk of being misunderstood, of becoming mired in prejudice, in ignorance, or fossilized into immobility."[9]

A committed political activity is not the only consideration governing the writer's contribution. Weiss's plays also demonstrate the importance of an international, broadly humanitarian outlook. Concerned authors should not confine themselves strictly to ideological matters, Weiss suggests, but they must provide critical commentary on many issues of contemporary significance. As Sartre has observed, "The real work of the committed writer is . . . to reveal, demonstrate, demystify, and dissolve myths and fetishes in a critical acid bath."[10] All Weiss's heroes address themselves to the task of improving their societies' political consciousness by improving mankind's consciousness of humanitarian ideals. Additionally, they offer constant criticism of institutions, customs, values, and political trends in order to illuminate the current situation.[11]

Committed art is not intended to generate ameliorative measures, legislative acts, or practical institutions like earlier propagandistic or "reformist" plays about syphilis, duels, alcoholism, whorehouses, and the like. Instead the committed writer works at the level of fundamental attitudes and he attempts—as Sartre would advise—to awaken the free choice of individuals in order to make social responsibility and authentic existence possible. He makes himself accessible to all readers and audiences; he does not limit himself to a select group, a narrow band of partisans. "All of us," Weiss remarked, "are concerned with the struggle to change society and to revolutionize art, we all find ourselves in this dilemma."[12]

The Writer's Artistic Contribution

Despite the need for commitment to leftist causes which Weiss's plays demonstrate, he also stressed that the committed writer has an aesthetic responsibility to himself. He must be certain that his choice and treatment of subjects are not governed by topical or strictly propagandistic factors. These are usually hallmarks of the second-rate artist. Instead he must rely upon artistic intuition.

His work must stem from serious personal engagement with the issues. The writer must sustain a delicate balance between personal and public concerns in his art.

Weiss's most successful plays, *Marat/Sade* and *Hölderlin,* are cases in point. Weiss's long fascination with the subjects of these dramas and his desire to make those subjects relevant to modern concerns accounted for the inspiration of those plays. As he remarked about the tragic features of Hölderlin's career: "Certainly this is pitiful . . . but the conflict is just as authentic today as yesterday. The author of the play himself struggled hard against such suffering. Naturally the choice of this theme indicates that the author has been puzzled by it . . . but I don't want it to be regarded as entirely personal."

The work of the committed writer, therefore, must be personal as well as political. The writer must ensure that his theme has contemporary applications. Hölderlin's situation, for example, "is the same scene of action familiar to Trotsky, to Che Guevara. The inhumanity, the ignorance and brutality of a world which finally crushed him without understanding him, is the same world which gradually overpowered many contemporary revolutionaries." At the same time, the writer must constantly challenge himself as he writes. He must experience self-growth in exploring his subject. "I value this play more as something from my former work," Weiss remarked about *Hölderlin,* "as the foundation for my own explorations, a rebellion; something to push away the contradictions and obstacles in my field of view."[13]

No matter how successfully the writer may struggle to overcome such "contradictions and obstacles," he must always be prepared to entertain a strong attitude of uncertainty towards his analyses and proposals. All of Weiss's major dramas focus heavily upon the problem of absurdity and its influence upon historical development, and they recognize socialism within this context of absurdity. Weiss presents what Herbert Lindenberger has called "the ambiguities inherent in all political situations," ambiguities indispensable for good historical playwriting.[14] Thus there must be a certain amount of stoicism in the committed writer's attitude towards his work; the tragic fates of Weiss's heroes imply that a socially concerned author will be condemned to working towards the solution of insoluble issues. His work will always remain partial because the "contradictions and obstacles" against which he struggles arise from man's existential condition, and to a large extent they are unable to be corrected.

The writer's most significant contribution to the socialist cause is his ability to think prophetically, to perceive how political objectives might be realized in the future. Weiss's documentary plays as well as his three portraits of revolutionary writers are all written from a standpoint which places the material within a broad historical perspective. This is most apparent in Weiss's treatments of Trotsky and Hölderlin, which suggest the eventual vindication of the hero's (and author's) beliefs in a later historical period. Weiss accurately traced the reasons behind the political failure of these two men, but he also showed how both had perceived the germs of the future. Most importantly, Weiss showed both men acting in accordance with those futurizing ideals despite the contradictions which inhibited and ultimately destroyed them. Their words and deeds had been, in Artaud's phrase, "the hand signalling through the flames." Weiss presented them as such, "standing alone with revolutionary consciousness, awaiting a kind of restorative period."[15]

The Purpose of Writing

The "revolutionary consciousness" of Peter Weiss's heroes is something which is also shared by the audiences of his plays. We must regard the situations of Marat, Sade, Trotsky, and Hölderlin with the same hope that a restorative period will emerge, coupled with our realistic skepticism about the possibilities of our immediate present situation. The failures of Weiss's political martyrs do not discredit the value or the need for rational planning in the political arena. On the contrary, in Weiss's historical plays we see what Herbert Blau has called "the brain admirably and joyously and muscularly in action . . . the critical mind back in the center of the drama—whatever spectres, devils, and darkness inhabit the periphery and the netherworld of conscious behavior."[16] Despite the frustration and the failure of Weiss's historical protagonists, we know that certain men have noticeably altered (if not advanced) human progress by a few degrees. New ages have been "ushered in," even if at first they did resemble the blood-spattered whores of whom Brecht's Galileo spoke.

In the final analysis it is this affirmation of meaning and value in Weiss's dramas, this expression of the Brechtian thesis that "the world is changeable," which makes his plays most distinctive. Weiss's qualified optimism separates his plays from the all-too-partisan statements of playwrights like Peter Hacks,[17] from the overly negative criticism expressed in such plays as Arthur Kopit's *Indians* and in Peter Brook's famous production of *Marat/Sade*. It is this political impact of Weiss's plays which distinguishes them from the popular heroical excursions into history which we frequently see in films and in such plays as John Osborne's *Luther;* from the stylistic emphasis which often strives for mere theatrical surprise like Peter Shaffer's *Royal Hunt of the Sun;* and from recent avant-garde and absurdist works depicting historical subjects from highly personal, subjective, and fragmented standpoints, like Robert Wilson's *Life and Times of Joseph Stalin* or Wolfgang Hildesheimer's *Maria Stuart*.

The inspiration for Peter Weiss's dramas is best described by Erwin Piscator who commented upon the "atrocious anti-Schopenhauer optimism" which he found in the finest work of modern historical playwrights. Though Weiss's plays include modern absurdist perspectives in their treatments, the plays stress the importance of *searching for and inventing meaning* when undertaking political reform. As in Brecht's plays, truth may be concrete in Weiss's dramas, but it is also elusive, and it is the hero's struggle to uncover the truth which

Weiss's plays celebrate. His plays demonstrate a consistent faith in the possibility of historical change through historical understanding. Such dramas, Piscator observed, "will be a force for change. . . . From objective recognition a passionate avowal of values can develop."[18]

More than any other historical playwright, Weiss has been able to summarize in his work the major concerns of other writers who have dealt with the subject of historical change, and in *Hölderlin* Weiss offered a partial—if personal—solution to his problem of playing a meaningful role in society. At the close of his career, therefore, Peter Weiss seemed to remain personally satisfied with a dualistic attitude towards change: revolutionary art and limited revolutionary action.[19]

Peter Weiss saw in his writing his own reflection as he moved towards a better understanding of the world and himself through historical images. At this point one is reminded of Kierkegaard's observation in *Fear and Trembling* on the nature of that mysterious relationship between the poet and the heroes he celebrates. Kierkegaard's words seem to encapsulate the mission Weiss felt with regard to his audiences, and to himself, as he wrote for a public which needed—and which still needs—inspired leadership in order to move into the future:

> If a consciousness of the eternal were not implanted in man; if the basis of all that exists were but a confusedly fermenting element which, convulsed by obscure passions, produced everything, both the great and the insignificant; if under everything there lay a bottomless void never to be filled—what else were life but despair? . . . And therefore it is not thus; but just as God created man and woman, He likewise called into being the hero and the poet or orator. The latter cannot perform the deeds of the hero—he can only admire and love him and rejoice in him. And yet he also is happy and not less so; for the hero is, as it were, his better self with which he has fallen in love, and he is glad he is not himself the hero, so that his love can express itself in admiration. . . . This is his achievement, his humble work, this is his faithful service in the house of the hero.[20]

For Peter Weiss, writing was a form of action. It was, no matter how slow, a force for change and it could, in Artaud's words, "influence the aspect of formation in things." For Weiss, the playwright who recreated historical periods and who celebrated the future possibilities of socialist planning, the immediate present was a nightmare of oppression, a world in need of change. He had to exist within it when he could not dwell within the complex web of his own ideas and imagination. "I never count on anything that lies in the future," he remarked to an observer in 1966. "I have been disillusioned too often since boyhood in Berlin. But my point is that even if the world is a madhouse like Charenton and nobody wants to belong in it, this is still where we are and the least we can do is to take a stand for or against madness. I want my plays, my new kind of theater, to force the inmates to declare themselves."[21]

Appendix A

Biographical Outline of Weiss's Career

1916	Born in Nowawes, a suburb of Berlin.
1918–29	Lives in Bremen with his family.
1929–34	Lives in Berlin with his family.
1932	First attempts at graphic art under Eugen Spiros. Small exhibition of watercolors and charcoal sketches.
1934	Emigrates to London with his family. His sister, Margit, killed in an auto accident.
1936	Small gallery exhibition of his paintings in London. Emigrates with his family to Warnsdorf, Czechoslovakia.
1936–38	Studies at the Academy of Art, Prague, under Willi Novak.
1938	In Switzerland for seven months with Hermann Hesse.
1939	In Gothenborg, Sweden, lives with his family, works in his father's textile factory.
1940	Takes up residence in Stockholm. Works part-time for his father and tries to live as a painter.
1941	First exhibition of his paintings in Stockholm.
1942	Weiss's first marriage, to a Swedish painter.
1944	Birth of Weiss's first daughter; divorced from his wife.
1945	Gains his Swedish citizenship.
1946	First book published, prose–poems in Swedish: *Fran ö till ö.*
1947	First postwar journeys to Paris and to Germany, as a Swedish newspaper correspondent. *Der Vogelfreie,* a novel, completed. First contact with Peter Suhrkamp, publisher.
1948	*Die Besiegten,* a volume of prose–poems in Swedish, published in Stockholm. Enrolled in the Swedish Academy for painting, film, and cinema production studies. Completion of *The Tower.* Beginning of *Vanishing-Point,* and membership in *Gruppe 47.*
1949	Stockholm radio broadcast of *The Tower.* Weiss meets Gunilla Palmstierna.

1951	*Das Duell* completed, a volume of surrealist short stories.
1952	*The Insurance* and *Shadow of the Coachman's Body* completed. First experimental film studies undertaken; continues work in film until 1960.
1953	*Das Duell* privately published.
1955	Essay on "Avantgarde Film" published.
1959	*Leavetaking* begun. Death of his parents.
1960	*Coachman's Body,* with Weiss's illustrations, published by Suhrkamp. The beginning of Weiss's career as a published writer. Numerous essays and short stories undertaken.
1962	*Leavetaking* and *Vanishing-Point* published. Weiss puts aside painting and graphic arts as "too static" a medium, and turns his attention to the stage. Major speech and essay on Strindberg presented in Berlin. *Night with Guests, Mockinpott,* and *Marat/Sade* begun.
1963	*Three Wayfarers* and translation of Strindberg's *A Dream Play* published. *Night with Guests* produced at Schiller Theater in Berlin. Charles Veillon Prize for *Vanishing-Point.*
1964	*Marat/Sade* produced in Berlin. Weiss in Frankfurt for the war crimes trials; begins his work on *The Investigation.*
1965	*The Investigation* produced in 16 European theaters simultaneously; premiere performance at Berlin's Freie Volkbühne, directed by Erwin Piscator. *Marat/Sade* opens in the Martin Beck Theater on Broadway. "Ten Working Points" essay published. Lessing Prize awarded in Hamburg; Weiss receives the Literary Prize from the Swedish Academy.
1966	Heinrich Mann Prize from the German Academy of Art. Weiss delivers a speech at Princeton University, his first contact with the United States. Publication of "Vietnam: Eleven Points." *Marat/Sade* wins the Tony Award as the best play of the season. Peter Brook's version of *Marat/Sade* is filmed. *Vietnam Discourse* and *Lusitanian Bogeyman* begun, *Mockinpott* continued.
1967	*Lusitanian Bogeyman* premiere at the Scala Theater in Stockholm. *Vietnam Discourse* completed.
1968	*Lusitanian Bogeyman* opens in New York at the Negro Ensemble Company. *Vietnam Discourse* produced in Frankfurt. *Mockinpott* produced in Hannover. Weiss travels to North Vietnam. Two volumes of collected plays and first volume of collected essays published. "Material and the Models" and "Vietnam Notes" published. Weiss begins work on *Trotsky.*
1969	Weiss prepares second volume of collected essays.
1970	*Trotsky in Exile* produced in Düsseldorf. Weiss begins work on *Hölderlin.*

1971   Second volume of collected essays published. *Hölderlin* produced in Stuttgart.

1972   *Hölderlin* published. Schiller Prize for Literature from the German Academy of Art.

1975   First part of the *Ästhetik des Widerstands* published. Initial adaptation of Kafka's *The Trial* produced in Bremen.

1976   Retrospective exhibition of selected painting in Rostock and Stockholm.

1977   Additional exhibitions of Weiss's retrospective paintings in Berlin, Munich, and Paris.

1978   Second part of the *Ästhetik des Widerstands* published.

1980   Major retrospective of all Weiss's graphics work and films in the Bochum Museum.

1981   Catalogue of the Bochum retrospective published, containing also a collection of family portraits, biographical interview with Weiss, and major commentaries on his career by friends and critics. Publication of the final part of the *Ästhetik des Widerstands*.

1982   *The New Trial,* the second adaptation of Kafka's work, produced at the Royal Dramatic Theater, Stockholm, co-directed by Weiss and Gunilla Palmstierna, March 12. Büchner Prize awarded by the (Darmstadt) German Academy of Literature and Poetry, May 3. Weiss dies in Stockholm, May 10.

Appendix B

Interview with Gunilla Palmstierna-Weiss

Gunilla Palmstierna-Weiss is well known in Europe as a designer for numerous theater and opera companies. She is also, of course, the woman who shared Peter Weiss's life for nearly thirty years, and who designed the sets and costumes for all of his plays. No critical attention has been paid to Gunilla's contribution to Weiss's dramas, despite the fact that she collaborated with him on the writing of all the plays. The following comments were made during an interview with her at her home on Lidingö Island, near Stockholm, on August 8, 1986.

RE: Gunilla, critics have written so much about Peter Weiss's plays, on just about every aspect of the plays, since the success of the *Marat/Sade*. In your opinion, what do you think most of these critics have missed in their discussions of your husband's work?

GP: Yes, well . . . I think that there are many levels of meaning in Peter's plays which people often fail to see. If you see the political level, this is the most apparent, but there are many more levels even in the so-called propaganda plays. For example, *Trotsky* is such a play. In this play the first level is intellectual, of course. And there is the political level, but the third level is also that of the artist—the way of the artist. He put in the scene with the dadaists as a contrast, to show another kind of revolution. And in a way this is something that goes through all his plays: the need to be a political and an artistic person, to show that these are really the same thing. One can't just have *only* politics, one can't just have *only* art. It has to be a combination where one revolution depends on the other. So very often I think the critics haven't seen that. They say, "That damned communist" or something, even after his death and certainly during his life. I think that many critics have been very one-sided towards Peter, fitting him into their little boxes. If he doesn't fit, then they don't see the levels underneath.

RE: Would you say that this happened with the *Hölderlin?* I like this play very much.

GP: Yes, I would say that *Hölderlin* is one of his best plays.

RE: Has *Hölderlin* been very successful since the time it was first performed?

GP: Yes, here in Sweden. In Germany, of course not.

RE: Why is that?

GP: Well I think it is too difficult for the Germans, not only as directors and actors but also audiences, to see all their heroes (Goethe, Schiller and others) in a new way. They have their own ideas of these people and so you cannot discuss them, you cannot change their ideas. Here in Stockholm where we have a *distanz* to it, you could just do it as a play. Now here, too, the critics were not very nice, but it was an enormous success with audiences in Stockholm. And the theater wanted to remove it from their repertoire because of these critics, but audience groups circulated a petition and so they had to restore it. So I would say that the audiences could see what was going on in the play, but the critics could not. That was very interesting.

RE: Aside from critics' "boxes," as you say, their preconceptions, why else does this happen that they fail to see what is happening onstage?

GP: Well of course there are those who do see the plays correctly. But also you must understand that Peter in his writing has been in a way one step ahead of others, ahead of his time. You have, for instance, the Angola play [*Song of the Lusitanian Bogeyman*]. That was first performed here in Sweden. We had one director at the beginning but he was let go. So we both sort of took over his work. And so that was really the first free group making political theater in Europe before all these other political groups started to work here. But the critics hated the whole idea of it, and therefore our group was killed by the reviews. Now of course, after ten years, people recognize all this, but for Peter and me it just didn't work out at the time because the critics just didn't see what was going on.

RE: Did the same thing happen with other plays, that you feel they were ahead of their time?

GP: Well, I think that is what happened with *Trotsky* too. *Trotsky* came at a time that was very turbulent in Germany and that worked against Peter: East Germany and West Germany, the left and the right, the anarchist and the centralist. Passions clashed at the performance. You know, he was forbidden for two years to go to East Germany because of that, because he presented his play during their "Lenin Year" and they didn't appreciate that. In a way he was perhaps childish or naive to think that just by writing *Trotsky* he could open their eyes.

RE: How did Peter feel about the reception of his plays in the United States?

GP: Well at first, of course, *Marat/Sade* was an enormous success. It came at the right time for America. And then you had *The Investigation* and that also had a good reception. Then I think we didn't hear very much what was going on over there except that politically he was being put in a corner, as a communist. And so the other plays weren't very successful there, that was his opinion.

RE: Were there any American playwrights or theater groups whom Peter admired?

GP: Yes, there were, a long time ago. There were the Becks and their group, The Living Theatre. Then there was also your Bread and Puppet Theatre. These groups performed over here and Peter liked their work.

RE: Gunilla, I'd like to ask you about Peter's travels, his contact with other cultures and political systems. Did he travel a good deal?

GP: No, he hardly ever travelled. He didn't like it.

RE: But to the openings of his plays in Germany? And he did travel once to Asia?

GP: Yes, we did travel together to the openings of the plays that we had worked on together, and that was for all his plays except the *New Trial* by Kafka. But the only openings of his plays that he attended very much were the different productions of *Hölderlin* in Germany. And there of course he was very disappointed. In Berlin he said, "They made a damned opera out of it. Four hours of singing and you couldn't understand anything." In Stuttgart he said, "Well, it was very decent but. . . ." And so he concluded, "In a way it's better that I don't see what is done and it's better that I no longer sit near the director because it kills me. Because the director has an idea of what he or she wants and I can't get through what I want."

RE: You and Peter worked with Hans Perten at the Volkstheater of Rostock, which produced many of his plays?

GP: Yes, they did all Peter's plays, except the *Trotsky*.

RE: How did Peter feel about their work?

GP: He was ambivalent. In a way it was very good because here was a director who said, "You are our house writer" [resident playwright]. And that doesn't happen very often, you know. But at the same time Peter could see this theater's limitations. It was a marvelous group of actors, assembled by Hans Perten, but none of them were very outstanding. They were good as a group, an ensemble. But here in Stockholm, you know, you can see excellent productions, with top actors. In Rostock you have a theater with actors who are not really the best, but the group works very well together and you could sometimes get beautiful productions out of this. And also they are a very devoted group, towards Peter. For all his plays they always wanted Peter to come, and they made great preparations for this, and of course Peter loved all of this.

RE: Did Peter actually write a new ending for *Marat/Sade* for this group?

GP: Yes he did. Of course we are very close friends with them. He wrote the new ending for Rostock but then he later changed it because he saw that it did not work, theatrically and also politically.

RE: Gunilla, a number of critics have mentioned Peter's comment at the time that in the Rostock production, where Marat was shown to be the "winner" in the debate, that Peter said this was the most correct interpretation of his play. Could you explain Peter's comment a little more?

GP: Well, you know, one has to see it from another point of view. Peter lived a very long life without any success, and then there came this man in Rostock who was producing all of his plays and Peter was very enthusiastic when his shows were well done. And, yes, he did say in a speech in Rostock, "This is the best production I have seen." I will say that Peter also said that in other places. But you see in Rostock they used Peter's statement in a political way, and because they were friends, because they were producing all of his plays, Peter just let them go on saying that. Later he told me, "I could care less if people are using my words that way, but for new productions I want to rewrite the ending." And he did, *Marat* has been rewritten seven times, especially the ending. Small things, but important. I have so many of Peter's notes here which we wrote down together and one day I plan to write all about it. But I've been working so much these days, there just hasn't been time.

RE: Gunilla, I know Peter travelled to Asia for research on Vietnam, and he spoke frequently of the underdeveloped nations. Did he travel very much to Third World nations?

GP: Well we took a long trip together to Cambodia and North Vietnam. And there are many Vietnamese living here in Stockholm who were and who are still close friends. Not just politically, you see, but also friendship. And so Peter did have much contact with things in Vietnam during those years. Then we went to Cuba together and Peter was very interested in Latin America. He stayed for a long time in Cuba, but he really couldn't stand to travel too much to those parts of the world because of his health. We were invited to Latin America and to Chile, but he always said it was impossible to work and to travel. You lose so much time.

RE: Did Peter contemplate writing more plays on the Third World nations, like the *Vietnam Discourse* or *Lusitanian Bogeyman?*

GP: Well in *Hölderlin,* the character of Empedocles was built upon the historical figure of Che Guevara. But Peter did not want to write more about these countries because after 1968 he was really finished with those kinds of plays, that kind of writing. You must remember that after *Hölderlin,* the novel took nine years of his life. He wanted it to be only three years, but it took much longer.

RE: Did Peter ever express much disappointment that the plays on Angola and Vietnam were not commercially as successful as his play on Marat or even as *The Investigation* was?

GP: Commercially he couldn't care less. He always said, "Money doesn't make anyone happy, it only makes life a little more convenient!" He lived very simply of course, so if he had enough money that he could continue writing, then it was all right. But of course he was very disappointed that critics didn't like the plays. And like any writer, he never remembered the good things that were said, he only remembered the bad critics. But you know, with *Vietnam Discourse* he had another *kind* of success because at the time there was the youth movement here in Europe. Peter had a marvelous time working with all the young people on that play, mostly in Germany. We went to many demonstrations there and he gave many speeches. So for him it was an introduction into the world of young people. Other than that, he was very disappointed. But you should keep in mind that political life in Germany is much harder than it is here. It's more controversial, more violent, tougher. If you stuck your neck out and screamed about Vietnam they branded you a communist and revolutionary. The headlines would kill you. And Peter encountered much of this in the German press, and I'd say the press has been very unfair to him because they have always been looking for something political.

RE: One doesn't always receive that impression from reading the reviews of his plays in the German press.

GP: Yes, but it was *his* impression. And he was also disappointed that *Vietnam Discourse* was not produced in more theaters. Of course, from a theatrical standpoint it is a difficult play to produce. It was done at the Berliner Ensemble, for instance, and Peter was very disappointed because they just took a part of it, made it like a Brechtian synopsis and changed it. So it was really not his play. But of course he never criticized the Berliner Ensemble—or any group in East Germany—because he knew that in the West it would be used by the conservatives. So in a way Peter's situation was very difficult, but in another way, of course, he could always return to neutral Sweden.

RE: While we're mentioning the Berliner Ensemble, can you speak a little bit about Brecht? What did Peter admire about Brecht?

GP: Oh, there were so many things . . . but I think mostly the language. Brecht's language was short, precise, and Peter liked this very much. Together with Brecht's music, of course. Peter had an enormous feel for music and for the sounds of words. He liked Brecht's frankness, his way of going straight to the political problem. And he liked Brecht's way of working with *Verfremdung,* that the actors didn't try to identify with their characters. Here in the West, actors identify absolutely with the character they are playing. And Brecht's way of working was very different.

RE: Did Peter feel that his own plays suffered from that kind of problem with the actors?

GP: Oh yes. I think that during his entire career we only had Konrad Swinarski, and he knew Brecht's way of working. It was marvelous for Peter then. Swinarski also had a good sense of feelings, of emotions, just as Brecht did. Peter knew all of Brecht's work—also Brecht's political writings, his poems, and of course his songs. Peter loved Brecht's songs.

RE: Of course, Brecht had his own theater group and he could experiment with his plays for many months as he wrote them.

GP: Yes, and this is what Peter wanted to do more and more, to direct his plays. *Trotsky* is a good example. He always wanted to direct it differently. Here in Stockholm we had a very weak director and it was really Peter and I who did this production, as everyone here knows. Peter had the chance then to experiment with the play, and with his other plays he never had this opportunity. When we directed *The New*

Trial here in Stockholm [1982] he would say to me, "Now a new stage is beginning for us, to direct and experiment with our plays." You see, he knew from the beginning that *Trotsky* was not finished, and if he had had a theater to try it out, that is what he would have done.

RE: What sort of "trying out" do you mean?

GP: Well, you write for a certain theater, for certain actors that you know. So you can create lots of experiments with it before you start the real rehearsals. That's what Brecht did, and that's what Peter wanted. That he missed enormously.

RE: Gunilla, you collaborated with Peter on all his plays, didn't you?

GP: Yes, I designed them all except for *Night with Guests,* and the Kafka play which we directed together.

RE: Did you help him with more than just the designs?

GP: Oh yes, I did. For instance, all of the stage directions in the plays, these are my contribution. Also Peter and I would discuss each and every line in his plays, from the very beginning. And he, of course, was always commenting on my design, my pictures. We were always very involved together in this.

RE: This is something that no critics have ever mentioned in their discussions of Peter's work.

GP: Yes, and it's a terrible discouraging thing for me that I am not being credited with this. Peter spoke of it to everyone, you see. On every photograph he put me in as the designer, but the publisher removed it and said, "You are his wife, and as his wife you're mentioned too often!" I could bring a lawsuit, but one just doesn't do that sort of thing. Anyway it has been very insulting to me, and I haven't had the time to write about this, to do anything about it. Because when I haven't been working with Peter, I was working a lot with Ingmar [Bergman], for twenty years. That took much time too. So it has all been very insulting.

RE: Gunilla, was there something about the way Peter wrote plays that you found exciting or challenging as a designer?

GP: Well, I would say the way that he documented them, his sources. Even *Marat* was full of documents, and that was very good for both of us. I spent about two months in the Bibliotheque Nationale finding not only pictures but also things about Marat. And then he'd use this material as he worked. More and more now you find playwrights doing this, but it was new at the time, the documents. And you know,

I also like the way Peter's plays analyze what their characters are doing, they force people to think.

RE: You mean the audiences?

GP: No, the designers, directors, actors. I have had to analyze his plays very carefully. Every color, for example, you have to know what a color means to people in a certain society, in every country. You must discover details about social classes. I like this kind of investigation of a play.

RE: How did Peter feel about your work?

GP: Well of course, he liked what I did. And you know, we could never have worked together the way we did without backgrounds that were so much alike. And our social, our political and artistic views were alike too.

RE: Did he criticize your work as much as you criticized his?

GP: Oh yes. And that is what I miss enormously now. Even when I was working for other directors we always discussed my work. Our ateliers were next to each other, he'd come into mine or I'd go into his. We'd always drink coffee together and he'd read over some lines to me. Or he'd come into my atelier and look at what I was doing, and he'd say, "I like that," or "This is garbage!" He wasn't always nice! But it was always, always very good.

RE: Gunilla, in your acceptance speech for the Büchner Prize awarded to Peter, you spoke of a "new phase" in his work which was just beginning at the time of his death. Can you mention some of Peter's plans for the future at that time?

GP: Yes, well, *Trotsky* was one thing he wanted to do. He wanted to rewrite *Trotsky*.

RE: Did he want to shorten it?

GP: No, no, not to shorten it. He wanted—and I think he was absolutely right—to put more of the dadaists into it. You know, the dadaists started a similar movement on Lenin's same street in Zurich. And Peter wanted to make a better balance between them, to show a revolution in art following upon a revolution in society.

RE: Did he really feel that Trotsky was tolerant of artists?

GP: Yes, he did. And most critics think that Peter himself was a Trotskyite, but you could never put Peter into any corner because he was unfaithful—in the right way—to everybody and every movement.

RE: Was Peter planning any new plays, perhaps with other strong central heroes like the plays on Trotsky or Hölderlin?

GP: Well, the central character for Peter, for all his life, was always Dante. I would say that Dante remained a hero for him until the bitter end. When he came back from Berlin just a few days before his death, he was starting to write again about Dante. He wanted to find a new way to write about the *Purgatorio*. If one looks back, after *Marat/Sade,* he did want to write a great play about Dante. And he did, he wrote a prose-poem that started with Dante, and then Peter began to write about the *Inferno*. Out of this came *The Investigation*. Next he tried to write about hell again, and that became the Angolan play, the *Bogeyman*. So you can say that Dante was a model for Peter, like a carrot held before the horse.

RE: So you feel he actually might have written a play on Dante had he lived?

GP: Well, he had an idea for a play and I don't know if he was only joking, but we discussed it a great deal. This was just two days before he died, I said to him, "If you look at your plays, they are all men's plays. All your heroes are men. And this is understandable, that you can identify with them because they are men. But for heaven's sake, write a play with women. For many reasons. There are not many writers who have done that. Secondly, in the big theaters, women are going without roles." And so he thought of Dante and he said, "OK! I'll write the *Purgatorio* and sitting in there will be many well-known men—Brecht, Beckett, and many others." And I said, "Why no women?" And he said, "I've learned after thirty years with you that women have already gone through their purgatory and therefore we men have to sit there and think over what's going on. Then in heaven and hell I'll have the women on both sides." I don't know if Peter would ever have finished it, but he was talking of it.

RE: Is there anything else you could mention about his plans?

GP: Well, if you have read his early work, before he was accepted as a playwright, you will see that it was heavily influenced by surrealism, and also by psychoanalysis. Peter wanted to make a combination of this psychological with the political way of looking at society. You know, Peter did not have very much success as a painter when he was beginning. He tried to learn to write in Swedish but after two books he was not accepted. And so he said, "Well, I must do something." He thought that he was defeated and during that time he made some experimental films. We did those together, but the critics didn't say very good things. In my opinion, if Peter had had more success with his films during this in-between period he would have been a filmmaker. He could do the writing, the music, the pictures—he could put it all together, and I think he would have been very happy. Anyway that's my theory. Later in 1982 after he came back from Berlin he said, "Now I'm ready to make film again!" So he had lots of plans.

RE: Gunilla, is there anything we have not spoken about here that you would like to bring out about Peter's work?

GP: Well, I have read in so many newspapers that Peter came back from Berlin and he was depressed, that he had made his great novel [*The Aesthetics of Resistance*] and then he died. He was finished. But this is not true. He was tired, yes, he had a very turbulent time in Berlin, but he was not depressed. I think sometimes people die "too early" and then critics invent theories out of that—that it was suicide, or that he was going to move from Stockholm to Berlin. But this is all nonsense. And also you know many critics write only about the serious things in Peter's work. They think he never had another side. You should mention Peter's views on democracy and political matters. He couldn't have learned these things if he hadn't lived in Sweden. Also his views on women's emancipation. The figures in his last book, the women, they couldn't have been written without this influence from the Scandinavian countries. I think this is very important because one forgets about Sweden, one thinks of Peter as a German writer because he wrote in German. But Peter only used language as a tool. And of course, after 38 years Peter had assimilated much from Scandinavia which influenced the way he wrote, and especially about democracy. I think Germany had very little influence on that. In his last book Peter put in many ideas from discussions we had among our small group of friends here in Sweden—artists, writers, and others, very hard-working artists. This last book is in a way a synthesis of all those conversations which this little group has had over the last thirty years. Without this group, this influence, Peter would never have written the way he did, had he lived in Germany.

RE: Gunilla, is there one piece of advice, perhaps, that you would like to give to theater people who read Peter's plays? Something to help them understand better Peter's work?

GP: Yes. The music. If you read Peter, read him aloud. This is very important for directors that they hear his plays like music, like a musical composition. The sound of Peter's words.

Notes

Chapter 1

1. *Leavetaking and Vanishing-Point,* tr. Christopher Levenson (London: Calder and Boyars, 1966), pp. 108–14.

2. Ibid., p. 153.

3. Ibid., p. 275.

4. Ibid., p. 127.

5. This appraisal of Weiss's early paintings is partially substantiated by Peter Suhrkamp, Weiss's publisher, who first met the author in 1947 when he was asked to read some of Weiss's short stories. Suhrkamp recalls commenting to Weiss that "the images in this remain visions of an inner world, whose reality is not shared by others." *Theater heute,* special issue, December 1972, p. 82.

6. Peter Weiss, "Avantgarde Film," *Akzente* 10 (April 1955), pp. 316–17.

7. *The Shadow of the Coachman's Body,* tr. E. B. Garside and Rosemarie Waldrop (New York: Delacorte, 1970), p. 27. Cf. also Jean Genet: "This journal is not merely a literary diversion. The further I progress, reducing to order, what my past life suggests, and the more I persist in the rigor of composition—the chapters, the sentences, the book itself—the more do I feel myself hardening in my will to utilize, for various ends, my former hardships. I feel their power." *The Thief's Journal,* tr. Bernard Frechtman (Evanston, Ill.: Greenleaf, 1965), p. 66. Weiss's initial attempt "to make seeing into an occupation" occurred five years earlier with the reportage published in Swedish as *De Besegrade* (translated in German in 1965 as *Die Besiegten*).

8. *Coachman's Body,* pp. 6–12.

9. Quoted in Ian Hilton, *Peter Weiss: A Search for Affinities* (London: Wolff, 1970), p. 16.

10. *Coachman's Body,* pp. 6–25.

11. Ibid., pp. 42–43. In a most revealing comment to an interviewer in 1979, Weiss pointed out that *Coachman's Body* dates from a period in his life during which he was "re-discovering" the German language after having lived in Sweden for so long. His difficulty with writing in German thus became an artistic means of representing the opacity of human experience in the novel.

12. Ibid., pp. 56–57.

13. *Conversation of the Three Wayfarers,* tr. E. B. Garside and Rosemarie Waldrop (New York: Delacorte, 1970), p. 61.

14. "Surreales und doch nicht unwirkliches Panoptikum." Quoted in the first edition of *Das Gespräch der drei Gehenden* (Frankfurt a.M.: Suhrkamp, 1963), p. 2.

15. John Milfull, "From Kafka to Brecht: Peter Weiss's Development towards Marxism," *German Life and Letters* 20, no. 1 (1966), p. 64.

16. Quoted in Martin Esslin, *The Theatre of the Absurd* (New York: Doubleday, 1961), p. 61.

17. A valuable discussion of the existential condition represented in these early prose works, especially with regard to Weiss's sense of being an exile, can be found in Kathleen A. Vance, *The Theme of Alienation in the Prose of Peter Weiss* (Las Vegas: Peter Lang, 1981), pp. 16–20.

18. "Avantgarde Film," pp. 307–8, emphasis mine.

19. Weiss referred to this function of writing in a 1965 interview with A. Alvarez: "I myself wanted to write in order to clear out for myself possibilities of how one could live, how one could find a way of life which makes it possible to go on in a more positive way." "The Truths That Are Uttered in a Madhouse," *New York Times Magazine,* 26 December 1965, p. 3. In an interview with Burkhardt Lindner less than a year before his death, Weiss restated this same point.

20. *Three Wayfarers,* p. 120. Weiss's conclusion is almost a direct translation of a passage written by Henry Miller in his 1939 essay "The Tailor Shop." The sameness of situation, wording, and bridge metaphors in the two selections suggests the extent of Miller's influence on Weiss, a point which will be explored in the following chapter. Cf. Henry Miller's *Black Spring* (New York: Grove, 1963), p. 110.

21. Peter Demetz, *Postwar German Literature* (New York: Schocken, 1970), p. 50.

22. All quotations from the play are taken from the translation by Michael Benedikt and Michel Heine in *Postwar German Theatre,* eds. Benedikt and Wellwarth (New York: Dutton, 1967).

23. This prologue is found in the collected edition of Weiss's plays, *Dramen I* (Frankfurt a.M.: Suhrkamp, 1968), p. 259.

24. *Leavetaking and Vanishing-Point,* p. 101.

25. Ibid., p. 22.

26. Ibid., p. 75.

27. The image of the artist as acrobat was certainly not Weiss's invention; the idea was used frequently by Thomas Mann and, notably, Andreyev who "made it into the type of the artist–actor or buffoon, 'he who gets slapped.'" The sense of alienation which permeates Weiss's play is simplified by this image on account of its dehumanizing connotations: the artist as clown, as puppet, as object or thing. "The allegory of the artist–acrobat suggests the tendency to dehumanize the human and to mechanize the vital." Quoted in Renato Poggioli, *The Theory of the Avant-Garde,* tr. Gerald Fitzgerald (New York: Harper and Row, 1968), p. 143. It is a motif which recurs throughout all Weiss's work, especially in *Marat/Sade* and *Mockinpott* where the puppetization of characters suggests problems of a political-historical nature.

28. Peter Demetz, for example, in *Postwar German Literature,* p. 133.

29. "Notes on *The Insurance,*" *Dramen I,* p. 260.

30. "In our age, shadowed by mushroom clouds and moon rockets, the technocratic nightmares of the Expressionists appear astonishingly prophetic, and much more realistic than at the time they were conceived. Distortion served the Expressionists as an x-ray eye for detecting . . . the direction in which history was moving." Walter Sokel, *An Anthology of German Expressionist Drama* (Stanford, Calif.: Stanford University Press, 1959), p. xxiii.

31. *Leavetaking and Vanishing-Point*, p. 162. Weiss's fascination with this period would be reflected in his portrayal of these same artists (always in terms of their political commitment) in the later play on Leon Trotsky and in his major novel, *Ästhetik des Widerstands*.

32. In conversation with Walter Wager, ed. and trans., *The Playwrights Speak* (New York: Delacorte, 1967), p. 192.

33. All quotations from the play are taken from *Dramen I*.

34. *Leavetaking and Vanishing-Point*, p. 162.

35. "Avantgarde Film," p. 305.

36. Paul Gray, "A Living World," *Tulane Drama Review* 11, no. 1 (T-33) (Fall 1966), p. 108.

37. Quoted in Hilton, *A Search for Affinities*, p. 193. Weiss produced five films during this period, some of them shorts such as *Hallucinations* (1953) and *Faces in Shadow* (1956), but also one full-length feature, *The Mirage* (1958), which dealt with a day spent in exploring the everyday activities of a large metropolitan city. When a series of his films were screened in New York in 1966, Bosley Crowther described them as displaying "a pervasive predilection for solemn and tormenting themes of personal alienation, hallucinations, sensory shifts and erotic agitation within abstract emotional voids." *New York Times*, 29 January 1966, p. 13.

38. "Avantgarde Film," pp. 298–99.

39. Brecht's influence on Weiss is a complex subject which deserves a much more extensive treatment than is possible here. While pointing out the major points of contact between the two writers, I do not attempt any systematic analysis of their methods or theories. A consideration of their different approaches to social change is included at the end of chapter 5.

40. "Avantgarde Film," p. 306.

41. Weiss, "Against the Laws of Normality," *Akzente*, 4 August 1962, p. 323.

42. Ibid., p. 327.

43. Ibid., p. 329.

44. Program note to the original production, published in *Dramen I*, pp. 261–62. The search for new and more vital performance environments has been a significant area of experimentation by theater artists of the 1960s. Weiss was one of the first to embark on this course in *Night with Guests* in 1963, and his interest in carnival Punch and Judy still holds many unexplored possibilities. Compare in this respect Brooks McNamara's article on "The Scenography of Popular Entertainment" where he singles out the amusement park as a unique performance space offering "a chaotic, jarring, and somewhat sinister environment, created with unrestrained fantasy architecture and 'flash.'" Variety, energy, mystery, and a high degree of audience involvement are principal features of the fairway which Weiss wanted for his play. *The Drama Review* 18 (T-61) (March 1974), p. 24.

45. "On Directing Night with Guests," *Dramen I*, p. 262. Weiss's contact with Asiatic performance styles probably dates from the late 1940s, although he certainly would have discovered references to Asiatic theater companies in his studies of the post-World War I European avant-garde. We do know, however, that as early as 1949 in Stockholm Weiss attended a performance of the Ram Gopal Indian dancers. It was at that event that he first met Gunilla Palmstierna, later to become his wife and lifelong scenic designer/collaborator.

46. The play is consistent, however, with many themes from Weiss's childhood. In *Leavetaking* (pp. 46–48) Weiss points out, "I learned that beneath logic there was another form of con-

sistency, the consistency of inexplicable impulses . . . I belonged to a community of the bewitched for whom everything was strange and phantom-like. I belonged to a group of wanderers who had gone into the land of horror. The gruesome was my special province."

47. Ian Hilton also makes this observation about the artistic polish of *Night with Guests*. The year 1963 marked an important turning point in Weiss's career because he was no longer abandoning half-completed works as he had done previously. The *Report on Institutions and Customs of the Grisons* was one such project, begun in 1953 and subsequently set aside, and the fragment of *Three Wayfarers* remained unfinished although it had originally been intended to form part of a longer novel. Hilton points out in this respect that "Weiss is planning with more confidence and on a grander scale, as he himself believes in his potential as an artist. The standpoint of doubtfulness may still be present at least in part, but artistically he is getting a clearer idea of what he himself can and wants to achieve." *A Search for Affinities,* pp. 44–45.

Chapter 2

1. "Author's Note On the Historical Background to the Play," *The Persecution and Assassination of Jean-Paul Marat as Performed by the Inmates of Charenton under the Direction of the Marquis de Sade,* trans. Geoffrey Skelton (New York: Atheneum, 1965), p. 106.

2. Alvarez interview, p. 14.

3. *Vanishing-Point,* pp. 110–13, emphasis mine.

4. Ibid., pp. 132–33.

5. Ibid., p. 172. Weiss's fascination with the "proletarian class" stemmed from his boyhood when he had been impressed by the Bolshevik revolution and by films like *Potemkin*. It was a fascination he would retain until the end of his career, and which would eventually receive full expression in his three-part novel, *Ästhetik des Widerstands*. Weiss called this book "a wishful biography" in which he speculated about how his values and outlook would have been very different if he had been born into the lower classes.

6. Ibid., pp. 184–86.

7. Ibid., p. 150. Weiss would return to Kafka's novel nearly 15 years later and write a dramatic adaptation entitled *Der Prozess* in 1975. It was later revised and restaged by Weiss and Gunilla Palmstierna in Stockholm in 1982, shortly before his death.

8. Ibid., p. 108, emphasis mine.

9. Ibid., p. 245–47.

10. Quoted in Karlheinz Braun, ed., *Materialien zu Peter Weiss' "Marat/Sade"* (Frankfurt a.M.: Suhrkamp, 1967), p. 92.

11. In addition to these plays which are familiar to Western audiences, there were a number of dramas which received local attention in Germany: Wolfgang Graetz, *Verschwörer* (1965); Hans Helmut Kirst, *Aufstand der Offiziere* (1966); Felix Lützkendorf, *Dallas: 22 November* (1965). There were also a large number of German dramas produced prior to 1966 which treated political themes but without the use of historical figures: Max Frisch, *Andorra* (1962); Martin Walser, *Eiche und Angora* (1962) and *Der schwarze Schwan* (1964); Carl Zuckmayer, *Die Uhr schlägt eins* (1961); and Reinhard Raffalt, *Der Nachfolger* (1962).

12. *Materialien zu "Marat/Sade,"* p. 103.

13. This epilogue was part of the original production, and was omitted in the published English translation.

14. These sections of the epilogue are found only in the original Berlin production and the acting version used by the Royal Shakespeare Company production, "version E" as described in the *Materialien zu "Marat/Sade,"* pp. 56–57. All other quotations from the play are taken from the translation by Geoffrey Skelton.

15. Otto Best, *Peter Weiss: Vom existenzialistischen Drama zum marxistischen Welttheater* (Bern: Francke, 1971), pp. 101–2.

16. Numerous critics have mentioned this feature of Weiss's work, finding the problems of modern political writers stated not only in *Marat/Sade* but in the other plays as well. Volker Canaris expressed this idea most succinctly in his introduction to the Suhrkamp anthology of criticism on Weiss, where he noted the tremendous controversy which Weiss's plays have provoked among European critics. Canaris stresses that this controversy "clearly indicates that Weiss has brought directly upon the stage the socio-political contradictions of our world." In *Über Peter Weiss,* ed. Volker Canaris (Frankfurt a.M.: Suhrkamp, 1970), p. 8.

17. Hans Mayer, "Peter Weiss und die zweifache Praxis der Veränderung," *Theater heute* 13, no. 5 (May 1972), p. 19.

18. In conversation with Volker Canaris, in *Der andere Hölderlin: Materialien zum Hölderlin-Stück von Peter Weiss,* eds. Volker Canaris and Thomas Beckermann (Frankfurt a.M.: Suhrkamp, 1972), p. 150.

19. "Author's Note On the Historical Background of the Play," p. 108.

20. *Materialien zu "Marat/Sade,"* p. 116. Consider also Weiss's 1965 description of Beckett: "He lives in a kind of embryo in a world that is too big and cruel for him. . . . I'm of the opinion that art must have the power to change society, or it will fail in its purpose," ibid., p. 198.

21. Alvarez interview, p. 3.

22. Milfull, p. 67.

23. *Materialien zu "Marat/Sade,"* pp. 112–14.

24. Ernst Wendt, "Peter Weiss zwischen den Ideologien," *Akzente* 12 (1965), p. 421.

25. There is a certain amount of truth in Weiss's criticism of Peter Brook. The impression evoked in Brook's audiences, as reported by reviewers in such magazines as *Commonweal, Nation, New Republic,* and *Saturday Review,* was one of grotesque insanity and absurdity, a spectacle of chaos. Wilfrid Sheen, "Bathtub Nights," *Commonweal,* 21 January 1966, pp. 476–77; Howard Clurman, "Marat/Sade," *Nation,* 17 January 1966, pp. 82–84; Robert Brustein, "Embarrassment of Riches," *New Republic,* 22 January 1966, pp. 23–28; Henry Hewes, "The Weiss/Brook," *Saturday Review,* 15 January 1966, p. 45.

26. Cf. a 1966 interview with Brook regarding his staging of Weiss's play: "I think that what we do on the stage, for better or worse, is exactly what the author himself was setting on the stage of his mind, seeing in his vision. This is why I am very jealous of any attempt to divide his work from mine. I feel that any criticism of his play and that any praise of the production is a praise of his vision." In conversation with Joseph Roddy, "Marat/Sade Stuns Broadway Playgoers with Sanity from the Asylum," *Look,* 22 February 1966, p. 110.

27. Peter Brook, *The Empty Space* (New York: Atheneum, 1968), p. 45.

28. Interview with Michael Gibson in *Tulane Drama Review* 17, no. 3 (T-59) (September 1973), p. 49. Brook's assessment of his *Marat/Sade* production received strong support from several of the most important theater critics. Margaret Croyden's comments upon his work are

perhaps the most insightful: "The real issue is not whether Brook uses Brechtian or Artaudian techniques, or whether he overstepped his role as director (as if this could be measured), but that Brook added his own aesthetic techniques *in visual, concrete metaphors,* and that these metaphors grew not only out of Artaudian theory, but out of the Weiss text. In the end this is what is creative and daring about Brook's work. He refuses merely to illustrate or stage the text; he evokes what is beyond the text." *Lunatics, Lovers and Poets: The Contemporary Experimental Theatre* (New York: McGraw-Hill, 1974), pp. 237–38. Brook's production won a Tony award in 1966 as the best play of the New York season.

29.   Interview with Paul Gray, "A Living World," p. 111. Cf. Also Peter Brook and Ronald Bryden's comments upon the use of Artaud in the drama: *Peter Brook's Production of William Shakespeare's "A Midsummer Night's Dream,"* ed. Glenn Loney, authorized acting version (Chicago: The Dramatic Publishing Co., 1974), pp. 12–19.

30.   *Materialien zu "Marat/Sade,"* p. 101.

31.   There is also a fourth historical perspective which bears upon the dramatic action at various times: the actual statements of the eighteenth-century characters themselves (Voltaire, Lavoisier, etc.) which are deftly intermingled with the madhouse dialogue.

32.   William Oliver, "*Marat/Sade* in Santiago," *Educational Theatre Journal* 19, no. 4 (December 1967), p. 488.

33.   Max Spalter, "Five Examples of How to Write a Brechtian Play That Is Not Really Brechtian," *Educational Theatre Journal* 27, no. 2 (May 1975), p. 230.

34.   Interview with Oliver Clausen, "Weiss/Propagandist and Weiss/Playwright," *New York Times Magazine,* 20 October 1966, pp. 130–31.

35.   Pablo Neruda, *Memoirs,* tr. Hardie St. Martin (New York: Farrar, Strauss, and Giroux, 1977), pp. 262–63.

36.   *Materialien zu "Marat/Sade,"* p. 112.

37.   Ibid., p. 109.

Chapter 3

1.   Alvarez interview, p. 3.

2.   Walter Wager, *The Playwrights Speak,* p. 190.

3.   Alvarez interview, p. 14.

4.   Paul Gray interview, p. 114.

5.   *Materialien zu "Marat/Sade,"* p. 108.

6.   Wager, *The Playwrights Speak,* p. 200.

7.   *Materialien zu "Marat/Sade,"* p. 110.

8.   Wager, *The Playwrights Speak,* p. 202. Although Weiss never referred to the madhouse situation in the Charenton play as an unsatisfactory approach to political issues, it is certainly possible that he was beginning to feel this way, particularly after the controversy over Peter Brook's production. As the critic Carl Rosen pointed out about *Marat/Sade,* 19 years after its premiere, "The confrontation between the playwright, Sade, and his dramatic persona, Marat, is ironically overshadowed by the madhouse which encloses and inevitably negates them both." *Plays of Impasse: Contemporary Drama Set in Confining Situations* (Princeton University Press, 1983), p. 99.

9. Weiss's postscript to the Alvarez interview, *New York Times Magazine*, 26 December 1965, p. 14.

10. *Materialien zu "Marat/Sade,"* p. 103.

11. Paul Gray interview, pp. 110–11.

12. Quoted in Wager, *The Playwrights Speak,* p. 194.

13. "My Place," ed. and trans. Christopher Middleton, *German Writing Today* (New York: Penguin, 1967), p. 28.

14. Ibid., pp. 20–22.

15. Paul Gray interview, p. 110.

16. Wager, *The Playwrights Speak,* p. 201.

17. All quotations from the play are taken from the translation by Jon Swan and Ulu Grosbard (New York: Atheneum, 1968).

18. Author's note on *The Investigation,* unnumbered page in the translated edition.

19. "Die Ermittlung in Westberlin," in Canaris, *Über Peter Weiss,* p. 93.

20. Demetz, *Postwar German Literature,* p. 132.

21. Ernst Wendt, "Was wird ermittelt?" *Theater heute* 6, no. 12 (December 1965), p. 14.

22. Joel Carmichael, "German Reactions to a New Play About Auschwitz," *American-German Review,* No. 3 (1966), pp. 30–32. It is interesting to note that Weiss's experimental dramaturgy aroused such a storm of bad press on account of his manipulation of the historical records. Christopher Innes, writing of the avant-garde 16 years after *The Investigation,* praised Weiss's approach to history despite the play's historical inaccuracy. Cf. Innes, *Holy Theatre: Ritual and the Avant-Garde,* pp. 222–24, where Innes discusses how the drama's real meaning comes from the mythical connotations in the play's *patterning,* not from historical analysis or the conventional elements of dialogue or dramatic situation.

23. "The Meaning of Silence," in *The Storm over "The Deputy,"* ed. Eric Bentley (New York: Grove, 1968), p. 28. The same might also be said of the internationally broadcast TV miniseries (liberally interspersed with commercials) during the late 1970s.

24. Demetz, *Postwar German Literature,* p. 132.

25. Theodore Adorno, "On Commitment," tr. Francis McDonagh, *Performing Arts Journal* 3, no. 3 (Winter 1979), pp. 60–61. Weiss's theatrically exciting manner of presenting atrocities in his plays was a subject of heated controversy among German theater critics during the 1960s.

26. Wager, *The Playwrights Speak,* p. 205.

27. In *Tip-Magazin* (West Berlin), No. 7 (1980). Cf. Siegfried Zielinski, "The New Weiss *Investigation,*" *Theater* 12 (Fall/Winter 1980).

28. It is unclear just when Weiss became convinced that neither the USSR nor the eastern European Soviet bloc nations were incapable of offering any significant contributions to the cause of human rights and political freedom in the Third World. What we do know is that by the end of the sixties this opinion was fixed in Weiss's mind. In a 1979 interview Weiss spoke of his boyhood fascination with Soviet Russia and his eventual disillusionment with Stalinist policies at the time of the Moscow trials in the mid-1930s. Weiss was certainly aware of the dismal conditions of artistic and political censorship imposed by Russia and the satellite na-

tions between 1950 and 1980, and in his drama on Trotsky in 1969 he levelled strong criticism against what he felt to be the betrayal of socialist ideals on the part of the Soviets. Following the success of *Marat/Sade,* a number of his plays had been produced in East Germany and he continued to develop a "working relationship" with artists in the GDR, particularly with Hager and Abusch, the dramaturgs at the East Berlin Deutsches Theater. But he resisted writing for these theaters or collaborating with them when offered the chance. Late in 1971, for example, he turned down an offer by Hager and Abusch to collaborate on a revised version of *Hölderlin.* He felt that the socialist nations had truly condemned his independent stance as an author, that he had been "unable to form any productive relationships" within the GDR; he called the GDR a repressive system "which to me seemed only to lead into a political vacuum." And as late as 1980 Weiss joined with other European intellectuals in condemning the Soviet invasion of Afghanistan. Cf. Weiss's *Notizbücher 1971–1980* (Frankfurt a.M.: Suhrkamp, 1981), pp. 24–25. Weiss's reception by and his feelings towards the Eastern bloc nations during the sixties and seventies is a subject requiring more detailed study than we can provide here.

29. "10 Arbeitspunkte eines Autors in der geteilten Welt," *Materialien zu "Marat/Sade,"* p. 118.

30. Tr. Heinz Bernard, *Theatre Quarterly* 1, no. 1 (January–March 1971), pp. 41–43.

31. This idea represented only a temporary resting place for Weiss at mid-decade. By the end of the 1960s Weiss would again return to absurdity and present such heroes as Trotsky and Hölderlin swallowed up in the abyss as they tried to influence the course of history. One is reminded here of Herbert Blau's comment that "the voice of the Absurd . . . and its demonic presence never really disappears—no more than empathy—from the drama of Brecht. The truth may be concrete, but it is also elusive; and the chaos is never used up." *The Impossible Theatre* (New York: Macmillan, 1964), p. 102.

32. Cf. Piscator's comment on documentary realism made in 1966 shortly before his death: "We had been degraded to war materiel; what wonder that we became materialists! Determined to alter the world by revealing it in exact descriptions!" March 1966, postscript to a reprint of *Das politische Theater* (1929; reprinted, Berlin: Rodewald, 1968), unnumbered page.

33. All quotations from the play are taken from the translation by Lee Baxendall (New York: Atheneum, 1970).

34. Quoted in Richard C. Webb, "Ritual, Theatre, and Jean Genet's *The Blacks,*" *Theatre Journal* 31, no. 4 (December 1979), p. 457.

35. Ibid., p. 459, emphasis mine.

36. All quotations from the play are taken from the translation by Geoffrey Skelton (New York: Atheneum, 1970).

37. "*Vietnam-Diskurs* in Rostock," in Canaris *Über Peter Weiss,* p. 110.

38. "Kritik am *Vietnam-Diskurs,*" in Canaris *Über Peter Weiss,* p. 116.

39. For this suggestion I am indebted to a discussion with Weiss by Henning Rischbieter in *Theater heute* 8, no. 3 (March 1967), pp. 6–7. Weiss's plays on Angola and Vietnam are the best examples of his inability during the mid-sixties to distinguish between the importance of individuals and the importance of social classes in bringing about historical change. As a dramatist he was probably inclined to weight his arguments in favor of the individual as the prime mover of revolution—a very un-Marxian approach. Weiss's lack of success with mass heroes in these plays was one factor which possibly encouraged him to return to a central dramatic figure in the plays which followed.

40. Peter Demetz's phrase in *Postwar German Literature*, p. 132. Weiss's views of the original Stockholm production as well as of later extravagant productions in East and West Germany reflect the same confusion in the playwright's goals. Reviews of these shows can be found in *Theater heute* 8, no. 11 (November 1967), pp. 12, 13, and in the special issue of December 1968, pp. 40–41. It is curious to note that as early as 1965 Weiss had been aware of this difficulty in presenting certain political subjects in his plays. In an interview with Michael Roloff following the Berlin production of *Marat/Sade* he remarked: "I am at odds with my own estheticism, you see; one is easily tempted to put too much effort and time into fiddling with form." "Interview with Peter Weiss," *Partisan Review* 32, no. 2 (Spring 1965), p. 230.

41. Henning Rischbieter, "Peter Weiss dramatisiert Vietnam," *Theater heute* 3, no. 3 (March 1967), p. 7.

42. All quotations from the play are taken from Christopher Holmes's translation in Michael Roloff, ed., *The Contemporary German Theater* (New York: Avon, 1972).

43. *Dramen I*, p. 264.

44. Henning Rischbieter, "Peter Weiss' *Wie dem Herrn Mockinpott das Leiden ausgetrieben Wird* in Hannover," *Theater heute* 6 (1968), p. 32.

45. Robert Corrigan, "Some Thoughts On Roman Drama," in *The Theatre In Search of a Fix* (New York: Delta, 1973), p. 73.

46. The Charenton inmates had actually been the initial step for Weiss in presenting mass heroes onstage. Although several roles were particularized—Corday, Duperret, Roux—the chorus generally functioned as a group of mass antiheroes. Because of their revolutionary fervor they were portrayed as depraved, bloodthirsty lunatics incited by other madmen like Marat.

47. For a more complete analysis of Weiss's search for dramatic heroes during this period, see Reinhard Baumgart's excellent article "In die Moral entwischt? Der Weg des politischen Stückeschreibers Peter Weiss," *Text + Kritik* 37 (January 1973), pp. 14–15.

48. Blau, *The Impossible Theater*, pp. 81–82. It is likely that Blau was referring here to Genet's *The Screens* which does not attack colonialism directly as does *The Blacks*, mentioned earlier in this chapter. In *The Screens*, as Martin Esslin points out, Genet's focal point is the general human problem of political oppression, the "outcasts of society fighting a desperate battle against the powers that be—the authorities, *les justes*." *The Theatre of the Absurd*, p. 164.

49. Hans Schwab Felisch mentions this point in his review of the original production of *Trotsky* in the *Frankfurter Allgemeine Zeitung:* "The new play by Weiss is a work which reflects the convictions of the author. . . . It is a self-description of Peter Weiss himself." Quoted in Lew Ginsberg's article, "'Selbstdarstellung' und 'Selbstentlarvung' des Peter Weiss," *Über Peter Weiss*, p. 138.

Chapter 4

1. It is clear from his notes how closely Weiss identified with the Vietnamese during his stay there. His comments about North Vietnamese literary figures on pp. 47–51 of the *Notizen* establish numerous parallels between their situation and his own. The German critic Otto Best has traced the literary similarities between Weiss's *Vanishing-Point and Leavetaking* and Weiss's descriptions of North Vietnamese literature in the *Notizen*. Cf. Best's chapter, "The Concept of an Holistic World" in *Peter Weiss*, pp. 168–71.

2. *Notizen zum kulturellen Leben der Demokratischen Republik Viet Nam* (Frankfurt a.M.: Suhrkamp, 1968), p. 9.

3. Ibid., p. 134.

4. Ibid., p. 80.

5. Quoted in Reinhard Baumgart, "In die Moral entwischt?" p. 8. Weiss and Enzensberger fought a heated literary battle over this question of the political engagement of leftist authors. A complete account of their correspondence was published in Enzensberger's quarterly magazine *Kursbuch* 6 (1966) (Berlin).

6. "Offener Brief an die *Literaturnaja Gaseta,* Moskau," in Canaris, *Über Peter Weiss,* pp. 146–47.

7. Ibid., p. 142.

8. Ibid., p. 150.

9. Ibid., p. 145.

10. Ibid., p. 150.

11. "The New International," (New York), March 1935, p. 40.

12. "Open Letter to the *Literaturnaja Gaseta,*" in Canaris, *Über Peter Weiss,* p. 145.

13. "10 Arbeitspunkte," p. 119.

14. All quotations from the play are taken from Geoffrey Skelton's translation (New York: Atheneum, 1972).

15. Interview with Canaris, *Materialien zum "Hölderlin"-Stück von Peter Weiss,* ed. Volker Canaris (Frankfurt a.M.: Suhrkamp, 1972), p. 145.

16. In addition to the dramatic value of more fully developed characters, this mixture of historical figures with a first-person narrator represents a significant philosophical change in approach from his prose works written before 1963. *Shadow of the Coachman's Body* and *Conversation of the Three Wayfarers* were also written from the perspective of a first-person narrator, but they lacked an objective world in which the reader could anchor himself. They expressed ambiguity and confusion. In *Trotsky* the narrator/dramatic hero achieves meaning *despite* his confusion by involving himself in direct action, and Weiss takes care to surround his writer—hero with factual and quasidocumentary characters and circumstances. In the first part of Weiss's final work, *Ästhetik des Widerstands,* he follows this same approach in an attempt to make his narrator "an historical presence and therefore more real." Kathleen A. Vance, *The Theme of Alienation in the Prose of Peter Weiss,* p. 188.

17. Interview with Canaris, *Materialien zum "Hölderlin,"* p. 145. Nonetheless, Weiss and the director did cut the script substantially for the Düsseldorf production.

18. Hans Mayer referred to Weiss's concept as "a drama within and between time-frames . . . the concretization of events through time and space, history being ignored like geography." Mayer was speaking of Weiss's relativization of historical time in *Hölderlin, Trotsky,* and *Marat/Sade* as an alienation device. Mayer's stress upon "timelessness" in these plays suggests that Weiss was less interested in events than in philosophical reflection upon events—an important change in direction from the agit-prop dramas he wrote at mid-decade. "Peter Weiss und die Zweifache Praxis der Veränderung," p. 19.

19. Robert Payne, *The Life and Death of Lenin* (New York: Simon and Schuster, 1964), pp. 271–72.

20. In certain respects Weiss's view was fair to Trotsky, though he omitted to mention Trotsky's narrow view of artistic possibilities. The most that Trotsky publicly conceded to the avant-

garde was to grant them a minor role in the revolution's initial phase of destruction. Thus Russian futurism, as Trotsky explained it, "was the pre-vision of all that (the immanent social and political crises, the explosions and catastrophes of history to come) within the sphere of art." Poggioli, *Theory of the Avant-Garde*, p. 69.

21. Interview with Paul Gray, *The Drama Review* 2 (T-33) (Fall 1966), p. 114. Weiss's naive "lack of understanding" about this issue reflects his political attitudes in 1966 when the statement was made. By 1969, however, he was prepared to demonstrate the danger of such political intolerance through the Zurich coffeehouse scene which strongly criticized the repressive tendencies in the early Bolshevik leaders.

22. The British playwright Tom Stoppard also used the confrontation between the Bolsheviks and dadaists in Zurich in his 1974 comedy *Travesties*. While Stoppard developed the historical situation into an entire play, however, he treated the issue of committed art only fancifully, using it as a comical background to explore the egoistical, half-witted mentality of the British Foreign Service which was his main target.

23. Interview with Paul Gray, p. 108.

24. *Materialien zum "Hölderlin,"* p. 142.

25. Ibid. Actually Weiss had paid a two-month visit to Tübingen in 1928, staying with his family in the home of his maiden aunt during his summer vacation.

26. Ibid., pp. 146–47.

27. Ibid., p. 147.

28. All quotations from the play are translated from the first acting edition (Schiller-Theater production), as published in *Theater heute* 12, no. 11 (November 1971).

29. *"Introduction"* to *Friedrich Hölderlin: Poems and Fragments*, tr. Michael Hamburger (Ann Arbor: University of Michigan Press, 1967), p. 4.

30. Reported by Siegfried Melchinger, "Der Fall Hölderlin und der Fall Peter Weiss: Szenenlogik und szenische Imagination in *Hölderlin*," *Theater heute* 12, no. 11 (November 1971), p. 26.

31. "Peter Weiss' Rückzug in den Idealismus: Anmerkungen zu seinem *Hölderlin*," *Materialien zum "Hölderlin,"* p. 204.

32. "Der Fall Hölderlin," p. 28.

33. Rischbieter, "Postskriptum," *Theater heute* 12, no. 11 (November 1971), p. 36. Rischbieter's comment is supported by Weiss's own sarcasm towards the Schiller Theater's staging, which he described as follows: "Bombastic staging. A mixture of *Die Meistersinger* and *Aida*. A director's theater. . . . Can I persuade them to just haul away the scenery?" *Notizbüchern 1971–1980*, p. 13.

34. *Materialien zum "Hölderlin,"* p. 147.

35. Poggioli, *The Theory of the Avant-Garde*, p. 46.

36. Tom Driver, *Romantic Quest and Modern Query* (New York: Delacorte, 1970), p. 368.

37. *Materialien zum "Hölderlin,"* p. 146.

38. Georg Hensel, "Hölderlin's Stiefeletten über Marat's Leisten," *Theater heute* 12, no. 11 (November 1971), p. 25.

39. *Materialien zum "Hölderlin,"* p. 148.

40. This connection between the work of the artist and that of the revolutionary is also expressed in Weiss's criticism of Goethe as an artist removed from human affairs, aloof from the political struggles of his times, and therefore dangerous since such artists easily become tools of the ruling classes. Thus Weiss shows Goethe and Schiller leading the police onstage to break up the student rally in Jena in scene 4. In an interview with Heinz Ludwig Arnold in 1981, shortly before his death, Weiss explained his ideas on art in order to clarify the meaning expressed by the title of his last major work, *Ästhetik des Widerstands:* "An aesthetics," Weiss remarked, "which has nothing to do with traditional ideas about aesthetics, namely the study of what is beautiful, harmonious, perfectly fashioned, expressive, and finished; but rather an aesthetics which includes everything pertaining to human struggle, to a struggle leading to a higher consciousness. People are portrayed in political struggles, but these are too narrowly conceived and need to be enlarged . . . so that out of this political struggle there emerges unmistakably a cultural transformation, an enrichment of people in terms of their cultural worth or value. . . . We are living today in this situation. As intelligent artists, we are completely caught-up in this situation." "Der ewige Kampf um die Befreiung," *Nürnberger Nachrichten,* 2 October 1982, p. 17.

41. Ronald Gray, *Brecht the Dramatist* (Cambridge: Cambridge University Press, 1976), pp. 177–78.

42. Alvarez interview, p. 3.

43. Darko Suvin, "The Mirror and the Dynamo: On Brecht's Aesthetic Point of View," *Brecht,* ed. Erika Munk (New York: Bantam, 1972), pp. 85–92.

44. Volker Canaris referred to this point in the following terms: "Peter Weiss has never spoken more directly through his stage characters than he has in this remark." *Über Peter Weiss,* p. 8.

45. "Rede in englischer Sprache gehalten an der Princeton University USA am 25 April 1966, unter dem Titel: 'I Come Out of My Hiding Place,'" in Canaris, *Über Peter Weiss,* p. 9.

46. Interview with Michael Roloff, *Partisan Review* 2 (1965), p. 227. In a 1979 interview with Peter Spielmann, Weiss described his exile as "an inner emigration within an emigration." *Der Maler Peter Weiss* (Berlin: Frölich und Kaufmann, 1982), p. 25.

47. Cf. Lee Baxendall's essay on Brecht's experiences in America: "Brecht In America," in *Brecht,* ed. Erika Munk, pp. 33–60.

48. "Georg Büchner, Peter Weiss und der ästhetische Widerstand," *Zeitschrift für Literatur,* No. 20 (January 1983), p. 26.

49. "10 Arbeitspunkte," p. 116.

50. Martin Esslin, "Brecht at Seventy," in *Brecht,* ed. Erika Munk, pp. 77–78.

51. Walter Sokel, "Brecht's Split Characters and His Sense of the Tragic," in *Brecht: A Collection of Critical Essays,* ed. Peter Demetz (Englewood Cliffs, N.J.: Prentice-Hall, 1962), p. 137.

52. Esslin, "Brecht at Seventy," p. 78.

53. "Fünf Schwierigkeiten beim Schreiben der Wahrheit," *Versuche,* 9, p. 87.

54. "The Industrialization of the Mind," in *The Consciousness Industry: On Literature, Politics, and the Media,* ed. Michael Roloff (New York: Seabury, 1974), p. 4.

55. Otto Best, *Peter Weiss,* p. 166.

56. Alvarez interview, p. 3.

57. Ernst Schumacher, *Drama und Geschichte: Bertolt Brecht's "Leben des Galilei" und andere Stücke* (Berlin: Henschelverlag, 1968), p. 196. In a more recent study of Brecht's work, James K. Lyon makes a similar point about Brecht's handling of characters. Lyon points out how Brecht never used either a worker or a world historical individual as the protagonist of any of his plays (with the exception of Galileo). This stands, of course, in sharp contrast to Weiss who created figures like Marat, Trotsky, and Hölderlin who functioned in just this way. Cf. Lyon's *Bertolt Brecht in America* (Princeton: Princeton University Press, 1980), p. 242.

Chapter 5

1. Interview with Canaris in *Materialien zum "Hölderlin,"* p. 147.

2. In conversation with Jürgen Lodemann, "Jeder Mensch, der denken kann, kann auch weiterdenken," *Deutsche Volkszeitung*, No. 38 (17 September 1981), p. 22.

3. Vance, *The Theme of Alienation in the Prose of Peter Weiss*, p. 176.

4. Interview with Oliver Clausen, "Weiss/Propagandist and Weiss/Playwright," *New York Times Magazine*, 2 October 1966, p. 128.

5. *Between Existentialism and Marxism*, tr. John Mathews (New York: Morrow, 1974), p. 117.

6. Ibid., p. 285.

7. William Oliver, "*Marat/Sade* in Santiago," *Educational Theatre Journal* 19 (December 1967), p. 489.

8. Interview with Canaris in *Materialien zum "Hölderlin,"* p. 142.

9. Ibid., p. 148.

10. Jean-Paul Sartre, *Between Existentialism and Marxism*, tr. John Mathews (New York: Morrow, 1974), p. 29.

11. Max Frisch is another German playwright who has commented on this need for broad theoretical criticism from concerned authors at a time when direct political action is either impossible or ineffective: "We cannot write the arsenal of weapons out of the world but, the more clearly we write, the more concretely, the more we can cause chaos in the arsenal of catchwords that are needed in every camp to wage war." Quoted in Arrigo Subiotto, "The Swiss Contribution," in *The German Theatre: A Symposium*, ed. Ronald Hayman (London: Wolff, 1975), p. 175.

12. Interview with Canaris in *Materialien zum "Hölderlin,"* p. 146.

13. *Materialien zum "Hölderlin,"* p. 129.

14. Herbert Lindenberger, *Historical Drama: The Relation of Literature to Reality* (Chicago: University of Chicago Press, 1975), pp. 109–10.

15. Interview with Canaris, *Materialien zum "Hölderlin,"* p. 146.

16. Blau, *The Impossible Theatre*, p. 103.

17. "We are working with a cheery humor for we're creating the socialist future, as we well know." Peter Hacks, "Busy for Harvests and Holidays," *Theater heute* 6, no. 6 (June 1965), p. 23.

18. "Introduction" to *The Deputy*, in Eric Bentley, ed., *The Storm over "The Deputy"* (New York: Grove, 1964), p. 15.

19. This conclusion, derived from my studies of his *dramatic* heroes, holds true as well for the three major works of fiction Weiss completed after *Hölderlin*, the novel *Ästhetik des Widerstands*, and both unsuccessful versions of Kafka's *Trial*. Shortly before his death in 1982 Weiss remarked, "I can sell my novel, *The Aesthetics of Resistance*, on the street myself, but that would take so much time and life is so short. What I want more is that my plays receive good productions, and have a strong effect on audiences. . . . Things are happening so quickly these days, and we have no more time to spare." In conversation with C. Bern Sucher, "Die letzte Arbeit eines vertriebenen Dichters," *Neue Musikzeitung,* No. 3 (June 1982), p. 27.

20. *Fear and Trembling,* tr. Lee M. Hollander (New York: Doubleday, 1960), pp. 125–26.

21. Clausen interview, "Weiss/Propagandist and Weiss/Playwright," p. 134.

Bibliography

Works by Peter Weiss

Abschied von den Eltern. Frankfurt a.M.: Suhrkamp, 1968.

Ästhetik des Widerstands. Frankfurt a.M.: Suhrkamp, 1981.

"Avantgarde Film." In *Rapporte I*, pp. 7–35.

Die Besiegten. Tr. from the Swedish by Beat Mazenauer, with a Foreword by Gunilla Palmstierna. Frankfurt a.M.: Suhrkamp, 1985.

"Brief an H. M. Enzensberger." In *Rapporte II*, pp. 35–44.

"Che Guevara." In *Rapporte II*, pp. 82–90.

Diskurs über die Vorgeschichte und den Verlauf des langdauernden Befreiungskrieges in Viet Nam als Beispiel für die Notwendigkeit des bewaffneten Kampfes der Unterdrückten gegen ihre Underdrücker sowie über die Versuche der Vereinigten Staaten von Amerika die Grundlagen der Revolution zu vernichten. In *Dramen II*, pp. 267–458.

Dramen. 2 vols. Frankfurt a.M.: Suhrkamp, 1968.

Die Ermittlung. In *Dramen II*, pp. 7–199.

Fluchtpunkt. Frankfurt a.M.: Suhrkamp, 1967.

"Gegen die Gesetze der Normalität." In *Rapporte I*, pp. 72–81.

Gesang vom Lusitanische Popanz. In *Dramen II*, pp. 201–65.

Das Gespräch der drei Gehenden. Frankfurt a.M.: Suhrkamp, 1968.

"Gespräch über Dante." In *Rapporte I*, pp. 142–69.

Hölderlin. Frankfurt a.M.: Suhrkamp, 1972.

Der Maler Peter Weiss: Bilder, Zeichungen, Collagen, Filme. Berlin: Frölich und Kaufmann, 1982.

"Das Material und die Modelle: Notizen zum dokumentarischen Theater." In *Dramen II*, pp. 464–72.

"Meine Ortschaft." In *Rapporte I*, pp. 113–24.

Nacht mit Gästen. In *Dramen I*, pp. 89–111.

Notizbücher 1971–1980. Frankfurt a.M.: Suhrkamp, 1981.

"Notizen zum kulturellen Leben der Demokratischen Republik Viet Nam." Frankfurt a.M.: Suhrkamp, 1968.

"Offener Brief an die *Literaturnaja Gaseta*, Moskau." In *Über Peter Weiss*. Ed. Volker Canaris. Frankfurt a.M.: Suhrkamp, 1970, pp. 141–50.

"Offener Brief an den Tschechoslowakischen Schriftstellerverband." In *Rapporte II*, pp. 73–81.

"Postskriptum" [to the Alvarez interview]. *New York Times Magazine*, 26 December 1965, p. 14.

Rapporte. 2 vols. Frankfurt a.M.: Suhrkamp, 1968–71.

"Rede in englischer Sprache gehalten an der Princeton University USA am 25. April 1966, unter dem Titel: *I Come Out of My Hiding Place*." In *Über Peter Weiss*. Ed. Volker Canaris. Frankfurt a.M.: Suhrkamp, 1970, pp. 9–14.

Der Schatten des Körpers des Kutschers. Frankfurt a.M.: Suhrkamp, 1960.

Trotzki im Exil. Frankfurt a.M.: Suhrkamp, 1970.

Der Turm. In *Dramen I,* pp. 7–33.

Die Verfolgung und Ermordung Jean Paul Marats dargestellt durch die Schauspielgruppe des Hospizes zu Charenton unter Anleitung des Herrn de Sade. In *Dramen I,* pp. 155–255.

Die Versicherung. In *Dramen I,* pp. 35–87.

Von Insel zu Insel. Tr. from the Swedish by Heiner Gimmler. Berlin: Frölich & Kaufmann, 1984.

"Vorübung zum dreiteiligen Drama *Divina Commedia.*" In *Rapporte I,* pp. 125–41.

Wie dem Herrn Mockinpott das Leiden ausgetrieben wird. In *Dramen I,* pp. 113–53.

"10 Arbeitspunkte eines Autors in der geteilten Welt." *Materialien zu Peter Weiss' "Marat/Sade."* Ed. Karlheinz Braun. Frankfurt a.M.: Suhrkamp, 1967, pp. 114–19.

English Translations of Peter Weiss's Work

How Mr. Mockinpott Was Cured of His Sufferings. Tr. Christopher Holmes. *Contemporary German Theatre.* Ed. Michael Roloff. New York: Avon, 1972.

The Investigation. Tr. Jon Swan and Ulu Grosbard. New York: Atheneum, 1968.

Leavetaking and Vanishing-Point. Tr. Christopher Levenson. London: Calder and Boyars, 1966.

"The Material and the Models: Notes towards a Documentary Theatre." Tr. Nicholas Hern. *Theatre Quarterly* 1, no. 1 (January 1971), pp. 41–43.

"My Place." Tr. Christopher Middleton. *German Writing Today.* Ed. Christopher Middleton. Baltimore: Penguin, 1967.

The Persecution and Assassination of Jean Paul Marat as Performed by the Inmates of Charenton Under the Direction of the Marquis de Sade. Tr. Geoffrey Skelton. New York: Atheneum, 1966.

The Shadow of the Coachman's Body and Conversation of the Three Wayfarers. Tr. E. B. Garside and Rosemarie Waldrop. New York: Delacorte, 1970.

Song of the Lusitanian Bogeyman. Tr. Lee Baxendall. New York: Atheneum, 1970.

The Tower. Tr. Michael Benedikt. *Postwar German Theatre.* Ed. Michael Benedikt and George Wellwarth. New York: Dutton, 1967.

Trotsky in Exile. Tr. Geoffrey Skelton. New York: Atheneum, 1972.

Vietnam Discourse. Tr. Geoffrey Skelton. New York: Atheneum, 1970.

Interviews with Peter Weiss

Alvarez, A. "Truths That Are Uttered in a Madhouse." BBC Interview reprinted in *New York Times Magazine,* 26 December 1965, pp. 3–14.

Anon. "Die Bundesrepublik ist ein Morast." *Der Spiegel* 12 (1968), p. 182.

Anon. "Peter Weiss' Entscheidung." *Theater heute* 6, no. 10 (October 1965), pp. 14–16.

Anon. "Warum gehen Sie denn ins Theater?" *Theater heute* 10 (1966), p. 13.

Arnold, Heinz Ludwig. "Der ewige Kampf um die Berfreiung." *Nürnberger Nachrichten,* 2 October 1982.

Canaris, Volker. "Gespräch mit Peter Weiss," *Der andere Hölderlin: Materialien zum "Hölderlin"-Stück von Peter Weiss.* Eds. Thomas Beckermann and Volker Canaris. Frankfurt a.M.: Suhrkamp, 1972, pp. 142–48.

Clausen, Oliver. "Weiss/Propagandist and Weiss/Playwright." *New York Times Magazine,* 2 October 1966, pp. 28–133.

Gibson, Michael. "Interview with Peter Weiss." *The Drama Review* 17, no. 3 (T-59) (September 1973), pp. 47–50.

Gray, Paul. "A Living World." *The Drama Review,* 2, no. 1 (T-33) (Fall 1966), pp. 106–14.

Lindner, Burkhardt. "Herakles, Hodann und das Archiv des verzweifelten Aufbegehrens." *Frankfurter Rundschau,* Feuilleton, 5 September 1981, p. 3.

Lodemann, Jürgen. "Jeder Mensch, der denken Kann, Kann auch Weiterdenken." *Deutsche Volkszeitung,* No. 38 (17 September 1981).

Michaelis, Rolf. "Es ist eine Wunschautobiographie: Peter Weiss im Gespräch mit Rolf Michaelis über seinen politischen Gleichnisroman." *Die Zeit,* No. 42 (10 October 1975).

Rischbieter, Henning. "Peter Weiss dramatisiert Vietnam." *Theater heute* 3 (March 1967), pp. 6–7.

Roddy, Joseph. "Marat/Sade Stuns Broadway Playgoers with Sanity from the Asylum." *Look,* 22 (February 1966), p. 110.

Roloff, Michael. "Interview with Peter Weiss." *Partisan Review* 2 (1965), pp. 17–20.

Schumacher, Ernst. "Gespräch mit Peter Weiss." *Theater der Zeit,* No. 16 (1965), pp. 4–6.

Ster, Dieter. "Gespräch mit Peter Weiss." *Theater heute* 5, no. 12 (December 1964), pp. 44–45.

Wager, Walter. "Interview with Peter Weiss." *The Playwrights Speak.* Ed. Walter Wager. New York: Delacorte, 1970, pp. 189–212.

Books and Articles on Peter Weiss

Anon. *"Marat/Sade* Forum." *Tulane Drama Review* 10 (Summer 1966) pp. 214–38.

Baumgart, Reinhard. "In die Moral entwischt? Der Weg des politischen Stückschreibers Peter Weiss." *Text + Kritik* 37 (January 1973), pp. 8–18.

Beckermann, Thomas and Canaris, Volker, eds. *Der andere Hölderlin: Materialien zum "Hölderlin"-Stück von Peter Weiss.* Frankfurt a.M.: Suhrkamp, 1972.

Best, Otto. *Peter Weiss: Vom existenzialistischen Drama zum marxistischen Welttheater.* Bern: Francke, 1971.

Braun, Karlheinz, ed. *Materialien zum Peter Weiss' "Marat/Sade."* Frankfurt a.M.: Suhrkamp, 1967.

Brustein, Robert. "Embarrassment of Riches." *New Republic* 22 (January 1966), pp. 23–28.

Canaris, Volker, Ed. *Über Peter Weiss.* Frankfurt a.M.: Suhrkamp, 1970.

Carmichael, Joel. "German Reaction to a New Play about Auschwitz." *American-German Review* (February–March 1966), p. 30–31.

Clurman, Howard. *"Marat/Sade." Nation,* 17 January 1966, pp. 82–84.

Crowther, Bosley. "Films by Peter Weiss." *New York Times Magazine,* 29 January 1966, p. 13.

Gerlach, Rainer, ed. *Peter Weiss.* Frankfurt a.M.: Suhrkamp, 1984.

Ginsberg, Lew. "'Selbstdarstellung' und Selbstentlarvung des Peter Weiss." Tr. by Hermann Pörzgen. In *Über Peter Weiss.* Ed. Volker Canaris. Frankfurt a.M.: Suhrkamp, 1970, pp. 136–40.

Hensel, Georg. "Hölderlin's Stiefeletten über Marat's Leisten." *Theater heute* 12, no. 11 (November 1971), pp. 24–26.

Hewes, Henry. "The Weiss/Brook." *Saturday Review,* 15 January 1966, p. 45.

Hilton, Ian. *Peter Weiss: A Search for Affinities.* London: Wolff, 1970.

Jens, Walter. "Die Ermittlung in Westberlin." In *Über Peter Weiss.* Ed. Volker Canaris. Frankfurt a.M.: Suhrkamp, 1970, pp. 92–96.

Mayer, Hans. "Peter Weiss und die zweifache Praxis der Veränderung." *Theater heute* 13, no. 5 (May 1972), pp. 18–20.

Melchinger, Siegfried. "Der Fall Hölderlin und der Fall Peter Weiss: Szenenlogik und szenische Imagination in *Hölderlin." Theater heute* 12, no. 11 (November 1971), pp. 26–28.

Milfull, John. "From Kafka to Brecht: Peter Weiss' Development towards Marxism." *German Life and Letters* 20, no. 1 (1966), pp. 61–72.

Oliver, William. *"Marat/Sade* in Santiago." *Educational Theatre Journal* 19 (December 1967), pp. 486–501.

Palmstierna, Gunilla. "Georg Büchner, Peter Weiss und der ästhetische Widerstand" (Acceptance speech on the award of the Büchner Prize for Literature). *Zeitschrift für Literatur,* No. 20 (January 1983), pp. 25–27.

Rischbieter, Henning. "Da ist das Deutsche Drama!" *Theater heute* 5, no. 6 (June 1964), pp. 21–25.

————. "Peter Weiss' *Wie dem Herrn Mockinpott das Leiden ausgetrieben wird* in Hannover." *Theater heute* 6 (1968), pp. 32–33.

————. "Postskriptum." *Theater heute* 12, no. 11 (November 1971), p. 36.

Schreiber, Ulrich. "Peter Weiss' Rückzug in den Idealismus." In *Der andere Hölderlin: Materialien zum "Hölderlin"-Stück von Peter Weiss.* Eds. Thomas Beckermann and Volker Canaris. Frankfurt a.M.: Suhrkamp, 1972.

Schumacher, Ernst. "*Vietnam-Diskurs* in Rostock." In *Über Peter Weiss.* Ed. Volker Canaris. Frankfurt a.M.: Suhrkamp, 1970, pp. 106–11.

Sheen, Wilfrid. "Bathtub Nights." *Commonweal,* 21 January 1966, pp. 476–77.

Sucher, C. Bernd. "Die letzte Arbeit eines vertriebenen Dichters." *Neue Musikzeitung* (Munich), No. 3 (July 1982).

Vance, Kathleen A. *The Theme of Alienation in the Prose of Peter Weiss.* Las Vegas: Peter Lang, 1981.

Vormweg, Heinrich. *Peter Weiss.* Munich: Beck, 1981.

Warneken, Bernd Jürgen. "Kritik am *Vietnam-Diskurs.*" In *Über Peter Weiss.* Ed. Volker Canaris. Frankfurt a.M.: Suhrkamp, 1970, pp. 112–30.

Wendt, Ernst. "Was wird ermittelt?" *Theater heute* 6, no. 12 (December 1965), pp. 38–41.

————. "Peter Weiss zwischen den Ideologien." *Akzente* 12 (1965), pp. 415–25.

————. "Die *Marat/Sade*" und andere Grausamkeiten." *Theater heute* 5, no. 10 (October 1964), pp. 32–37.

Wiegenstein, Roland. "Peter Weiss' *Die Ermittlung:* The Auschwitz Trial Onstage." *American-German Review* 7 (December 1965), pp. 33–35.

Zielinski, Siegfried. "The New Weiss Investigation." *Theater* 12 (Fall/Winter 1980), pp. 79–82.

Related Material

Adorno, Theodore. "On Commitment." Tr. Francis McDonagh. *Performing Arts Journal* 3, no. 3 (Winter 1979), pp. 58–67.

Sokel, Walter, ed. *An Anthology of German Expressionist Drama.* New York: Doubleday, 1963.

Artaud, Antonin. *The Theatre and Its Double.* Tr. Mary Caroline Richards. New York: Grove, 1958.

Baxendall, Lee. "Brecht in America, 1935." In *Brecht.* Ed. Erika Munk. New York: Bantam, 1972, pp. 33–60.

Bentley, Eric, ed. *The Storm over "The Deputy."* New York: Grove, 1964.

Blau, Herbert. *The Impossible Theater.* New York: Macmillan, 1964.

Brecht, Bertolt. *Versuche.* 15 Issues. Frankfurt a.M.: Suhrkamp, 1957–59.

Brook, Peter. "Looking for a New Language." *Performance* 1, no. 1 (December 1971), pp. 72–75.

————. *The Empty Space.* New York: Atheneum, 1968.

Busacca, Basil. "Brecht and the Destruction of Theater." *Medieval Epic to the "Epic Theater" of Brecht.* University of Southern California Studies in Comparative Literature. Los Angeles: University of Southern California Press, 1968, pp. 185–201.

Cohn, Ruby. "*Marat/Sade:* An Education in Theatre." *Educational Theatre Journal* 19 (December 1967), pp. 478–85.

Conliffe, W. G. "The Would-Be Novelist: An Interpretation of Peter Weiss' *Der Schatten des Körpers des Kutschers.*" *Modern Language Notes* 86 (1971), pp. 414–19.

Corrigan, Robert. *The Theatre in Search of a Fix.* New York: Delta, 1973.

Croyden, Margaret. *Lunatics, Lovers and Poets: The Contemporary Experimental Theatre.* New York: McGraw-Hill, 1974.

Demetz, Peter. *Postwar German Literature*. New York: Shocken, 1970.

————, ed. *Brecht: A Collection of Critical Essays*. Englewood Cliffs, N. J.: Prentice-Hall, 1962.

Deutscher, Isaac. *The Prophet Armed: Trotsky 1879–1921*. New York: Oxford, 1954.

————. *The Prophet Unarmed: Trotsky 1921–1940*. New York: Oxford, 1959.

Driver, Tom. "The Meaning of Silence." In *The Storm Over "The Deputy."* Ed. Eric Bentley. New York: Grove, 1964, pp. 28–30.

————. *Romantic Quest and Modern Query*. New York: Delacorte, 1970.

Enzensberger, Hans Magnus. "The Industrialization of the Mind." In *The Consciousness Industry: On Literature, Politics and the Media*. Ed. Michael Roloff. New York: Seabury, 1974.

Esslin, Martin. *The Theatre of the Absurd*. New York: Doubleday, 1961.

————. "Brecht at Seventy." In *Brecht*. Ed. Erika Munk. New York: Bantam, 1972, pp. 68–79.

Fraser, John. *Violence in the Arts*. New York: Cambridge, 1974.

Freed, Donald. "Peter Weiss and the Theatre of the Future." *Drama Survey* 6 (1967–68), pp. 119–71.

Garten, H. F. *Modern German Drama*. New York: Grove, 1962.

Genet, Jean. *The Thief's Journal*. Tr. Bernard Frechtman. Evanston: Greenleaf, 1965.

Genno, Charles N. "Peter Weiss' *Marat/Sade*." *Modern Drama* 13 (December 1970), pp. 304–15.

Gray, Ronald. *Brecht the Dramatist*. Cambridge: Cambridge University Press, 1976.

Hacks, Peter. "Tätig für Felder und Feste." *Theater heute* 6, no. 6 (June 1965), pp. 22–24.

Hampton, Charles C., Jr. "Verfremcluhanseffekt." *Modern Drama* 14, no. 3 (December 1971), pp. 340–54.

Hainaux, Rene and Bonnat, Yves, eds. *Stage Design throughout the World since 1960*. New York: Theatre Arts, 1972.

Hayman, Ronald, ed. *The German Theatre: A Symposium*. London: Wolff, 1975.

Hölderlin, Friedrich. *Poems and Fragments*. Ed. and tr. Michael Hamburger. Ann Arbor: University of Michigan Press, 1967.

Hristic, Jovan. "Commentary." *Contemporary Drama* 3, no. 3 (Fall 1969), pp. 222–27.

Innes, C. D. *Erwin Piscator's Political Theatre*. Cambridge: Cambridge University Press, 1972.

————. *Holy Theatre: Ritual and the Avant-Garde*. Cambridge: Cambridge University Press, 1981.

Ionesco, Eugene. *Notes and Counter-Notes*. Tr. Donald Watson. New York: Grove, 1964.

Isaac, Dan. "Theatre of Fact." *The Drama Review* 15, no. 3a (T-51) (Summer 1971), pp. 109–35.

Kernan, Alvin B., ed. *The Modern American Theatre*. Englewood Cliffs, N. J.: Prentice-Hall, 1967.

Kierkegaard, Søren. *Fear and Trembling*. Tr. Lee M. Hollander. New York: Doubleday, 1960.

Krasso, Nicolas, ed. *Trotsky: The Great Debate Renewed*. St. Louis, MO.: New Critics Press, 1972.

Lamont, Rosette C. "From *Macbeth* to *Macbett*." *Modern Drama* 15, no. 3 (December 1972), pp. 231–53.

Lindenberger, Herbert. "*Danton's Death* and the Conventions of Historical Drama." *Comparative Drama* 3, no. 2 (Summer 1969), pp. 99–110.

————. *Historical Drama: The Relation of Literature to Reality*. Chicago: University of Chicago Press, 1975.

Linnell, James. *Bertolt Brecht, Leopold Jessner 1918–1933: An Investigation of Theatrical Style*. Ph.D. Dissertation, University of California, Berkeley, 1968.

Loney, Glenn, ed. *Peter Brook's Production of William Shakespeare's "A Midsummer Night's Dream."* Chicago: Dramatic Publishing Company, 1974.

Lyon, James K. *Bertolt Brecht in America*. Princeton: Princeton University Press, 1980.

McCluhan, Marshall. *Understanding Media: The Extensions of Man*. New York: Signet, 1964.

McNamara, Brooks. "The Scenography of Popular Entertainment." *Drama Review* 18, no. 1 (T-61) (March 1974), pp. 16–24.

Meyerhoff, Hans, ed. *The Philosophy of History in Our Time.* New York: Doubleday, 1959.

Miller, Henry. *Black Spring.* New York: Grove, 1963.

Miller, Leslie. "Peter Weiss, Marat, and Sade: Comments on An Author's Commentary." *Symposium* 25, no. 1 (Spring 1971), pp. 39–58.

Müller, Klaus-Detlef. "Der Philosoph auf dem Theater." *Text + Kritik,* Brecht Special Issue, 1972, pp. 45–71.

———. *Die Funktion der Geschichte im Werk Bertolt Brechts.* Tübingen: Niemeyer, 1967.

Munk, Erika, ed. *Brecht.* New York: Bantam, 1972.

Nelson, Robert. *A Play within a Play, The Dramatist's Conception of His Art: Shakespeare to Anouilh.* New Haven: Yale University Press, 1958.

Neruda, Pablo. *Memoirs.* Tr. Hardie St. Martin. New York: Farrar, Strauss and Giroux, 1977.

Neugroschel, Joachim. "Peter Weiss' Search for Identity." *American-German Review* 3 (October-November 1966), pp. 34–36.

Oliver, William. "Theatre Aesthetics In Crisis." *Educational Theatre Journal* 21, no. 1 (March 1969), pp. 17–27.

Payne, Robert. *The Life and Death of Lenin.* New York: Simon and Schuster, 1964.

Perry, R. C. "Historical Authenticity and Dramatic Form: Hochhuth's *Der Stellvertreter* and Weiss' *Die Ermittlung.*" *Modern Language Review* 64 (1969), pp. 829–39.

Piscator, Erwin. *Das politische Theater.* 1929. Reprint. Berlin: Rodewald, 1968.

———. "Introduction to *The Deputy.*" Tr. Eric Bentley. In *The Storm Over "The Deputy."* Ed. Eric Bentley. New York: Grove, 1964.

Poggioli, Renato. *The Theory of the Avant-Garde.* Gerald Fitzgerald. New York: Harper and Row, 1968.

Rosen, Carl. *Plays of Impasse: Contemporary Drama Set in Confining Situations.* Princeton: Princeton University Press, 1983.

Rühle, Gunther. "Die zehn Taten des Erwin Piscator." *Theater heute* 12, no. 11 (November 1971), pp. 3–7.

Sartre, Jean-Paul. *Between Existentialism and Marxism.* Tr. John Mathews. New York: Morrow, 1974.

Schumacher, Ernst. *Drama und Geschichte: Bertolt Brechts "Leben des Galilei" und andere Stücke.* Berlin: Henschelverlag, 1968.

———. "*Die Ermittlung* von Peter Weiss: Über die Szenische Darstellbarkeit der Hölle auf Erden." *Sinn und Form* 17, no. 6, pp. 930–47.

Shaw, Leroy R. *The Playwright and Historical Change.* Madison: University of Wisconsin Press, 1970.

Sokel, Walter. "Brecht's Split Characters and His Sense of the Tragic." In *Brecht: A Collection of Critical Essays.* Ed. Peter Demetz. Englewood Cliffs, N. J.: Prentice-Hall, 1962, pp. 127–37.

Spalter, Max. "Five Examples of How to Write a Brechtian Play That Is Not Really Brechtian." *Educational Theatre Journal* 27, no. 2 (May 1975), pp. 224–32.

Subiotto, Arrigo. "The Swiss Contribution." In *The German Theatre: A Symposium.* Ed. Ronald Hayman. London: Wolff, 1975, pp. 171–77.

Suvin, Darko. "The Mirror and the Dynamo: On Brecht's Aesthetic Point of View." In *Brecht.* Ed. Erika Munk. New York: Bantam, 1972, pp. 80–100.

Thurm, Brigitte. "Geschichte für die Gegenwart." *Theater der Zeit* 4 (1971), pp. 44–46.

Triesch, Manfred. "Peter Weiss, Marat, and de Sade." *American-German Review* 6 (1964), pp. 9–11.

Trotsky, Leon. "The New International." Handbill. New York, March 1935.

Webb, Richard C. "Ritual, Theatre, and Jean Genet's *The Blacks.*" *Theatre Journal* 31, no. 4 (December 1979), pp. 443–59.

Weiss, Samuel A. "Peter Weiss' *Marat/Sade.*" *Drama Survey* 5 (Summer 1966), pp. 123–30.

Wellwarth, George. *The Theatre of Protest and Paradox.* New York: New York University Press, 1967.

White, J. "History and Cruelty in Peter Weiss' *Marat/Sade.*" *Modern Language Review* 63 (1968), pp. 437–48.

Willett, John, ed. and tr. *Brecht on Theatre.* New York: Hill and Wang, 1966.

Wirth, Andrzej. "Günter Grass and the Dilemma of Documentary Drama." *Dimension,* Special Issue on Günter Grass (1970), pp. 22–36.

Wulbern, Julian. *Brecht and Ionesco: Commitment in Context.* Urbana: University of Illinois Press, 1971.

Zipes, Jack. "Ends and Beginnings: West German Theatre Now." *Performance* 1, no. 4 (September–October 1972), pp. 54–62.

Index

Absurdity, xi-xii, 7-8, 13, 14, 17, 20, 24, 27, 30-31, 33-39, 50, 53, 57, 58, 71, 76, 89, 94, 109, 119, 130, 138-40, 161-62n.31
Adamov, Arthur, 7, 18
Aesthetics of Resistance, xiii, xv, 96, 115, 120, 134, 166n.40
"Against the Laws of Normality," 18-19
Agit-prop, xi, 55, 57, 59, 114, 115
Alienation: existential, xv, 3, 7, 100-101, 108-9, 122, 156nn.17,27; theatrical, 17, 19, 61, 76, 99, 105, 116-17, 150, 164n.18
Allegory, 9-12
Andersch, Alfred, 9
Artaud, Antonin, 13, 16, 17-18, 139, 140; and *Marat/Sade,* 21, 26, 34, 37
Asiatic Theatre, 20, 61
Ästhetik des Widerstands. See Aesthetics of Resistance
Auschwitz, 1, 43-54, 78, 132

Beckett, Samuel, 5, 17, 18, 21, 48, 159n.20
Berliner Ensemble, xv, 61, 113, 117, 150
Die Besiegten, 141
Bread and Puppet Theatre, 61, 147
Brecht, Bertolt, xiv, 16, 17, 21, 29, 57, 59, 61, 65, 73, 75, 111-17, 139, 150, 157n.39, 167n.57; "Five Difficulties in Writing the Truth," 115; *Galileo,* 113, 117, 139; *Good Woman of Setzuan,* 75; *Mahagonny,* 113; *Mann ist Mann,* 73; *Threepenny Opera,* 113
Brook, Peter, 35, 37, 61, 114, 139, 142, 159-60nn.25,26,28
Büchner, Georg, 31-32, 99, 113, 152

Chaplin, Charles, 77
Comedy, 5, 14-15, 32, 71-78
Cinema, 4, 8, 13, 14, 17-18, 21, 23, 45, 81, 95, 111, 119, 141, 154, 157n.37
Circus and Carnival, 19-20, 70-76, 157n.44
Conversation of the Three Wayfarers, xii, 3, 6-9, 58, 170

Dadaism, 88, 95, 110, 126, 145, 152
Dante, xiii, 46, 153
Directing: directorial interpretations of plays, xiv-xv, 27, 33-34, 37, 45, 76-77, 105, 107, 146-47, 150, 154, 159-60nn.25,26, 165n.33; Weiss's experience, xiii, 21, 59, 61, 91-92, 150-51; working with directors, 21, 23, 114, 147-51
Documentary technique, xv, 7, 13, 44-48, 53, 56-71, 77, 91, 92-95, 112, 115, 117, 120-23, 133-39, 151, 162n.32, 164n.16
Doggerel, 20, 44, 63
Das Duell, 142
Dulac, Germaine, 8, 18
Dürrenmatt, Friedrich, 9, 15, 26

Die Ermittlung. See The Investigation
Existentialism, 10, 12, 16, 19, 26, 33-34, 37-38, 54, 113, 116, 123, 135-36, 138-40, 156n.17
Expressionism, 4, 13, 15-16, 89, 91-94, 97, 117, 156n.30

Fairbanks, Douglas, 2
Fascism. *See* National Socialism
Film. *See* Cinema
Fluchtpunkt. See Vanishing-Point
Fran ö till ö, 2, 141
Frisch, Max, 9, 16, 167n.11

Genet, Jean, 25, 63, 79, 163n.48; *The Blacks,* 63; *The Thief's Journal,* 155n.7
Gesang vom Lusitanischen Popanz. See Song of the Lusitanian Bogeyman
Das Gespräch der drei Gehenden. See Conversation of the Three Wayfarers
Goldoni, Carlo, 78
Gozzi, Carlo, 78
Grass, Günter, 114
Grosz, Georg, 15
Gruppe 47, 141
Guevara, Che, 19, 55, 85, 99, 138, 149

Hacks, Peter, 139, 167n.17
Hallucinations, 4
Handke, Peter, 77–78
Hesse, Hermann, 11, 141
Hildesheimer, Wolfgang, 139
Hochhuth, Rolf, 27, 44
Hölderlin, xiii, 31, 67, 79–80, 97–111, 115–16, 119, 121–40, 142–43, 146–49, 153
Hölderlin, Friedrich, 4, 19, 27, 31, 98–99, 105, 107, 108
Hörspiel. See Radio Drama
How Mr. Mockinpott Was Cured of His Sufferings, xiii, 5, 23, 55, 71–80, 91,104, 120, 134–35, 142
Huelsenbeck, 13, 88

The Insurance, xii, 13–17, 18, 19, 71, 142
The Investigation, xiii, 27, 43–55, 58–59, 61, 63, 77–78, 91, 115, 120, 129, 131, 135, 142, 147–53, 161n.22
Ionesco, Eugene, 16, 17, 18, 26

Kabuki, 20
Kafka, Franz, xiii, xv, 3, 7, 26, 61, 61; *The Trial,* xiii, 25, 142
Kayser, Georg, 13, 14
Kierkegaard, Søren, 140
Kipphardt, Heinar, 27
Knittelvers. See Doggerel
Kopit, Arthur, 139

Living Theatre (Julian Beck), 61, 97, 147

Madness, 3–4, 14, 18–19, 24, 27–40, 91, 98–99, 103–5, 110, 116, 125–28, 131–34, 140
Mann, Thomas, 156n.27
Marat/Sade. See The Persecution and Assassination of Jean-Paul Marat as Performed by the Inmates of Charenton Under the Direction of the Marquis de Sade
Marceau, Marcel, 77
Marx, Karl, xiii, 33, 83, 85–89, 98, 104–10, 124, 126, 135, 162n.39
"The Material and the Models: Notes towards a Definition of Documentary Theatre," 56–71, 142
Miller, Henry, 7, 17, 18, 25–26, 85, 156n.20
Moritat, 19–20
Murnau, Claude, 2
"My Place," 50

Nacht mit Gästen. See Night with Guests
National Socialism, xii, xiii, 1, 11, 24, 43–55, 85, 113, 125, 129–30
Naziism. *See* National Socialism
Neruda, Pablo, 40

Night with Guests, xii, 5, 19–21, 71, 76, 114, 142, 151
Notes on Vietnam, 81–83
Novak, Willi, 11, 141

Orwell, George, 25
Osborne, John, 139

Palmstierna-Weiss, Gunilla, xiii, xiv, xv, 21, 37, 45, 59, 67, 89–91, 113, 141, 145–54, 157n.45
Pantomime, 13, 16, 32, 49, 45, 59–63, 71, 76
Parable, 9–12, 71, 73, 76–78, 115, 117
Peer Gynt (Ibsen), 103
The Persecution and Assassination of Jean-Paul Marat as Performed by the Inmates of Charenton Under the Direction of the Marquis de Sade, xi–xiii, 5, 16, 18, 20–45, 48, 53, 57, 63, 70–71, 76–80, 84, 88, 91–97, 105–7, 109, 112, 116–23, 124–40, 141–42, 145, 147–49, 151–52, 153
Perten, Hans, 33–34, 37, 63, 147–48
The Physicists (Dürrenmatt), 15
Piscator, Erwin, 57, 59, 114, 139, 142, 162n.32
Plato, 5
Porter, Edwin, 17
Propaganda, 33, 56, 57, 67–71, 78, 109, 115, 137, 145
Punch-and-Judy, 5, 19, 73, 76
Puppets, 5, 20, 45, 71–77, 82, 156n.27

Radio Drama, 9–10
Reinhardt, Max, 10
Revolution, xi–xiv, 4, 14–19, 24–40, 43, 45, 54–70, 76–79, 104–7, 108–14, 120–40, 145, 149, 152
Rostock (Volkstheater), 33–34, 37, 65–66, 147–48
Der Ruf, 9

Sartre, Jean-Paul, 84, 135–40
Der Schatten des Körpers des Kutschers. See The Shadow of the Coachman's Body
Schlemmer, Oskar, 14
The Shadow of the Coachman's Body, xii, 3–9, 12, 13, 58, 134, 142
Shaffer, Peter, 139
Socialism, xi, xiii, 7, 26, 32–33, 55–57, 71, 76–80, 89–99, 104–15, 125–40
Song of the Lusitanian Bogeyman, xiii, 5, 27, 55–71, 78, 112, 115–17, 120–21, 123, 132, 134, 142, 146, 148, 149
Stein, Gertrude, 14
Stoppard, Tom, 165n.22
Strehler, George, 77–78
Strindberg, August, 13, 17, 18–19, 20–21, 71, 85, 141; *The Father,* 19

Surrealism, 4, 6–8, 13, 15, 18, 39, 48, 95–96, 104, 107, 153
Swinarski, Konrad, 21, 34, 150
Symbolism, 7, 10, 38

Taboo, 2, 18
"Ten Working Points of an Author in a Divided World," 56, 142
Thief of Baghdad, 2, 18
Third World. *See* Underdeveloped Nations
Toller, Ernst, 14
The Tower, xii, 9–14, 27, 127, 128, 141
The Trial (Der Prozess) (Weiss), xiii, xiv, xv, 61, 114, 143, 147, 151
Trotsky, Leon, i, 4, 19, 27, 31, 33, 82–87, 95, 96, 97–98, 152, 164–65n.20
Trotsky in Exile, xiii, 16, 71, 79–98, 104, 107, 109–10, 112, 116–17, 119–21, 122–28, 130–34, 136–38, 142, 145–47, 150–53
Der Turm. See The Tower
Tzara, Tristan, 13, 88

Underdeveloped nations, 40, 43, 48, 54–71, 78–79, 81–89, 94–95, 97–98, 121, 125, 136,

148–49, 161–62n.28
US (Peter Brook), 61

Vanishing-Point, xii, 2, 13, 24, 141–42
Vaudeville, 13, 16
Die Versicherung. See The Insurance
Vietnam Discourse, xiii, 4, 27, 54, 55–71, 78, 82, 91, 98, 112, 115, 117, 120–21, 123, 134, 142, 149–50
"Vietnam: Eleven Points," 142
"Vietnam Notes," *See Notes on Vietnam*
Der Vogelfreie, 142

Walser, Martin, 9
Weiss, Gunilla Palmstierna. *See* Palmstierna-Weiss, Gunilla
Wie dem Herrn Mockinpott das Leiden ausgetrieben wird. See How Mr. Mockinpott Was Cured of His Sufferings
Wilson, Robert, 139–40

"Zehn Arbeitspunkte eines Autors in der geteilten Welt." *See* "Ten Working Points of an Author in a Divided World"